Huang Quanyu, PhD
Joseph W. Leonard, PhD
Chen Tong, MS, MGS

Business Decision Making in China

*Pre-publication
REVIEWS,
COMMENTARIES,
EVALUATIONS . . .*

"An important aspect of this book is the focus on historical aspects of Chinese culture, society, and structure. Without a basic understanding of these historical and cultural aspects that shape modern-day Chinese society, it is very difficult to comprehend and to function efficiently in those markets. The intricacies of Chinese business culture that impact greatly on the decision-making process of all parties involved can best be understood by learning about the intricacies and roots of Chinese culture, traditions, and way of life.

The chapter titled 'Tactics of Decision Making' is particularly interesting, as it focuses on current realities of business and strategies at work among players/negotiators."

Jeffrey L. Gabbour, MA
*Marketing Manager,
Robbins International, Inc.,
Cincinnati, OH*

"*Business Decision Making in China* is an excellent study of the formal structure of Chinese organization for decision making, as well as the philosophy behind Chinese thinking that motivates decisions by shaping the context in which action is taken."

Dr. John D. Stempel
*Director, Patterson
School of Diplomacy
and International Commerce,
University of Kentucky, Lexington*

More pre-publication
REVIEWS, COMMENTARIES, EVALUATIONS . . .

"This intriguing volume provides a wealth of information and insight that would be useful for those involved in business relations with China. It begins with a clear and comprehensive presentation of the structure and organization of various types of companies, then depicts the overall political and economic context of a China in transition from central planning to market socialism. Processes, characteristics, and tactics of decision making are explained in subsequent chapters, against a backdrop of assumptions drawn from American business textbooks and manuals. This results in a fascinating set of comparisons between American and Chinese social and cultural worlds.

What makes this book particularly valuable is the way in which its authors draw on a wide range of Chinese source materials to illustrate important aspects of the Chinese business context. Many classical sources are used, with stories that illuminate Chinese patterns of thought and action and help to explain present day behavior. There are also many historical illustrations, which give pointed insights into motivation and action. In addition, there are tips on how to read the Chinese press, from an insider accustomed to the peculiar requirements for de-coding it, and philosophical reflections on concepts of leadership and views of social relations in China.

The writers have made every effort to make explicit for Western readers a wide-ranging philosophy and psychology of human interaction that needs to be understood by all who hope for enduring and effective business relations with China."

Ruth Hayhoe, PhD
*Former First Secretary
of Canadian Embassy to China;
Associate Dean
for Graduate Studies,
Ontario Institute for Studies
in Education, University of Toronto*

International Business Press
An Imprint of The Haworth Press, Inc.

NOTES FOR PROFESSIONAL LIBRARIANS AND LIBRARY USERS

This is an original book title published by International Business Press, an imprint of The Haworth Press, Inc. Unless otherwise noted in specific chapters with attribution, materials in this book have not been previously published elsewhere in any format or language.

CONSERVATION AND PRESERVATION NOTES

All books published by The Haworth Press, Inc. and its imprints are printed on certified ph neutral, acid free book grade paper. This paper meets the minimum requirements of American National Standard for Information Sciences–Permanence of Paper for Printed Material, ANSI Z39.48-1984.

Business Decision Making in China

INTERNATIONAL BUSINESS PRESS
Erdener Kaynak, PhD
Executive Editor

New, Recent, and Forthcoming Titles:

International Business Handbook edited by V. H. (Manek) Kirpalani

Sociopolitical Aspects of International Marketing edited by Erdener Kaynak

How to Manage for International Competitiveness edited by Abbas J. Ali

International Business Expansion into Less-Developed Countries: The International Finance Corporation and Its Operations by James C. Baker

Product-Country Images: Impact and Role in International Marketing edited by Nicolas Papadopoulos and Louise A. Heslop

The Global Business: Four Key Marketing Strategies edited by Erdener Kaynak

Multinational Strategic Alliances edited by Refik Culpan

Market Evolution in Developing Countries: The Unfolding of the Indian Market by Subhash C. Jain

A Guide to Successful Business Relations with the Chinese: Opening the Great Wall's Gate by Huang Quanyu, Richard Andrulis, and Chen Tong

Industrial Products: A Guide to the International Marketing Economics Model by Hans Jansson

Euromarketing: Effective Strategies for International Trade and Export edited by Salah S. Hassan and Erdener Kaynak

How to Utilize New Information Technology in the Global Marketplace: A Basic Guide edited by Fahri Karakaya and Erdener Kaynak

International Negotiating: A Primer for American Business Professionals by Michael Kublin

The Eight Core Values of the Japanese Businessman: Toward an Understanding of Japanese Management by Yasutaka Sai

Implementation of Total Quality Management: A Comprehensive Training Program by Rolf E. Rogers

An International Accounting Practice Set: The Karissa Jean's Simulation by David R. Peterson and Nancy Schendel

Privatization and Entrepreneurship: The Managerial Challenge in Central and Eastern Europe by Arieh Ullmann and Alfred Lewis

U.S. Trade, Foreign Direct Investments, and Global Competitiveness by Rolf Hackmann

Business Decision Making in China by Huang Quanyu, Joseph Leonard, and Chen Tong

International Management Leadership: The Primary Competitive Advantage by Raimo W. Nurmi and John R. Darling

The Trans-Oceanic Marketing Channel: A New Tool for Understanding Tropical Africa's Export Agriculture by H. Laurens van der laan

Business Decision Making in China

Huang Quanyu, PhD
Joseph W. Leonard, PhD
Chen Tong, MS, MGS

International Business Press
An Imprint of The Haworth Press, Inc.
New York • London

Published by

International Business Press, an imprint of The Haworth Press, Inc., 10 Alice Street, Binghamton, NY 13904-1580

© 1997 by The Haworth Press, Inc. All rights reserved. No part of this work may be reproduced or utilized in any form or by any means, electronic or mechanical, including photocopying, microfilm, and recording, or by any information storage and retrieval system, without permission in writing from the publisher. Printed in the United States of America.

Cover design by Monica L. Seifert.

Library of Congress Cataloging-in-Publication Data

Quanyu, Huang
    Business decision making in China / Huang Quanyu, Joseph W. Leonard, Chen Tong.
       p.   cm.
    Includes bibliographical references and index.
    ISBN 0-7890-0190-X (alk. paper)
      1. Decision making–China. 2. Industrial organization–China. 3. China–Manufactures–Management–Decision making. 4. Government business enterprises–China–Management–Decision making. I. Leonard, Joseph W. II. Tong, Chen. III. Title.
HD30.23.H773 1997
658.4'03'0951–dc20

96-28274
CIP

CONTENTS

Executive Editor's Comments	ix
Foreword	xiii
John Thanopoulos	
Preface	xix
Martha S. Lee	
Acknowledgments	xxi

PART I: ORGANIZATIONAL STRUCTURES IN CHINA   1

Chapter 1. The Structures of Manufacturing Organizations   3

State-Owned Enterprises	3
Collective Enterprises	9
Joint-Venture Enterprises	12
Foreign-Owned Enterprises	21
Individual Companies	26
Discussion Questions	29

Chapter 2. The Structures of Service Organizations   31

Commercial Organizations	31
Foreign Trade Organizations	35
Financial Organizations	43
Discussion Questions	51

Chapter 3. The Structures of Governmental Organizations   55

Semigovernmental Organizations	55
Nongovernmental Organizations	57
Governmental Structures	59
Discussion Questions	66

PART II: THE OPERATION OF DECISION MAKING 69

Chapter 4. The Processes of Decision Making 71

Decisions Makers Concerned 71
The General Models of Decision Making 75
Steps of Decision Making 79
Discussion Questions 87

Chapter 5. Characteristics of Decision Making 89

Personalities 89
Basing Decisions on the Party's Policies
   and the Government's Viewpoints 97
Changeability 100
Inflexibility 106
Predictability 112
Unpredictability 118
Complexities 122
Simplicity 129
Radical Decision Making 130
The Golden Mean 133
Timing (Fast and Slow) 135
Poor Continuity 138
Discussion Questions 145

Chapter 6. Tactics of Decision Making 149

Yin and *Yang* (Unity and Opposite) 150
Military Strategy and Tactics from Sun Tzu 165
"Thick" and "Black" 202
Discussion Questions 213

PART III: THE ELEMENTS THAT IMPACT CHINESE DECISION MAKING 217

Chapter 7. Traditional Culture 219

Saving Face 219
The Individual and the Collective 234
Equality 246

Hierarchy	255
Social Role and Self	263
Modesty and Implication	270
Discussion Questions	276

Chapter 8. Modes of Thinking — 281

Unity of Opposites	281
Two Unbalanced Pairs	286
Discussion Questions	293

Epilogue — 295

Index — 299

ABOUT THE AUTHORS

Huang Quanyu, PhD, is President of H.C.K. International and Manager of the Community Leadership Program at Miami University, Oxford, Ohio. He has offered Sino-American business consulting for a number of corporations, conducted international business, and been involved with the Sino-American business conference, "To Close, To Link." Dr. Huang has published many papers and books in the United States, China, and Britain and is co-author of *A Guide to Successful Business Relations with the Chinese.*

Joseph W. Leonard, PhD, is a member of the faculty at Miami University's Richard T. Farmer School of Business Administration, where he teaches international business and strategic management. His research publications include numerous journal articles, book chapters, and other papers about Japanese, Chinese, and Korean business.

Chen Tong, MS, MGS, was a journalist and former Vice General Secretary of Guangxi (province) Federation of Social Science Societies. She has published eight books and approximately 100 articles in China, the United States, and Britain and is co-author of *A Guide to Successful Business Relations with the Chinese.* Ms. Chen is also a guest editor for several Chinese publishing houses and journals.

Executive Editor's Comments

In terms of both size of the market and purchasing power, East Asia is the most dominant market in the world. Within this region, two markets namely the Peoples' Republic of China and India–stand out. These two countries have achieved tremendous growth as of late. For instance, the PRC accounts for nearly 22 percent of the world's population and its rate of economic growth has been one of the highest in Asia as well as in the world, running at a rate of 11 to 13 percent–a remarkable performance. The country has also opened its doors to foreign investments, and over the last decade we have witnessed some of the most spectacular developments in the country, which have not been seen anywhere else in the world in the recent past.

The Chinese have learned how to work within centrally planned economy principles. Despite 43 percent of gross value of industrial output being obtained from state-owned enterprises, free market economy principles have been practiced considerably without which this high level of development and performance could not have materialized. In particular, managerial know-how and expertise gained in the southern province of Guandong and the entrepreneurial skills developed in Beijing and East China (in particular Nanjing and Shanghai) are being disseminated in other parts of vast Chinese land. Advances in technology, know-how, and investment do not show their positive impact unless they are supported by superior management practices. My first-hand observation of the Chinese industries is that this has also been the case. Chinese enterprises, both small and large, are trying very hard to change their outmoded managerial and decision-making practices. In this process, one must accept the yeoman's job multinational enterprises have performed.

In the light of the changing and transforming business environment of Chinese enterprises, a gradual change and adaptation is also taking place in business decision making in China. Having developed a very useful guidebook in 1994 on how to form successful business relations with the Chinese, Huang Quanyu, Joseph W. Leonard, and Chen Tong have now developed an outstanding book for our readers in *Business Decision Making in China*. The book contains eight chapters and each chapter treats an important aspect of managerial decision making by Chinese enterprises. The authors have examined the structures and characteristics of manufacturing organizations by using five different organization types available within the Chinese business environment. These are state-owned enterprises, collective enterprises, joint-venture enterprises, foreign-owned enterprises, and individual companies.

We are moving toward a service economy. This has also been the trend in China. The Chinese government is facilitating this process at different levels. Chapter 2 of the book examines in an insightful way the structures of service organizations in China during development. In particular, the role and function of foreign trade organizations and financial organizations are looked at. In addition, the role of service organizations in a socialist economy versus a free market economy is illustrated in a very clear and understandable fashion.

Whether it is a free market or centrally planned economy, government and its organizations play a pivotal role in the smooth functioning of the economy. In Chapter 3, the authors examine the structures of governmental organizations in China. Having analyzed the Chinese governmental structure, the authors study the functioning of semi-governmental and nongovernmental organizations. Chapter 4 looks critically at the structure of a Chinese manufacturer where the relationships between the Party secretary and the business manager are rather unique, which cannot be seen in any other organization in the Western companies.

The characteristics of Chinese managers' decision-making process, discussed in Chapter 5, are at the heart of this book. In particular, the power structure between the Party secretary and the company manager and personalities involved in decision making, the bases for their decisions and distinct characteristics, and the complexities of the decisions made make up the core of this chapter. While Chapter 5 gives a general outline of the focus of decision making, Chapters 6 and 7 discuss specific issues regarding decision making, namely tactical issues and the role and impact of the traditional Chinese culture. In particular, seven perspectives from the art of war of Sun Tzu are applied to today's business decision making. From Sun Tzu military principles, the authors conclude that "knowing yourself" (internal company self-analysis) and "knowing your enemy" (external market and competitive analysis) are the most critical factors for effective decision making in the contemporary market environment. An important dichotomy between the Western cultures and the Oriental Chinese culture is individualism versus collectivism, which shows its influence in the decision-making process. As well, the terms equality, hierarchy, social role, self, and modesty have different meanings and implications in Chinese decision making.

Finally, Chapter 8 discusses the modes of thinking and behavior norms in Chinese decision making. Such unique Chinese characteristics as unity of opposites, the importance of universality over individuality, and an emphasis on imaginative over abstract thinking have all been examined and their relation to decision making has been delineated.

This book by Huang, Leonard, and Chen is an outstanding addition to the international business literature. I sincerely congratulate the authors for bringing this volume to fruition. It is must reading for everyone who is interested in understanding how the Chinese mind works. A welcome addition to our International Business Press book series, the volume succinctly describes and analyzes Chinese-style business decision making and contrasts it with Western-style decision making. This book treats the subject in a very comprehensive and clear fashion. It will be a very useful textbook for undergraduate classes in management, cross-cultural communication, international business, marketing, and comparative management. Businesspersons, public policy makers, and business consultants would also find this book immensely useful, enabling them to understand the intricacies of Chinese decision making.

Have a happy reading and enjoy it.

Erdener Kaynak, PhD, DSc
Executive Editor, International Business Press
Professor of Marketing at The Pennsylvania State University

Foreword

A very successful businessperson once said, "To win a bridge game, a crucial means is to understand what decision your partner and opponents would make." The purpose of this work is to help readers to understand who is involved in business decision making in China, how decisions are made, and what the characteristics and strategies of Chinese decision making are. This book analyzes how and why business decision making in China is influenced by traditional culture and modes of thinking.

As we approach the twenty-first century, we wonder about the economic future of the earth, the respect for its fragile ecological realities, the social pressures on the human factor, the educational potentialities, and the political battles of the coming years. It is within this framework that noted scholars predict that China will be the most powerful economy on the planet within fifty years.

It is axiomatic that China, the most populous country, cannot be presented within the covers of any books. Its recorded history dates back to 1766 B.C. It has survived tyrants, monarchs, emperors, and great occupying forces. It has experienced purely capitalist and communist regimes. It has grown during times of incredible pressures, political upheavals, and moments of greatness and of extraordinary pain. It has taught the world philosophy, arts, sciences, business, and military strategy for more than 5,000 years. It is a unique mosaic of hundreds of cultures and languages. And, yes, in the eyes of most Westerners, it represents one single country.

It was, therefore, with academic curiosity that I accepted the invitation to provide comments on a manuscript on decision making in China. At that early stage, I was questioning the possibility of being presented with a single volume that summarizes the wisdom of entrepreneurial thinking, business acumen, and negotiation practices of more than one billion people. Eventually, I prepared this foreword. It was only natural. I have conducted business on four continents; studied in Greece, France, England, and the United States; and lectured in China, England, Greece, Holland, and the United States. I have worked with the Chinese. I felt that this text had significant messages to contribute. Moreover, the book capitalized on the authors' personal experiences and extensive knowledge of China and other Far East countries. It was not merely another review of the literature.

Let's start this foreword with a walk through the major issues that the book addresses. There are three parts. The first part deals with the "what," aiming to familiarize the reader with the present-day realities of the Chinese government structure, manufacturing operations, and service supports. The second part deals with the "how," illustrating the main influences of Chinese thinking as this has been projected through thousand-year-old teachings. The third part deals with the "why," presenting areas of concern that a businessperson aiming to approach the Chinese marketplace should observe.

Ideally, the reader of the first part should start by becoming familiar with the structures of governmental organization. In a vast country like China, it is imperative to examine the governing structures and their interrelationships (Chapter 3). The authors have classified the different governing bodies as "governmental," "semi-governmental," and "nongovernmental." Vivid illustrations, as in the case of the China Council for Promotion of International Trade, serve to point to the fact that China is still in a very fluid administrative state, where there is a lot of room for creative solutions that are magnified by a lack of exact procedures.

Vital to the understanding of the Chinese manufacturing operation is the division among the state-owned enterprise, the collective enterprise, the joint venture, the foreign-owned enterprise, and the individual company. The first, owned by the state, is in a rapidly evolving condition where the main question remains of who is really in control and what is the interrelation among the various influencing bodies, including the military and the Party. The second, owned equally by its members, has the peculiar characteristic that the member cannot sell it but clearly its structure is by far more flexible and functional. Still, the manager directly reports to higher authorities, thus enjoying a reduced administrative autonomy. The joint-venture option may be either with a state-owned or a collective enterprise.

This is a less bureaucratic concept, mainly due to its desirability in terms of foreign funding, technology, sourcing, and/or marketing advantages.

The two last options are the most intriguing solution for a knowledgeable foreign investor or an entrepreneurial Chinese person. Moreover, legislative experience of nearly twenty years permits the optimism that these enterprising forms will spearhead a new era where state-owned and collective enterprises will become the minor players of the upcoming century of Chinese realities.

The service infrastructure of the present Chinese realities appears to be based on governmental directives, most of them originating from the Ministry of Commerce and its departments and bureaus. However, since 1978, the dynamics of market demand have led the traditional state-supported service organizations to a more pragmatic outlook. For example, specialized foreign trade organizations assist trades from medical to silk, and financial organizations imitate foreign counterparts and practices.

It is believed that good international business sense necessitates in-depth understanding of the philosophical and religious tenets of the host country. The second part of this book deals with the major influences that shaped modern-day Chinese thinking.

This part starts by raising issues that are mute in the Western administrative forms. They include the conflict between power and authority, Party and military, director/manager of an enterprise and its local supervising committee. For a newcomer from the West, this can be very confusing. Who is really in control? Who makes the final decision? How will the decision be made? Is this decision going to hold?

It is different, very different, indeed, from the decision-making models found in Europe and in the United States. But it is logical and careful, with its own protocols of interaction. One should observe that the business decision-making models in China, to a great extent, originated in the early stages of the Soviet Union.

Not to mention the political implications, the fact that the Soviets had little experience in managing modern-era enterprises resulted in less than efficient structures, unable to accept innovation or to strive for optimization. This was the paradigm that the Chinese Communist Party accepted. Therefore, there is a business culture embedded in the minds of millions of Chinese bureaucrats. A culture of many checks and balances, of policies from above and counter-tactics from below, of a planned-economy mentality.

Nevertheless, the authors indicate the emerging modern Chinese enterprising thinking that includes autonomous decision making, marketing thinking, usage of internal and external information, and to a great extent, merging proven concepts of Western management with the Chinese traditional *modus operandi*. So, there is a trend–a trend where the old communist paradigms are dying and those of the West survive. No, this is not an easy conclusion.

The Chinese have been traders for thousands of years. They have perfected the art of business dealings and negotiations. Since they have a drastically different perception of the deity than we have in the West, they adopt a very realistic attitude toward the earthly world. However, they do believe and accept powerful leaders. They do follow command. A case in point is Mao Zedong, who twenty years after his death is adored by many almost as a deity. Moreover, basic tenets of life's understanding are embedded in their laws, history, and tales.

For example, the blind acceptance of Mao's strong leadership is attributed to the fact that for hundreds of years the Chinese have been conditioned to readily accept the government's policies and viewpoints. It is interesting that this manifested behavior is affected by two seemingly opposing tendencies: to accept change and to be inflexible. In the West we would have preferred to state our predispositions as being flexible and tolerant. In the Chinese thinking, however, the inflexibility construct aims to accept flexibility within a process that "does not rock the boat," that allows for gradual change, and that even ignores modern-era information collection in inclusion in the decision-making models.

The *yin* and *yang* concepts are anchoring these polarities: to be simple and complex, predictable and unpredictable, straightforward and double-faced, positive and negative. The second part of the volume offers a rare approach in learning about Chinese decision making. Very rarely do Western readers get the opportunity to review such truly vital perspectives of the Chinese enterprise and, therefore, to enhance their negotiation sensitivities.

For a moment, let's venture back to the issue of information collection. In the West, sound information is imperative for sound decision making. Not so in China: Mao was clearly misled (and probably he knew it) when extraordinarily good harvests were quoted during the Great Leap Forward. Still, decisions were made and predictability of events was instrumental in furthering Mao's causes.

It is worth noting that in today's China, predictions on business conditions should be based on current government policies–not on micro-information gathering. In China, business and politics are always intertwined. Moreover, seemingly simple thinking is profoundly complex, often having examined an incredible number of options occasionally resulting in very radical approaches.

However, even in the rapidly changing realities of today's China, the *yin* and *yang* concepts predominate. The understanding of extremes implies the understanding of a "golden mean" between these extremes. This is a critical characteristic of the Chinese thinking and the tenet that made possible the public ownership during the socialist years. The present text makes excellent points orchestrating these unique behaviors that milestone the Chinese approaches to business to life, indeed!

Given, therefore, the complexities, the vast hierarchical structures, the sensitivities, the protocols of behavior, and the respect to authority and power, one can wonder about the Chinese ability to quickly implement business decisions. Here the role of the "powerful leader" becomes important and the solution of importance is chosen. China is not a simple country to do business with, and visiting all parts of Chapter 5 are truly necessary.

In my view, however, Chapter 6 is of ultimate importance to any student of modern-era China. Unquestionably, most military wars had economic motivation. It is, therefore, not at all peculiar that prestigious American MBAs and Japanese advanced business curriculums require the study of *The Art of War of Sun Tzu*. This book goes far beyond Sun Tzu. Illustrations from the Zhou Dynasty (*The Book of Changes*), *Intrigues of the Warring States*, and *The Romance of the Three Kingdoms* (Han Dynasty) point to the fact that Chinese were exceptional military strategists for the duration of their history and not only during the Sun Tzu era.

Through many examples, the reader understands that these strategies are well-engraved in the Chinese thinking concepts. Concepts about "promotion and restraint" or relationships between actual military force and its manifestation, cannot be understood except by pure reference to the original parable and source. The interesting thing is that this reference is very natural to the authors. Two of the three authors are of Chinese origin and were taught this thinking from infancy. They relate to the issues and, by being effectively bicultural, they transmit their unique insights with clarity and depth.

Naturally, a standard walk through Sun Tzu is expected. The effect is unique. The readers get a good understanding of modernear Chinese thinking by studying the teachings that shaped it during thousands of years.

Only at the third part do the readers get exposed to more specific elements of the traditional culture of China, like the concepts of equality, of saving face, or collective determination versus individualistic aspiration, of the role of self versus that of hierarchy. At the end, the reader understands that concepts like the *yin* and *yang* do not relate only to Chinese business negotiations. They are very advanced behavioral structures that when seen in the historical evolutionary dimension, point to a complex negotiation pattern that should have broad applicability beyond China. Thus, the third part probes the implications and tackles the "so what's" raised from the facts and information presented in the first two parts.

I have attempted to present a synopsis of this very unique book, adding from time to time my own insights. I belive this serves two purposes. First, it provides a short understanding of this work. Next, it points to the usefulness of this effort. This is not another text on how to do business in China. It does not elaborate on the rather simplistic daily business affairs in Shanghai or in Beijing. It provides an in-depth understanding of the Chinese business mind, its evolution, and the factors that shape decision making in this vast land. To that extent, the text qualifies to be a "primer" in understanding the Chinese business mind, thus, becoming a unique reference book, and a tool for executive seminars and specialized graduate-level instruction.

John Thanopoulos, PhD
Professor of Marketing and International Business,
Director, International Business Programs
The University of Akron

Preface

Ever since China opened the door to foreign investment in the late 1970s, a steady stream of books on business in the Middle Kingdom has issued forth from publishers around the world. At first, the books sought to introduce China in general terms, typically covering culture, historical background, business practices, and economic developments in one volume geared toward newcomers. Gradually, the books targeting businesspeople became more specialized, and the mid-1990s saw the publication of works such as

> *Management in China During the Age of Reform* by John Child (Cambridge: Cambridge University Press, 1994), an examination of how economic reform changed management in the factories and boardrooms of China's state-owned enterprises;
>
> *Chinese Etiquette and Ethics in Business* by Boye Lafayette de Mente (Lincolnwood, Illinois: NTC Business Books, 1994), an analysis of the values and behavior of Chinese business people; and
>
> *The Management of Human Resources in Chinese Industry* by Malcolm Warner (New York: St. Martin's Press, 1995), a study of labor contracts, wage systems, and other human resource practices in large industrial enterprises.

Business Decision Making in China by Huang Quanyu, Joseph W. Leonard, and Chen Tong is an important new work in this generation of books addressing crucial business issues. In order to help practitioners, consultants, and government leaders involved with business in China, the book first explains the structure of various corporate and organizational forms–from state-owned enterprise and government ministries to joint ventures and nongovernmental organizations—as well as these organizations' relationships to each other. The book goes on to describe the principles and strategies of Chinese decision making, illustrating many actual decisions (as well as some mythical ones). Most important, *Business Decision Making in China* analyzes the whys and wherefores of decision patterns in China. The purpose is to elucidate the thinking of Chinese partners, suppliers, customers, and other business associates so that readers can adapt their own approaches toward business negotiations in order to save time and become more effective. The goal is achieved inasmuch as readers will find themselves pondering business situations and considering new alternatives to a degree never done before.

Business Decision Making in China is a companion text to *A Guide to Successful Business Relations with the Chinese: Opening the Great Wall's Gate* by Huang Quanyu, Richard Andrulis, and Chen Tong (Binghamton, New York: International Business Press, 1994). Both books benefit from lead author Dr. Huang's considerable experience as a consultant focusing on Chinese business. *Business Decision Making in China* contains fascinating anecdotes such as the reading of newspaper editorials with a view to determining favorable investments (cellular telephone systems, yes; commercial complexes, no); the umbrage taken by Chinese negotiators (with disastrous results both for themselves and their German hosts) when told that China could not produce a high-quality grinding head; and the unprofitable but face-saving decision taken by a rising tycoon in Macao.

Filled with thought-provoking examples and insightful stories from the Chinese classics, *Business Decision Making in China* is a guidebook for the intrepid explorers of China's business terrain—for those explorers who not only wish to avoid the pitfalls but also seek to understand and appreciate the landscape along the way.

Martha S. Lee
Senior Research Manager
The William Davidson Institute
University of Michigan Business School

Acknowledgments

This book could be viewed as a sister copy for the previous book, *A Guide to Successful Business Relations with the Chinese: Opening the Great Wall's Gate* (1994), by Huang Quanyu, Richard Andrulis, and Chen Tong. Therefore, we appreciate the efforts of its co-author, Dr. Richard Andrulis at Villanova University.

Many thanks to Quanning Huang, who as an assistant helped with the organizational structure of this book. Drs. Charles Teckman, Nelda Cambron-McCabe, Richard Quantz, and James Burchyett, of Miami University provided their encouragement and support. Special thanks to Dr. Daniel G. Short, Dean; Dr. Joshua L. Schwarz, Chair of the Department of Management; and to the faculty and staff of Miami University's Richard T. Farmer School of Business Administration.

This text was prepared in an environment of total support provided by many friends and colleagues including Drs. William DeMeester, Keith Peterman, Gary Bittner, John Levisky, Brian Glandon, Annette Logan, Melvin Kulbicki, Helaine Alessio, Valeria Freysinger, Robin Vealey, Linda Noelker, Wiley Eldon, Richard Hofmann, Suzanne Kunkel, Robert Applebaum, Lisa Groger, John Patton, Professor Richard Achtzehn, Mr. Robert Howard, Robert Karrow, Ms. Esther Yeagley, Marian Reichard, and Cheryl Smith.

When Huang Quanyu was studying in the United States, his father Huang Zhuyi, an English professor, was struggling with cancer in China. Without his father's encouragement and "secret" English education during the Cultural Revolution, Dr. Huang Quanyu would be unable to write this book in English. Grateful thanks must be given to his father who has passed away to another world.

Finally, we want to thank our families in the United States and China; without your support, we could not have published this book.

PART I: ORGANIZATIONAL STRUCTURES IN CHINA

Many of us may have had the experience of observing mechanics checking our cars. The engine was running; hundreds of parts were working. He magically touched something and all parts suddenly slowed down, or he pushed something and the engine abruptly roared. But without knowing the structure of our cars, he could do nothing to fix them. We can learn many things from this life experience: Architects need to know the structures of buildings, mechanical engineers should know the structures of machines, physicians must know human structures, administrators ought to know organizational structures, and the people who conduct business with China ought to know Chinese organizational structures regarding the operation of administration and decision making.

Before the People's Republic of China was established in 1949, the Chinese Communist Party led its armed forces, the People's Liberation Army (PLA), in more than twenty years of wars. The soldiers and officers of the PLA became the main cadres of the state. Therefore, the structures of Chinese organizations were influenced by the military organizations. On the other hand, the first socialist country in the world, the Soviet Union, had already had more than thirty years of experience to build its models of organizational structure. China also borrowed from the experience of the Soviet Union to form its organizational structures.

Chapter 1

The Structures of Manufacturing Organizations

STATE-OWNED ENTERPRISES

First of all, as we know, China is a socialist country; so, about 43 percent of gross value of industrial output results from Chinese state-owned enterprises.[1] The structures of the state-owned enterprises have very special characteristics. Figure 1.1 shows the current typical structure of state-owned enterprises in China.

Before we analyze and illustrate this chart, we need to clarify several points.

1. This is the most typical kind of Chinese manufacturer, which has between several hundred to several thousand employees.
2. The structures of a Chinese state-owned or collective enterprise are substantially different from a Western company. Most of them own a clinic or hospital, dining hall(s), store(s), housing/apartments/condominiums, nursery or kindergarten, elementary school or high school, barbershop, library, and theater, etc. These business enterprises operate as largely autonomous communities. As a result, the overall manager takes the role of a "prime minister" who needs to take care of and direct every affair in this "kingdom."
3. In the past, the Communist Youth League Committee could be a mass organization under the leadership of the manager. Now, it is more likely to be led by the Party leadership as a political organization.
4. The Women's Commission often shares an office with the enterprise union. This commission is in charge of birth control educa-

tion and women's affairs. The functions of the union differ substantially from American unions. The union of a Chinese organization (manufacturer) is usually in charge of recreation and some other activities including sports, art performances, games, movies, funerals, and the library.
5. The school(s), which may include a nursery, kindergarten, an elementary school, a high school, or even a university, have the dilemma of where to locate their positions within the overall enterprise structure. Some organizations put a nursery or a kindergarten under the leadership of logistics, some organize an elementary school or a high school under the direction of the propaganda department, some may put the school(s) under the authority of the union. There is no single model for the administration of the schools.
6. The logistics department is extremely complex. Since most employees live within the enterprise's walls, the logistics department manages the housing arrangements. In this autonomous community, the employees and their families require services such as food and medical treatment. Thus, providing a dining hall and establishing safeguards for the prevention of epidemics and common medical treatment are considered duties of the enterprise. A small or medium-sized factory usually places its clinic under the direct management of its logistics section.
7. Some manufacturers place their security departments under the Party leadership as Figure 1.1 indicates. Other enterprises may still keep security under the direct control of the managers.
8. The business relations between the varied departments and the workshops (work stations or shop floor) are subtle and complex. The various departments often give technical advice, suggestions, and even operating directions to the workshops. The departments report to the manager, and in some cases, they may direct the workshops by an order from the manager. The workshops report to the manager too, if necessary. While these workshops have some discretionary authority, all major decisions must be approved by the manager.

From Figure 1.1, we can see that the relationship between the Party secretary and the manager is unique. Who listens to whom?

FIGURE 1.1. Organizational Structure of a Typical State-Owned Enterprise in China

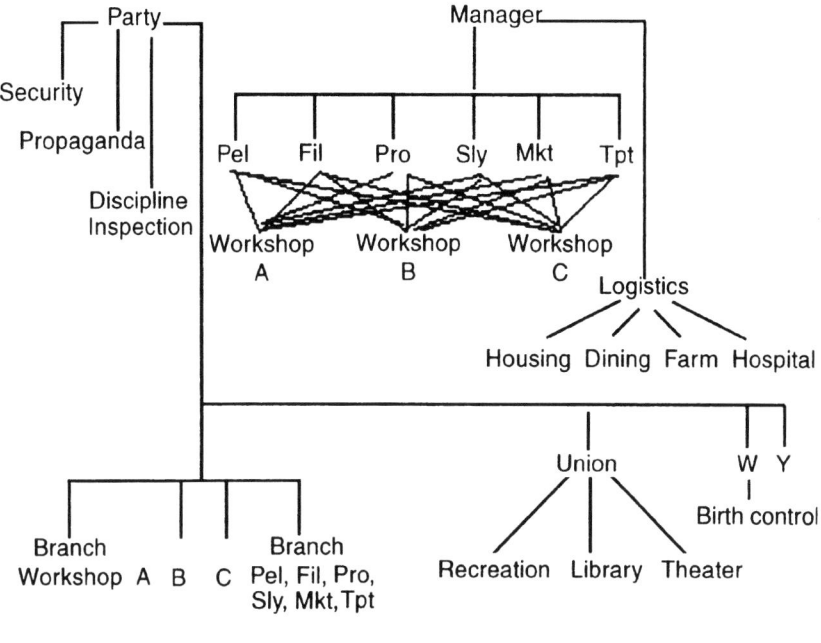

Notes: Pel = Personnel Section
Fil = Financial Section
Pro = Production Section
Sly = Supply Section
Mkt = Marketing Section
Tpt = Transport Section
W = Women's Commission
Y = Communist Youth League Committee (Branch)

Who is really in control of the manufacturing enterprise? From the figure it appears that they do not listen to each other, and the manager is essentially controlling the entire factory system. The manager is in power to manage personnel (through the personnel department), finance (through the financial department), manufacturing (through the production, supply, marketing, and transportation departments) and daily lives (through the logistics department, etc.) These four parts, personnel, finance, manufacturing, and daily lives, are the basic foundations of power for a manufacturer. Other than propaganda about political issues, the Party does not control the essential power in a Chinese manufacturing enterprise. In general, these conclusions are true. Nevertheless, the facts which we will address in the next chapters may be much more complicated in reality. For example, the personnel section is under the direct control of the manager, but the Party has a certain amount of authority (sometimes very strong) in arranging the cadres' positions. In brief, the manager has the legal authority to manage the manufacturer according to Chinese law. Figure 1.1 is reflective of the current situation in China. Since the People's Republic of China was established in 1949, the business organizations have moved through five stages of jockeying for power and control. Chapter 5 will delineate the characteristics of the power structure between the Party secretary and the manager.

The structures of Chinese organizations are influenced by the military organizational structures. A Chinese manufacturer is an independent entity, but it also has some of the characteristics of a military base, which also contains housing, dining, medical treatment, schools, stores, and recreation. Interestingly enough, during the Cultural Revolution, some manufacturing units were referred to as military units; for example, a mechanical repairing "company," a forge "platoon," and a carpentry "squad." Others were referred to by numbers: "company" one, "platoon" two, or "squad" three. The head of a workshop was called the "company commander," and a party secretary for a larger workshop was called the "battalion political instructor."

Chinese manufacturers ranging from 10,000 up to a 100,000 employees, while not common, do exist. These enormously large businesses are organized somewhat differently, as shown in Figure 1.2.

This can be better understood with the following clarifications:

1. There is a general manager's office and several vice general managers under the direction of the general manager, who is the symbol of the organization's headquarters.
2. The departments directly under the headquarters could include personnel, financial, production, supply, marketing, research, quality control, public relations, armed (includes the security section), logistics, transportation, and perhaps one or two others. The union and the women's commission are more

often under leadership of the Party. Each department could have several sections. For example, the personnel department may contain the education (for employees' children), training (for employees), human resource planning, performance appraisal, salary administration, etc. The marketing department may include advertising, marketing research, sales, and/or an international division. For these reasons, the detailed structure of the general manager's role could be complicated far beyond the scope of the illustrative figure.

3. Schools, including elementary, middle, high, vocational, technical, or even a university could be independent, or could be placed under an educational section of the personnel department.
4. Business A, Business B, and Business C could be the branch companies that manufacture different products, or make different component parts for further manufacturing use. For example, an automobile corporation may contain several branch companies (manufacturers) in which Business A makes the engine, Business B makes the body, and Business C makes electronic parts.
5. There could be a direct relation between departments A, B, and C and the business units A, B, and C. For instance, the financial department might report to headquarters but have business relations with A, B, and C. A, B, and C might report to headquarters, but have business relationships with the supply department, as well. These complex organizational structures have some similarities with matrix organizations in large Western corporations, but to think of them as the same is too simplistic.
6. Sections A, B, and C under the businesses A, B, and C could be personnel, finance, production, etc. Likewise, there would be direct business relationships between the sections A, B, and C and factories A, B, and C. For example, suppose that business A manufactures automobile engines, factory A is a foundry plant, factory B is a heat treatment mill, and factory C is a mechanical processing works. Then, the personnel section not only reports to the manager of business A, but also has business relationships with factories A, B, and C. Several other structural configurations are also possible.

7. The business relations between the varied departments and businesses A, B, and C are not relations between the higher level and the lower level. Generally speaking, the various departments only give technical advice, suggestions, and guidance to businesses A, B, and C. The business relations between the various sections and factories A, B, and C are similar to the business relationships between the various departments and the businesses A, B, and C.
8. In terms of the clarifications of 4, 5, and 6, we can simply add the first figure of this chapter as a detailed subchart for businesses A, B, and C. In fact, for some huge corporations, if businesses A, B, or C were still very large, we may even use Figure 1.1 as a subchart under factories A, B, or C.
9. Many corporations may put the Communist Youth League Committee under the leadership of the Party because the general managers have far too many tasks to oversee.
10. The Party committee of a giant corporation usually contains an organizational department that handles the files (archives) of the Party members and the promotions of the cadres who are Party members. Because most individuals in the cadres are Party members, this department has a deep and subtle relationship with the personnel department. Furthermore, it is not unusual for the director of the organizational department to also be the director of the personnel department. In general, the personnel department takes care of the common employees, and the organizational department is in charge of cadres and administrators. Hence, the organizational department is a critical department for the Party leadership, involving itself in general administration.

From Figure 1.2, we can see that the general manager is in a more powerful position and placed in direct control of finance, production, personnel, and daily life decision making. The only difference illustrated is that there are more organizational levels within a similar structure under the general manger. The relationship between the secretary of the Party committee and the general manager in a giant corporation is basically the same as that of the standard-sized manufacturer that we addressed previously. Yet there may be the

FIGURE 1.2. Organizational Structure of Large Chinese Manufacturers

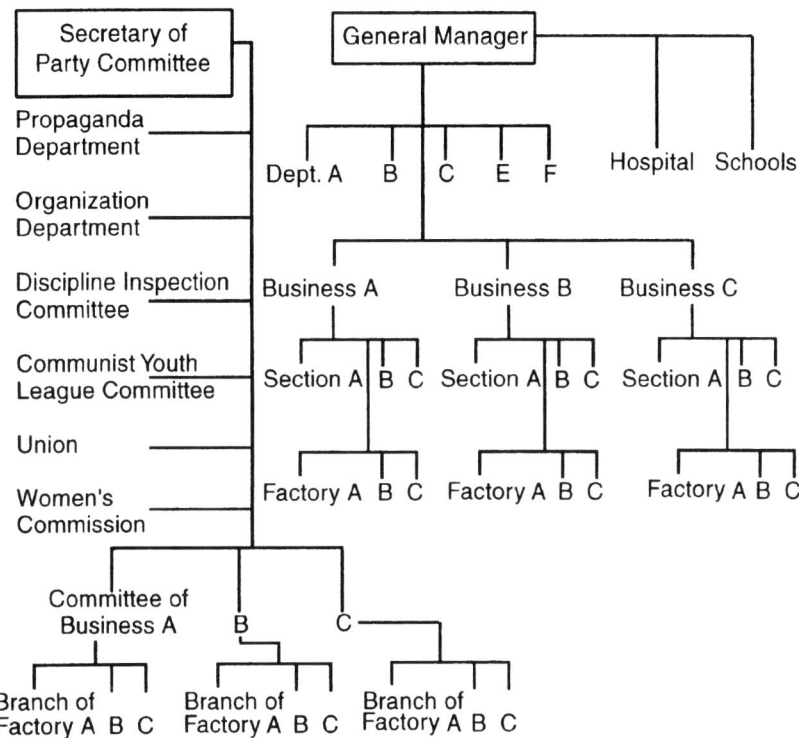

delicate distinction that there are more party members to organize a party committee in a giant corporation, thus having a stronger impact on the business decision making.

COLLECTIVE ENTERPRISES

Collective enterprises account for about 38 percent of China's gross value of industrial output.[2] The concept of collective enterprise, in a sense, is similar to the American public company because both are owned by a group of people. Nevertheless, there are some critical differences. First, the Chinese collective enterprises, in many cases, are equally owned by every member of certain groups.

In the Tong Xiang Flocking Factory, for example, it could be that everyone in Xiang[3] equally owns this factory. The American public companies are owned by various shareholders: some are major holders, others are small. Second, the American shareholders can indirectly or sometimes even directly influence top management through the corporate board of directors. Of course, a majority (more than 50 percent) of shareholders can theoretically dictate the strategic direction and administration of the company. The Chinese collective enterprises are equally owned by every member of certain groups, and directed by the leaders of the groups such as the Xiang government. An individual in a large group that may have more than 10,000 members could have no impact on overall administration. Indeed, the Chinese collective enterprises are almost the same as many church organizations in America. Every member of the church "equally" owns the church property that is managed by a set of administrators. An individual member of a huge church could probably have no influence on the administrative body, either. Third, the individual who "owns" the Chinese collective enterprises will be unable to sell what is "owned," just as a member of a church in America "owns" church properties, but cannot sell what he or she "owns." Certainly, the shareholders of an American corporation can buy or sell shares of the stock in the open market at any time.

The structure of a typical Chinese collective enterprise is illustrated in Figure 1.3.

FIGURE 1.3. Structure of Typical Chinese Collective Enterprise

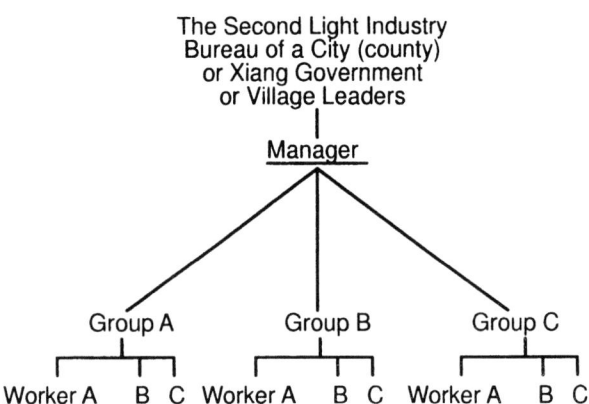

The following points explain the workings of the more standard-sized business:

1. This is a small Chinese collective enterprise consisting of fewer than 100 employees. This size enterprise has significant structural differences from the giant business enterprises previously discussed.
2. These small Chinese collective enterprises may have just one or two Party members, or sometimes no Party members. The higher authorities of the Chinese collective enterprises are village leaders, neighborhood committee leaders (in a city), Xiang/town government officials, or from the secondary light industry bureau of a city.
3. Another name of the second light industry bureau could be the "handicraft industry bureau." As the name implies, Chinese collective enterprises were formerly engaged in handicraft industries, which were labor intensive, and depended on a low level of technology, relatively inexpensive equipment, and little capital expenditures. This is why they were administered by the "second" light industry bureau. Of course, a few Chinese collective enterprises were involved in heavy industry and employed high levels of science and technology trades.

From Figure 1.3, we can see that this organizational structure is simple. The manager directly controls the leaders of the work groups or directly supervises the workers. The manager does not have a formalized departmental structure. Thus, the business functional activities such as personnel, finance, production, supply, and marketing are all carried out by the direct managerial authority of the single manager. This means that he or she must be a generalist and take on all the responsibilities. The manager directly reports to the higher authorities (e.g., village leaders, the neighborhood committee, the Xiang/town government, or the second light industry bureau.) This system has some limitations concerning span of control and autonomy. If the higher authorities have too many collective enterprises to direct, the managers will have stronger authority to make business decisions without the direct approval of the higher authority. On the contrary, when a higher authority has only a few collective enterprises to lead, the higher authority may often directly participate in business decision making for the collective enterprise.

Since reforming and opening in 1978, Chinese collective enterprises have been playing a larger role in China's economic development. As a result of inadequate technology, engineers, equipment, material resources, and funding, collective enterprises have shown stronger dynamics than the state-owned enterprises. The most famous Chinese collective enterprises were those of Daqiu village, which included the modern steel mills. Daqiu village's collective enterprises have conducted more than 200 million yuans (one U.S. dollar equals about 8.32 yuans) of output value, and have made Daqiu the richest village in China. The leader of Daqiu village's collective enterprise, Yu Zuomin, the secretary of the village Party, was jailed in 1995. It was reported that while he was making successful business decisions, he had illegally arrested an employee who was killed by Yu's trusted followers.

JOINT-VENTURE ENTERPRISES

Joint-venture enterprises in China can be categorized into several types: a foreign investor combines with a state-owned enterprise, a foreign investor combines with a collective enterprise, a foreign investor combines with a private enterprise, or a foreign investor combines with another foreign enterprise, or with an investor from Taiwan, Hong Kong, or Aomen (Macao). The first type is the most common—a foreign investor joins a state-owned enterprise. The second most popular joint venture is when the foreign investor combines with a collective enterprise. The reason for this is simple. By making use of its governmental background, a state-owned enterprise or a collective enterprise is able to provide what a foreign investor really needs, such as funds, governmental examination, and approval for land. Furthermore, there are two approaches for this kind of joint venture. In one approach there is already an existing state-owned enterprise or collective enterprise. The foreign investor brings funds, technology, and a market to combine with this enterprise to reform and/or remodel it. The other approach is that a foreign investor and a Chinese investor both invest funds to build a brand new enterprise—either for an international market or for the Chinese domestic market. Chinese investors prefer the first, and that is the current trend. Figure 1.4 illustrates the organizational structure of a joint-venture enterprise in which a foreign investor has combined with an existing state-owned enterprise.

FIGURE 1.4. Structure of Joint-Venture Enterprise: Foreign Investor Combined with State-Owned Enterprise

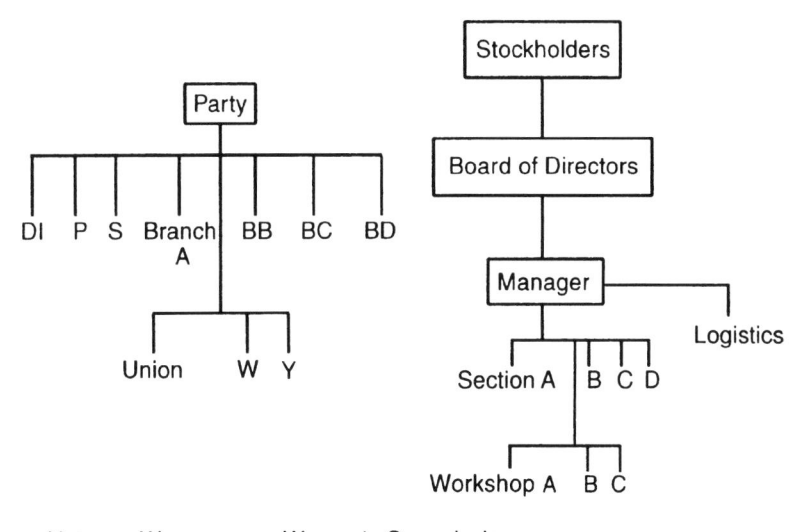

Notes:
W = Women's Commission
Y = Communist Youth League Committee (Branch)
DI = Discipline Inspection
P = Propaganda
S = Security
BB, BC, BD = Branch B, Branch C, Branch D

The following essential factors need to be explored:

1. This organizational structure of the joint venture is usually most appropriate for the enterprise in which the Chinese side holds 51 percent or more of the stock ownership.
2. This existing benchmark criteria is the typical state-owned enterprise to develop an organizational structure for the joint-venture enterprise. Compared to state-owned enterprises, the

most significant changes are the adding of the stockholders and the board of directors.
3. The stockholders are the Chinese government and the foreign investor(s). The board of directors has the supreme power to make final strategic decisions. While the board has a minimum of three members, it usually has five to nine. The proportion of board members on each side will depend on the proportions of the stock holdings. The board members are appointed by the stockholders, and their office term is four years. After four years, the members can continue their positions with an approval from the stockholders.[4]
4. The Sections A, B, C, and D could be personnel, finance, production, etc. To improve efficiency, the board has the power to reduce, increase, or combine these sections. Furthermore, the board can change the workshops or make other organizational changes.
5. In terms of "The Union Law of the People's Republic of China," the employees of a joint-venture enterprise have the right to organize their union. A joint-venture enterprise of 200 to 500 employees can have a full-time cadre; 501 to 1,000 employees must have two full-time staff members; 1,001 to 1,500 employees have four full-time positions; and, if an enterprise has less than 200 employees, one full-time position is required. The foreign representatives such as board members, foreign managers, or vice managers have no rights to join the union, but a foreign worker who is not a representative and who receives a salary will have the right to join the union. Since there has already been a union in the state-owned enterprise—the Chinese side of the joint venture—the board does not have the legal right to dissolve it. The employees also have the right to have or establish other collective entities such as the Women's Commission and the Communist Youth League Committee.[5]
6. The logistics section still has many important responsibilities. Many foreign investors do not like the logistics department because they feel that it is a staff function that not only increases the costs of the products but also makes the enterprise cumbersome and overstaffed. Therefore, some foreign investors try to merely organize a joint venture with a single workshop, not

the whole enterprise. Sometimes, the Chinese side may accept this idea. Nevertheless, the problems have not been resolved yet. Because the actual income of the employees in the joint-venture workshop is generally about three times that of the other employees in the same enterprise, the other employees and staff might not cooperate with those of the joint-venture workshop. Without others' assistance and cooperation, the joint-venture workshop can only accomplish little. For example, to provide for a successful workplace environment, assistance and cooperation from the financial section and supply section are extremely vital, and cooperation from the dining hall, hospital, and nursery or kindergarten are necessary, too. Suppose a kindergarten teacher does not take good care of children of the employees in the joint-venture workshop. Will those employees work hard and perform well? Obviously not! Furthermore, if the financial and supply sections do not offer the proper assistance and cooperation, how can any products be made in the joint-venture workshop?

7. According to "The Law of the People's Republic of China on Chinese-Foreign Joint Ventures," the manager or a vice manager could be either a foreign national or a Chinese. This decision is rendered by the board of directors. The board also has the authority to remove an unsatisfactory manager or vice manager. When the two or more groups have differences or conflicting perceptions about the manager's or vice manager's performance, a single side does not have the right to remove the manager or vice manager. If one group insists on removing the manager or vice manager, after an investigation, the board can make a termination decision with a two-thirds majority vote. Without a decision from the board, any appointment or removal from any single side is illegal.[6]

8. In a joint-venture enterprise, the Party leadership is obviously weaker than in other Chinese organizational forms. Nonetheless, since the Chinese government is the major stockholder, it may understandably have undue influence when it appoints its board members, and manager or vice manager. However, the Chinese governments (central and local) and Chinese people are sincerely striving to attract foreign investment, science and

technology, experts, and equipment, and the Chinese governments foresee great potential economic benefit from these foreign joint ventures. The governments have given serious respect—perhaps sometimes too much respect—to foreign investors. It will be interesting to see how the Chinese government continues to treat joint-venture enterprises.
9. Some large collective enterprises may have this kind of organizational structure when they become joint-venture enterprises.

In summary, the board is fully empowered to make business decisions in a joint-venture enterprise. With foreign funds, science and technology, markets, and administrative concepts, a joint-venture enterprise usually outperforms its state-owned counterparts.

Brand-new but similarly sized joint-venture enterprises that are being invested in by the Chinese government and one or more foreign investors will all have a comparable organizational structure. The key difference is that the role of the Party, however, may not exist as in Figure 1.4. Nonetheless, some Party members may arrange to be on the board and/or to play some other important roles in this newly proposed form. This is understandable because the Chinese Communist Party is the core of leadership that has been clearly stated in the Chinese Constitution, and every foreign investor who is going to invest in China must be prepared to deal with the Chinese Communist Party. In fact, many Westerners who have had an opportunity to deal with China have found that many Party members are very open, intelligent, and friendly, not the fierce and savage beasts that many Western people believe. As we know, the former Primary Minister of the People's Republic of China, Zhou Enlai, was a friend of Dr. Henry Kissinger, President George Bush is a friend of Deng Xiaoping, and Boris Yeltsin is President Bill Clinton's friend. Additionally, Mikhail Gorbachev, Hu Yaobang, and Zhao Ziyang are famous influential leaders known worldwide.

Some small foreign investors would like to find small collective enterprises or private companies to be their joint-venture partners. While this is not easy to arrange, with time and persistence, it can be done. Figure 1.5 shows a typical organizational structure of this kind of joint venture.

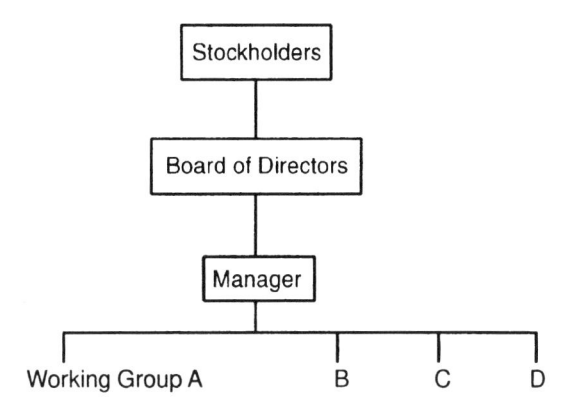

FIGURE 1.5. Structure of a Small Partner Joint-Venture Enterprise

```
                    ┌──────────────┐
                    │ Stockholders │
                    └──────┬───────┘
                           │
                 ┌─────────┴────────┐
                 │ Board of Directors│
                 └─────────┬────────┘
                           │
                      ┌────┴────┐
                      │ Manager │
                      └────┬────┘
          ┌────────────┬───┴───┬────────┐
  Working Group A      B       C        D
```

Based on Figure 1.5, we want to explain:

1. For this kind of joint-venture enterprise, the Chinese side usually is not concerned if it does not hold more than 50 percent of the stocks. The major shareholder could be either the Chinese local governments such as a neighborhood committee (in a city), a Xiang/town government, or a city government, or the foreign investor. When the partner of this joint-venture enterprise is a village, the village leaders are likely to play a critical role as shareholders.
2. There are usually three board members, and village leaders are likely to be directly involved in the managerial workings of the board of directors.
3. A small collective enterprise usually does not have a union or a Women's Commission. Nevertheless, since young people like to join activities together, the enterprise may need an organization such as the Communist Youth League Branch.
4. A small collective enterprise usually does not have logistical support mechanisms such as dining halls, clinics, schools, and/or housing. This is one of the concessions made to attract small foreign investors.
5. This kind of small collective enterprise usually does not require much start-up capital. The Chinese side usually is not concerned whether it holds a majority of the stock. As a result, a pre-existing Chinese enterprise is not necessary. Even though the

legal stipulation ("The Law of the People's Republic of China on Chinese-Foreign Joint Ventures" and the other relative regulations) requires that both groups of a joint venture must have capital funds invested, it is common for counties, Xiangs, towns, or villages to use a piece of land and their power as start-up capital in a joint venture with a foreign investor. (We will discuss this issue in more detail in a later chapter.) Many small foreign investors with a Chinese background (having relatives in China, having studied Chinese culture or lived in China, or having powerful connections and friends in China) prefer this kind of joint venture.
6. A technical section or department is not necessary because of the simplicity of its manual operations and/or simple equipment operations of the enterprise. Typical products of this type of joint venture would include toys, clothing, and even component parts and subassemblies to be used in another joint-venture enterprise.

To compare this with Figure 1.3, which details the organizational structure of a collective enterprise, we can conclude that both structures are very simple. In general, the joint venture should be more effective. Nevertheless, some undemocratic administrating such as unsafe working environments, overload of working hours, etc., may occur.

Many foreign investors are interested in the large existing state-owned enterprises. When an agreement of joint venture has been reached, the organizational structure as illustrated in Figure 1.6 could be a typical model.

Some explanations need to be made:

1. This is an organizational structure for a large joint-venture enterprise with more than 10,000 employees. For this form of joint-venture enterprise, the Chinese side might strongly desire to hold more than 50 percent of the stock. In some cases, they would prefer the enterprise to remain a state-owned organization rather than to hold less than 50 percent of the stock.
2. There can be more than eleven members of the board of directors. When there are as many as twenty-five or thirty-five members of the board, a standing board can be established. This standing board is composed of members from the regular board.

3. There is one general manager with several vicegeneral managers. The general manager and the first vicegeneral manager must include one Chinese citizen and one foreign citizen unless the foreign investor(s) agree that both managers can be Chinese. The members of the board can include the general manager, the vice-general managers, or other persons in senior positions.[7]
4. Departments A, B, C, and D are most often the financial and management department, the technical development department, the production and planning department, and the supply and marketing department. The financial and management department includes a manager and a general accountant. This department is in charge of finance, accounting, personnel, and other management (e.g., logistics) activities. The other three departments are structured similarly. A manager and a general engineer run the technical development department. A production manager and a sales manager are in charge of the production and planning department, and the supply and marketing department is similarly staffed.
5. Under the Party leadership, there is nothing shown under committee D, because this is a committee comprised of all departments, and some other units (e.g., the general manager's office, the union, the Women's Commission, the Communist Youth League Committee, the propaganda department, and the organizational department, etc.). Likewise, branch D is for sections A, B, C, and some others.

If the Chinese side and the foreign investor(s) agree to build a large, brand-new joint-venture enterprise, the basic organizational structure will be similar to the above chart except for the following points:

1. The role of the Party would probably be changed because a strong committee may not be established, but a smaller and weaker Party branch is likely to be established.
2. Schools, hospitals, and some other logistical parts may not exist.
3. The union, the Women's Committee, and the Communist Youth League Committee will be organized as mass organizations, not political organizations.

FIGURE 1.6. Structure of Joint-Venture Enterprise: Foreign Investor Combined with Large State-Owned Enterprise

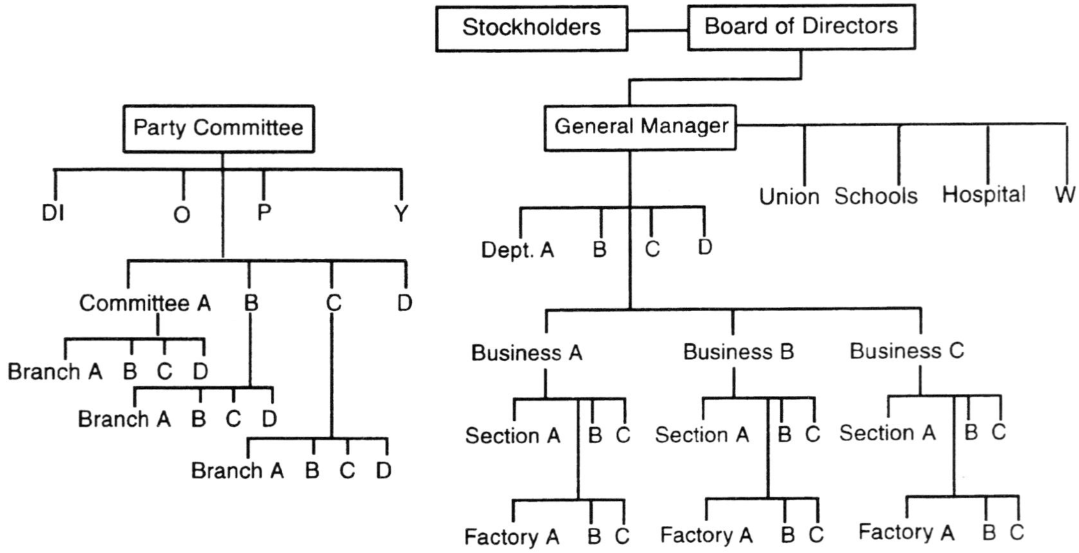

Notes: W = Women's Commission
Y = Communist Youth League Committee
DI = Discipline Inspection Committee
P = Propaganda Department
O = Organizational Department

20

FOREIGN-OWNED ENTERPRISES

Currently, there are a variety of foreign-owned companies conducting business in China. Owned by investors from various nations, these organizations have varying structures.

Before we illustrate the organizational structures of the foreign-owned enterprises, we would like to share a very interesting Chinese story, "Southern Orange and Northern Jyy,"[8] with our readers.

> Long, long ago, Yan-zi was once sent on a diplomatic mission to Chu State as a messenger of Qi State. The king of Chu State planned to shame him. When the banquet was bustling with noise and activity, two soldiers escorted a bound man across the hall. The king of Chu State asked them, "Who is he?" The soldiers answered, "He is a man from Qi State. He is a robber!" The king fixed his eyes on Yan-zi and asked, "Are the people of Qi State usually robbers?" Yan-zi smiled and said, "I once heard this from someone: 'Oranges raised south of the Huai River are oranges, while those raised north of the Huai River change into jyy. Though their leaves are alike, the taste of their fruits are different.' Why so? Because the natural environment and climate differs widely between the south and the north of the Huai River. The people of Qi State were not robbers when they were in Qi State, but as soon as they came to Chu State, they would become robbers. Does the natural environment and climate of Chu State make people become robbers?"
>
> The king smiled wryly and said, "Making a joke to a scholar is wrong. I am sorry!"[9]

Though this is a joke, it reveals a truth: an orange will be changed into a jyy if it is grown north of the river because of the different natural environment and climate. If an orange is so, what about an organization?

Let us study the organizational structure of a typical, but not large, Western-owned enterprise (Figure 1.7).

In general, there is not too much difference between the organizational structure of an American enterprise doing business in the United States and one doing business in China. There are, however, some subtle points that we must explain:

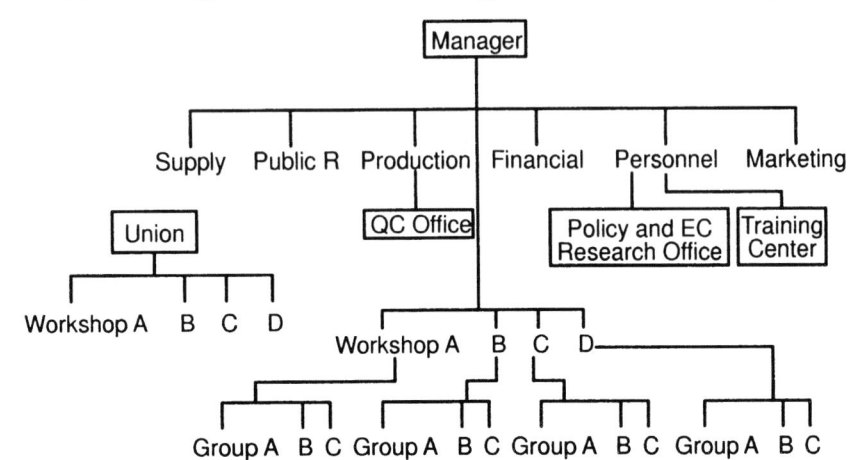

FIGURE 1.7. Organizational Structure of a Typical Western-Owned Enterprise

```
                                    Manager
         ┌──────────┬──────────┬─────┴────┬──────────┬──────────┐
       Supply   Public R   Production  Financial  Personnel   Marketing
                            [QC Office]           ┌─────────┐ ┌────────┐
       [Union]                                    │Policy and EC│ │Training│
                                                  │Research Office│ │ Center │
   ┌────┬───┬───┐                           
Workshop A  B  C  D        ┌────┬───┬───┐
                        Workshop A  B  C  D
                        ┌──┬─┐ ┌──┬─┐ ┌──┬─┐ ┌──┬─┐
                       Group A B C Group A B C Group A B C Group A B C
```

Notes: Public R = Public Relations
        QC Office = Quality Control Office
        Policy and EC Research Office = Policy and Enterprise
          Culture Research Office

1. The relative Chinese laws and regulations do not require a "board of directors" for a foreign-owned enterprise. Many small foreign-owned enterprises do not have their own boards. Of course, large foreign-owned enterprises that have their branches in different Chinese provinces may have their board of directors in China. Most small foreign-owned enterprises operate as branch or subsidiaries of larger foreign corporations. Thus, the board would be functioning at the corporate level, and it would not have direct impact in China frequently. In the case of a joint venture, however, a board of directors can serve the function of resolving contradictions or conflicts that may arise between any involved group.

2. Generally speaking, a foreign-owned enterprise that does not entirely supply its materials for production from foreign countries must have a very strong supply department. For most production materials, supply has been falling short of demand (China has been the largest purchaser of materials for production for many years). To further complicate commerce, some

means of production are strictly controlled by the state, which means that allocation is based on governmental controls, and price plays a secondary role or even no role whatsoever. Thus, having the cash funds does not ensure that an enterprise will be able to procure the needed products or services. There is a Chinese saying "The cleverest housewife cannot cook a meal without food—one cannot make bricks without straw." Therefore, without a strong supply department, a foreign-owned enterprise that does not entirely supply its materials of production from outside sources could face a very awkward situation.
3. In general, a foreign-owned enterprise that does not completely sell its products internationally must have a very strong marketing department. While China has had a buying market for a long time, there is no assurance that a Western company can find a market for its products in China. The selling aspect of the marketing function is often a critical success factor for foreign-owned enterprises attempting to sell their products in China. To facilitate this, many companies use the method of a commission for buyers. Commission for buyers is a very special way of selling in China. In 1994, the author, Huang Quanyu, and Dr. Richard Andrulis went to lecture at Guangxi Economic Administrative Cadres Institute in China. When the audiences asked questions about the method of commission for buyers, Huang Quanyu could not find a proper official English definition of it. In short, the way is to deduct a certain percentage of the sales volume to refund to the buyers, either under the table or openly. Namely, it could be labeled by an American nickname, a "kickback." Of course, for the very popular goods of the foreign-owned enterprises, the situation may be very different.
4. A foreign-owned enterprise that either must entirely supply its means of production from outside of China or not, and either must sell its products to the Chinese domestic market or not, must have a very powerful public relations department. Even if a foreign-owned enterprise completely supplies its production materials and sells 100 percent of its goods to an international market, the company still must deal with governmental organizations, must ship its products through Chinese shipping

companies, and must deal with the Chinese infrastructure (e.g., Chinese phone company, power company, water supplier, etc.). The public relationship, or "connection," is an extremely interesting, but delicate and complex issue. If some readers want to learn more about this complicated knowledge, please consult *A Gate to Successful Business Relations with the Chinese: Opening the Great Wall's Gate* by Huang Quanyu, Richard Andrulis, and Chen Tong, published by The International Business Press, an imprint of The Haworth Press in 1994. In brief, without a harmonious and friendly relationship with relative and vital organizations and persons, a company will face a quite difficult situation. For this reason, a very powerful and sophisticated public relations department is extremely critical.

5. Without human resources availability, a company cannot move a single business step. Hence, the personnel department is absolutely important as well. The activities of the personnel department in China are somewhat different from those in Western companies. Dr. Joseph W. Leonard explained those differences in his book chapter, "Strategic Influences on the Management of Human Resources: An Exploratory Analysis of Chinese versus United States Practices." For those readers seeking more details, please read it.[10] When compared to Western standards, most employees were raised and educated in very different cultural environments with markedly different social backgrounds, economic systems, and administrative situations. Thus, training becomes a key variable to bring the Chinese workforce up to desirable output levels. This is a delicate balancing act. Clearly, the Chinese employees could never be totally transformed into Western employees. They should not be completely changed into American employees either, because they possess original strengths that American employees might not have. For these reasons, the personnel department will have the unduly unique and consequential job of retraining; thus, many foreign-owned enterprises have their training centers under the leadership of the personnel departments.

6. A policy and enterprise cultural research office is necessary. China, with its social and economic changes, is currently "groping" for a whole new set of laws, policies, and regulations.

Accordingly, the laws and policies are very changeable. (We will discuss this in detail in Chapter 5.) For a foreign-owned enterprise, researching the policies is sensitive and critical work. As the story "Southern Orange and Northern Jyy" indicated, an American enterprise in China will be unable to be a 100 percent American enterprise because of the special Chinese cultural environment, and most of its employees would be unable to be completely changed into American-like employees–even though the enterprise operates the company according to American methods. As a result, the American company must research the culture of the country where the new enterprise is based. For many companies and many managers, this objective reality is independent from human will. The policy and enterprise cultural research office may be under the personnel department or some other departments, or may simply be an independent department.

7. While there would usually not be a Women's Committee or the Communist Youth League Committee, a union would be the norm. By the legal terms of "The Law of the People's Republic of China on Foreign-Owned Enterprises," a union has to be organized in a foreign-owned enterprise.
8. Foreign-owned enterprises usually do not have the logistical burdens that the Chinese state-owned and some joint-venture enterprises do. Although some may have dining halls and employee training centers, very few–if any–would provide hospitals, housing, or schools. Therefore, many Chinese couples would prefer one partner (husband or wife) to work for a state-owned enterprise in which their family would be well-taken care of, while the other could work for a foreign-owned enterprise for the inordinately higher salary, and also with a new chance for career opportunities.
9. The Party does not exist in a foreign-owned enterprise. But a foreign-owned enterprise does have to commence business relations with some governmental organizations. For example, to address a contract problem, the enterprise needs to associate with the governmental ministry of foreign economic relations and trade; to solve any business problem (supplying materials, electricity, transportation), the enterprise ought to deal with the governmental planning commission or economic commission; and to

tackle any common administrative problem, the enterprise will need to contact a relative governmental bureau, such as the light industry bureau, heavy industry bureau, etc. Of course, any governmental organizations or their affiliated organizations cannot interfere with any of the legal business activities of a foreign-owned enterprise.

In summary, the organizational structure of a foreign-owned enterprise in China does have some minor differences from one found in its native country. Those minor differences are not required by law, policy, or regulation from China. There are some necessary and critical adjustments for a foreign-owned enterprise that need to be well-understood in order to better adapt sound business practices in the Chinese cultural and social environment.

INDIVIDUAL COMPANIES

Over the past decade, private economy has been developing extremely rapidly in China. According to incomplete statistics, there are more than 12 million individual companies in China.[11] In the register capital in the Guangdong province, which borders on Hong Kong, about 30 percent of businesses are state owned, 16 percent are collectively owned, and about 53 percent are privately owned. Of course, this is a very special province in China, as it has been designated by the central government to serve as a facilitating model to test the free-market economic system. Thus, private ownership is certainly not so high in the other provinces and autonomous regions. There are approximately 1 million people who own more than 1 million yuans of property or capital, and about 100 people who have more than 100 million yuans—this amounts to more that 12 million U.S. dollars. For example, Mr. Mou Qizhong, the president of the private Nan De Group Cooperation, who is believed to be one of the richest men in China, owns more than 300 factories and companies in China, Hong Kong, Eastern Europe, and Russia. He intends to build highways, huge power stations, a university, and satellites. This level of affluence simply cannot be compared to the majority of individual companies in China. A typical individual company operating in China today follows the structural form shown in Figure 1.8.

FIGURE 1.8. Organizational Structure of a Typical Independent Company in China

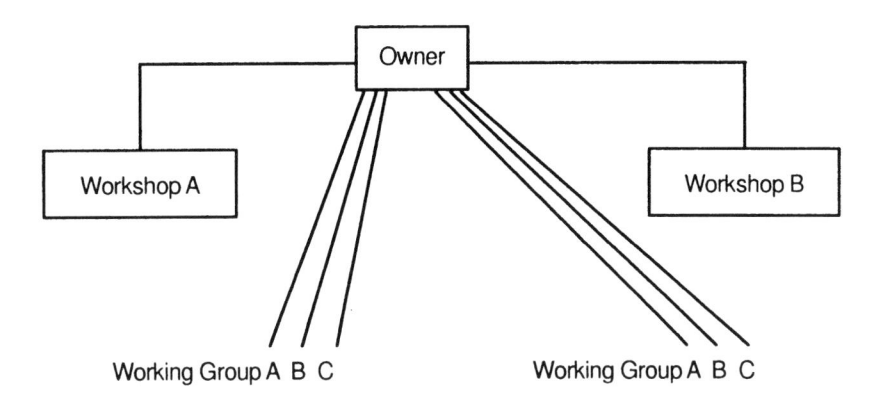

```
                          ┌─────────┐
              ┌───────────│  Owner  │───────────┐
              │          /│    \    \           │
              │        /  │     \    \          │
        ┌──────────┐ /    │      \    \   ┌──────────┐
        │Workshop A│      │       \    \  │Workshop B│
        └──────────┘      │        \    \ └──────────┘
                       /  │         \    \
                      /   │          \    \

     Working Group A  B  C         Working Group A  B  C
```

To explain this figure, we need to illustrate the following descriptive points:

1. We do not have the exact figures, but we believe that the vast majority of the 12 million Chinese individual companies are stores and restaurants with only a few employees. Obviously, small retailers and the like are not comparable to the types of organizational enterprises we have been discussing so far in this book. Nonetheless, there are a significant number of private manufacturers in China. We believe that most of these manufacturers employ from around ten to nearly one hundred employees. Figure 1.8 is representative of most of their situations.
2. The figure resembles a crab who is running horizontally, brandishing claws–doing whatever it wants. Indeed, this structure describes what an owner may be running in his or her private company. The author, Huang Quanyu, inspected a private company, Wu County Hardware Co., Ltd., in November 1994. The company had about twenty small machines in two large rooms that we unofficially called "workshops." The owner, Mr. Feng, had about sixty to eighty employees who were divided into different groups to operate different machines. There was a very small room, which looked like a janitor's room, just beside the gate. Mr. Feng was very proud to tell his visitors, "This is my office. That's good enough! I don't want to put money into my

office, I don't sit in my office anyway. I prefer to save money for more machines." Mr. Feng had only his nephew as an assistant. The nephew handled production and accounting and was also a truck driver. He did not have directors for those two bigger rooms or "workshops"; he directly arranged and supervised each and every employee's work. He and his nephew handled every affair from management, finance, personnel, supply, marketing, production, transportation, and public relations. He was running from this room to that room, yelling to somebody and then smiling at his visitor, Huang Quanyu. Although his company seemed to be a bit disordered, it was dynamic. He proclaimed to be able to make more than 3 million door hinges each year. Based on our observations, we believed him. This company is a very typical private manufacturer in China today.

3. The first generation of privately-owned enterprises since 1978 are nearly twenty years old. Most of the owners are still workers or managers. There are no shareholders controlling the enterprise. Some may collect or borrow money from their family members, relatives, or friends. Before the funds are returned, those people could be considered shareholders.

4. For larger private companies, and/or complicated family relationships, boards of directors may exist.

5. The organizational structure of a bigger private company may be similar to a brand-new joint-venture enterprise or a foreign-owned enterprise. However, if a bankrupt state-owned enterprise were annexed by a big private company, the logistical load might be transferred to this individual company.

6. Most of the first generation privately-owned manufacturers (many of whom now have more than ten years of private experience) are very likely to be familiar with technology, if not technical experts. Therefore, they should be able to control or master production techniques. Often they employ relatives to carry out the other important staff positions (e.g., the financial department and personnel department).

7. In a rigidly traditional American private enterprise, the oldest male–even though he may be so old that he showers with his hat or shoes on–has absolute authority to control the business. Since ownership of private companies in China has created the

first generation of "capitalists" since 1978, arbitrary rule (as by a patriarch) will appear after their second generation becomes actively involved in the business administration. For these reasons, these owner/managers of individual companies tend to be very open, flexible and dynamic. Thus, they are good candidates to become potential business partners for the Western businesspeople.

DISCUSSION QUESTIONS

1. In what ways are the organizational structures of Chinese businesses influenced by military structures?
2. Explain the significance of the Communist Party's influence on the organizational structure of businesses?
3. Very few Western business organizations provide for support units such as a hospital, store(s), housing, school(s), etc. How do these differences affect employees in China?
4. Discuss the roles of the Communist Youth League Committee and the Women's Committee. Do Western organizations have structures that serve similar roles?
5. Many Western businesses are significantly influenced by organized employee collective bargaining. Are there any structures in Chinese enterprises that are similar to Western labor unions?
6. Distinguish between state-owned enterprises and collective enterprises. Give an example or two of when one type might be more efficient or effective than the other?
7. Are smaller-sized (fewer than 100 employees) Chinese businesses more similar to their Western counterparts than are larger businesses? Discuss the implications?
8. Discuss the pros and cons of joint-venture enterprises from both a Chinese and Western perspective.
9. What is the role of China's foreign-owned enterprises? Do they have any similarities to Western organizations?
10. Discuss the function and role of boards of directors in China and for Chinese foreign-owned enterprises. How do the boards affect decision making?

11. The daily operations of the individual companies in China are not only the most dynamic but also the most unusual. Agree or disagree? Why?

REFERENCE NOTES

1. Harry G. Broadman, *Meeting the Challenge of Chinese Enterprise Reform,* (Washington, DC: The World Bank, 1995), 12.
2. Ibid, 12.
3. Xaing means a rural administrative unit under the county. Before 1978, a xiang was a "commune." A county usually can contain 10 to 20 xiangs.
4. Yang Canying, *Enterprise Administration Involving Foreigners*, (Tianjin, P.R. China: Nankai University Publishing House, 1993), 84-85.
5. Ibid, 89-90.
6. Ibid, 88.
7. Ibid, 84, 86, 87.
8. Jyy is a poor-quality orange.
9. Yuan Lin and Shen Tongheng, Eds., *The Stories of Chinese Idioms*, (Shen Yang: Liaoning People's Publishing House, 1981).
10. Joseph W. Leonard, Charles R Gowen, III, and Luo Zhang, "Strategic influences on the management of human resources: An exploratory analysis of Chinese versus United States practices," in Anant R. Negandhi and Peter Schran, Eds., *Research in International Business and International Relations*, Volume 4, (New York: JAI Press), 1990, 177-190.
11. Individual companies account for about 8 percent of China's gross value of industrial output.

Chapter 2

The Structures of Service Organizations

The service organizations, including commercial organizations, foreign trade organizations, and financial organizations, are state-owned or collective organizations. They are the main service organizations Western businesspeople need to deal with.

COMMERCIAL ORGANIZATIONS

The commercial system in China is much more officially organized than in America. First, let us examine the governmental structure of commercial organizations:

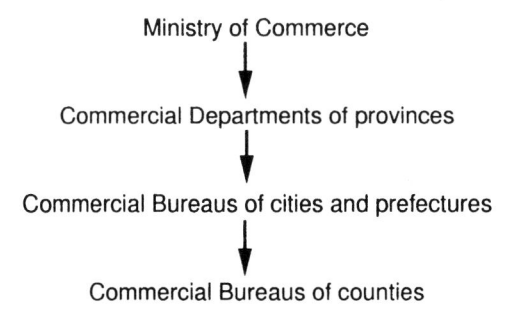

Ministry of Commerce
↓
Commercial Departments of provinces
↓
Commercial Bureaus of cities and prefectures
↓
Commercial Bureaus of counties

The Ministry of Commerce and the commercial departments of provinces basically tend to the daily official affairs. The commercial bureaus of cities, prefectures, and counties directly relate to various business companies.

For instance, as a governmental department responsible for the commercial activity, the commercial bureau of a small city with a population of around 100,000 has jurisdiction over a service corporation (hotels, beauty shops, barbershops); a catering corporation (various restaurants); a food corporation (grocery stores, food processing factories); a general merchandise corporation (department stores, general stores); a cigarette and wine corporation (cigarette and wine stores, and their processing); a hardware and electronics corporation (hardware stores and electronic stores); a local products corporation (local products stores), etc. The commercial bureau of a big city like Beijing, with a population of more than 10 million, will be much larger than the bureau of a small city. The small city commercial bureau may direct one catering corporation, but Beijing's commercial bureau may have ten catering corporations in order to manage thousands of restaurants.

The previous illustration might give the impression that the commercial bureaus and departments are very powerful in people's daily lives. This was quite true in a planned economic system. Before 1978, nearly all stores were state-owned or collective. In other words, almost everything you wanted or needed to purchase were from these governmental commercial stores. The various levels of governments tried to forecast people's consumption to replace a market demand with a planned economy. When soap was in short demand, households were limited to one piece of soap each month through the use of a special coupon ticket. When the demand for sugar exceeded the supply, consumption was likewise controlled. The commercial bureau also distributed meats and certain foods to the catering corporation according to a plan from the higher authority. In a parallel way, the catering corporation allocated the meats and foods to its restaurants. But, in general, the needs and demands of the market were ignored.

Since 1978, when the market economy was gradually implemented, private stores have sprung up like mushrooms; even the state-owned manufacturers are not controlled by governmental plans to supply products to meet market needs. The governmental commercial bureaus have been faced with a strong challenge from the market economy. In order to adapt to the change to a market economy and compete with private and foreign stores, the governmental commercial bureaus must transfer their business authority to the various corporations. Now, these commercial bureaus have gradually become real governmental organizations and let their corporations struggle to compete with various private and foreign companies. While this message may sound to many readers like the series of stories that led to the demise of the Soviet Union, since 1978 China has not suffered under the same level of distribution problems that occurred in the Soviet economy.

Let us take a food-producing corporation as an example of an organizational structure (Figure 2.1). Some explanations should be given.

1. During the period of a planned economy, the foods corporations and most other corporations were "taken care of" by the governments; they only implemented the governmental plans. The corporations did not need to be concerned about their profitability or losses. The goal was to move the goods from the warehouse to the relative stores, according to the governmental plans; employees received fixed salaries from the government. Questions such as "Were the goods sold?", "Were the customers' needs satisfied?", and "Was the system functioning efficiently?" were given little thought. No one needed to know! This was just like a Chinese saying, "The sole daughter of an Emperor does not need to worry about her marriage– Sole one vs. so many demands." But when the monopolization of the market ended, the corporations had to compete with countless flexible and dynamic private stores. To adapt to this challenge, these corporations have been assuming sole responsibility for their profits or losses. Many of them have started to enjoy a new life from the "throes" of this economic transference. Perhaps the old adage of "sink or swim" is applicable!
2. The foods corporation is just an example that we chose to illustrate these points. The situations and organizational structures of most other corporations are similar.
3. The corporation is state-owned. Some of its stores or processing factories, however, could be joint ventures. The reason for this is that their excellent locations or their unique skills at making traditional foods attract foreign investors.
4. If the Party members in the corporation were not enough to organize a large committee, the organizational department of the Party would become the organizational section, or this "Party

personnel function" would simply be moved to the higher authority—the commercial bureau.
5. Some of the corporations may have boards of directors.
6. The relationships between the corporations and the commercial bureaus are quite delicate and complex. As a governmental organization, the commercial bureau is the official responsible institution for the corporations, but the corporations have the independent authority to manage their own businesses. The commercial bureau can provide its suggestions, advice, or directions to the corporations, but it cannot interfere with the corporations' normal and legal business activities. The corporations, however, are state-owned companies, and the commercial bureau is the representative of the government. Accordingly, the commercial bureau is the theoretical legal counsel. Or to express it differently, the commercial bureau is the owner, and the general manager is entrusted or contracted to administer the corporation. The commercial bureau cannot interfere with the corporations' normal business activities, but in the personnel function, it has the authority to evaluate, select, appoint, or remove the general managers, the vice general managers, or the board members of the corporations.

FIGURE 2.1. Organizational Structure of Food-Producing Corporation

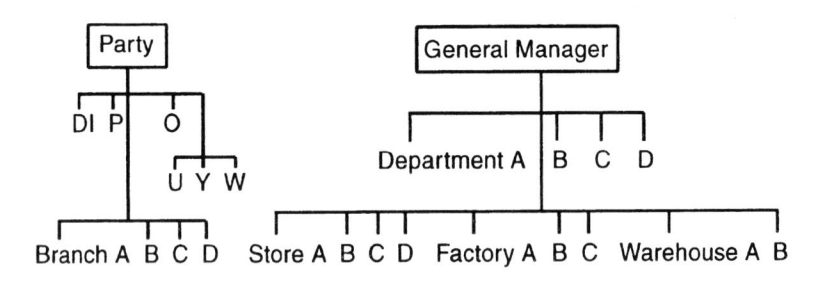

Notes: W = Women's Commission
DI = Discipline Inspection
P = Propaganda
O = Organizational Department (Section)
Y = Communist Youth League Committee

FOREIGN TRADE ORGANIZATIONS

Currently, there are at least four categories of state-owned foreign trade organizations in China: (1) the foreign trade organizations under the Ministry of Foreign Economic Relations and Trade, (2) the foreign trade organizations under the various ministries and committees of the state, (3) the foreign trade companies of the state-owned overseas organizations, and (4) the foreign trade organizations of various local governments.

We will first discuss the foreign trade corporations and their branch companies directly under the Ministry of Foreign Economic Relations and Trade.[1] These corporations are divided into many import/export corporations with specialized trades, e.g., China National Cereals, Oils and Foodstuffs Import and Export Corporation, China National Native Produce and Animal By-Products Import and Export Corporation, China National Textiles Import and Export Corporation, China Silk Import and Export Corporation, China National Arts and Crafts Import and Export Corporation, China National Light Industrial Products Import and Export Corporation, China National Chemicals Import and Export Corporation, China National Machinery Import and Export Corporation, China National Machinery and Equipment Import and Export Corporation, China National Metals and Mineral Import and Export Corporation, and China National Medicines and Health Products Import and Export Corporation, etc. Each specialized foreign trade corporation has branch companies in each province and autonomous region, and each of the branch companies of the province or autonomous region will have its subsidiaries in various important cities. For example, China National Silk Import and Export Corporation has its branch company, the Zhejiang (province) Branch of China National Silk Import and Export Corporation, which also has its subsidiaries, including the Ningbo (city of Zhejiang province) subsidiary of China National Silk Import and Export Corporation. In fact, some of them have singular and direct business and leadership relationships, particularly those that still keep their general headquarters' names, such as the Zhejiang Branch of China Silk Import and Export Corporation. Many of them have been transferred to localities to be put under double leadership requirements from their general headquarters or from the Ministry of Foreign Economic Relations and Trade, and from the local governments. Usually, the general headquarters or the Ministry of Foreign Economic Relations and Trade will give professional business directions, and local governments will be involved in personnel administration and appointing or removing senior leaders, as well as other official matters.

Their administrative structures could be as follows:

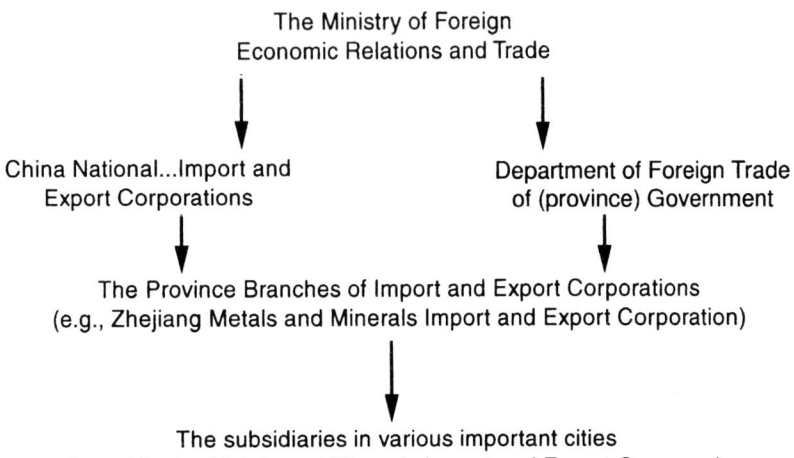

```
                    The Ministry of Foreign
                   Economic Relations and Trade
                    │                    │
                    ▼                    ▼
   China National...Import and    Department of Foreign Trade
      Export Corporations           of (province) Government
                    │                    │
                    ▼                    ▼
       The Province Branches of Import and Export Corporations
       (e.g., Zhejiang Metals and Minerals Import and Export Corporation)
                              │
                              ▼
             The subsidiaries in various important cities
        (e.g., Ningbo Metals and Minerals Import and Export Company)
```

The foreign trade organizations under the various ministries and committees of the state were created since the Movement of Reforming and Opening in 1978. For instance, China National Coal Import and Export Corporation was established in July 1982 with an approval from the State Council, and is under the leadership of the Ministry of Coal Industry. China Metallurgical Import and Export Corporation was founded in 1980, and is led by the Ministry of Metallurgical Industry. Many enterprises of this type are under double leadership authority from their own ministries and from the Ministry of Foreign Economic Relations and Trade. For example, China National Nonferrous Metals Import and Export Corporation, built in January 1981, is one that has been administered by the Ministry of Metallurgical Industry as well the Ministry of Foreign Economic Relations and Trade.

The foreign trade companies of the state-owned overseas organizations are extremely powerful, mysterious, and special organizations.

They are somewhere in-between the Chinese state-owned and foreign-owned enterprises. They can have the privileges that some special Chinese state-owned enterprises can have, such as importing or exporting some special items that a foreign enterprise is not allowed to obtain, and for which only some professional Chinese state-owned enterprise can legally trade. They also enjoy the priority policies that a foreign-owned enterprise can have, e.g., reducing and remitting taxation. The instances can be listed as the various companies of China International Economic Information Center, or China International Trust and Investment Corporation, etc. The foreign trade organizations are uniquely special in China. They were the places where children of senior cadres worked because of the privileges of foreign trade organizations. Of course, they are still the places for which those persons yearn. Particularly, the foreign trade companies of the state-owned overseas organizations are most popular. It is widely known that Deng Xiaoping's son, Deng Zhifang, and the former vice president of the People's Republic of China, Wang Zhen's son, Wang Jun occupy paramount positions in these kinds of organizations. Before the Movement of Reforming and Opening in 1978, the foreign trade organizations were the sole organizations with the authority to conduct import/export, and all international business in China. Even if a research institute needed to replace a special screw from a foreign machine, the institute had to import it through an import/export company. In brief, all matters, big or small, as long as they were related to international trade, had to be handled by the foreign trade organizations.

After 1978, many places in China were opened to foreign countries for the first time. Those local governments had a chance to directly deal with foreign companies but did not have the authority to engage in the import/export business. This structural configuration created many conflicts. As a result, many provinces and autonomous regions wanted their own import/export organizations. With the permission of the central government, the local governments established their own import/export companies one after another.[2] Now, it is not uncommon for even cities and counties to have their own import/export companies. Likewise, the same requests came from the various ministries and committees under the central government, and now they also have their own foreign trade organizations.

Let us examine the administrative structures between local governments and their own foreign trade organizations.

```
          The Committee of Foreign Economic Relations
          and Trade of Provinces or Autonomous Regions
              │                           │
              ▼                           ▼
The Provinces Foreign Economic      The Committee of Foreign Economic
Relations and Trade Corporations    Relations and Trade of Cities and
(e.g., Zhejiang Province Foreign    Counties Government
Economic Relations and Trade                │
Corporation)                                ▼
                                    The Corporation/Company of Foreign
                                    Economic Relations and Trade of
                                    Cities or Counties (e.g., Ningbo City
                                    Foreign Economic Relations and
                                    Trade Company)
```

After 1978, when China opened its doors to the outside world, many foreign companies have established joint-venture enterprises, or began their own manufacturing in China. Those joint-venture enterprises or foreign manufacturers must conduct their own international trade. Many of them were "internally" dealing with their parent corporations, branch companies, and subsidiaries that were in foreign countries in which the Chinese state-owned import/export companies should not and/or could not be involved. Logically and reasonably, these joint-venture enterprises or foreign manufacturers needed to have the authority to conduct international business; otherwise, it would not be profitable for them to engage in business operations in China. As a result, they have been granted import/export authority and some other priority policies.

Because the above four kinds of organizations have authority to conduct international trade, the former monopolization of international trade by the foreign trade organizations under the Chinese central government is broken. Nevertheless, through the state-owned foreign trade organizations, the central government still keeps certain special privileges to control certain items of import and/or export with "import permission certificates,"[3] "export permission certificates,"[4] or "quotas."[5] For example, there are seven goods (grains, steel, rubber, timbers, chemical fertilizers, tobacco, and chemical fibers/polyesters/etc.)

that are imported by those corporations carrying the name "China National," e.g., China National Chemicals Import and Export Corporation. Also, there are nineteen items (rice, beans, peanuts, frozen pork, cottons, cotton yarns, cotton cloth, cotton-polyester cloth, cotton-polyester yarns, drawnwork, tobaccos, tea, silk, crude oil, finished oils, coals, pearls, corns, and prawns/shrimp) that can only be exported through the state-owned import/export corporations with the name "China National" or their branch companies.

When the monopolization of international trade by the foreign trade organizations under the Chinese central government is broken, some disruptive issues appear in China. Some Chinese enterprises, joint ventures, and foreign-owned enterprises (such as those that are Taiwan- or Hong Kong-owned) that do not have the quotas to export textile products to the United States may try to ship those products to some third country, put new brand labels on them, then ship them to the United States. During the trade conflicts between China and the United States in 1995, the American trade representative addressed the issue with the Chinese Ministry of Foreign Economic Relations and Trade and discussed closing twenty-three manufacturers that illegally copied others' compact discs. But in fact, the Ministry of Foreign Economic Relations and Trade might not have the authority to directly interfere with those twenty-three manufacturers. On one hand, the monopolization of international trade from the central government is broken; on the other hand, chaos occurs to some extent.

Now let us discuss two kinds of typical organizational structures for state-owned foreign trade companies and corporations (see Figure 2.2).

The following points need to be explained:

1. This is usually a medium-sized import/export company.
2. The business departments are the organizational core that direct and conduct import/export business activities, such as planning, statistics, shipping, etc.
3. The function departments include the personnel and the financial departments.
4. The administrative departments contain the manager's office(s) and the secretarial section.
5. Logistical departments oversee dining halls, housing, kindergartens, etc., as is the same for other state-owned enterprises.

6. According to the article, "Party Committee Collective Leadership of Foreign Trade Enterprise" in *The Great Dictionary of Economy and Trade*, the union and the Communist Youth League are led by the Party committee. Though a Women's Committee was not mentioned in that article, usually the union, the Communist Youth League, and the Women's Committee are placed together. Thus, we included the Women's Committee under the leadership of the Party.
7. There should be the same geographical group A, B, and C under the commodity section B, C, and D, which we did not include (to avoid confusion) in the figure.
8. Some small foreign trade companies may organize by product groupings as opposed to territorial groupings. For example, they have hardware sections, tin sections, and copper sections, etc., but not an American group, an Asian group, and a European group under hardware and the other sections. Likewise, some may organize geographically, such as the American section, the Asian section, and the European section.

FIGURE 2.2. One Version of the Typical Organizational Structure for a State-Owned Foreign Trade Company

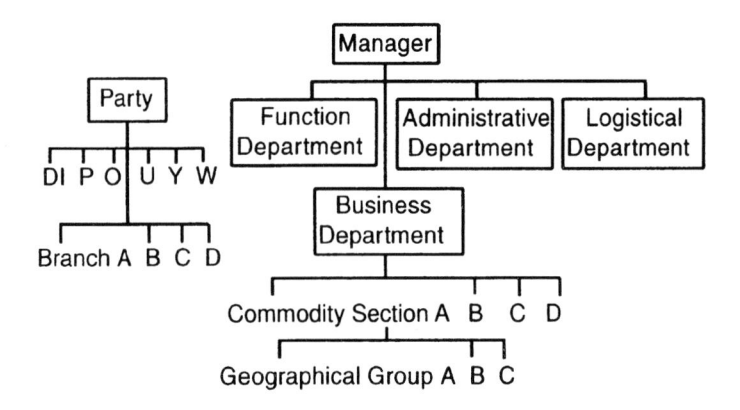

```
                              Manager
                                 |
         Party          ┌────────┼────────┐
          |       Function  Administrative  Logistical
    ┌──┬──┬──┬──┐ Department  Department   Department
    DI P  O  U  Y  W
                        Business
                        Department
    ┌──┬──┬──┐              |
    Branch A B C D      ┌───┼───┬───┐
                   Commodity Section A B C D
                                |
                           ┌────┼────┐
                   Geographical Group A B C
```

Notes: DI = Discipline Inspection
        P = Propaganda
        O = Organizational Department (Section)
        Y = Communist Youth League Committee
        W = Women's Committee

Figure 2.3 shows another organizational structure. We should also explain the following points:

1. This could be an organizational structure of a large foreign trade corporation, which may have its branch companies in different provinces.
2. The administrative department includes general managers' and/or vice general managers' offices, a secretarial section, the personnel department, and the logistical department.
3. There should be commodity sections A, B, C, and D under commodity departments B, C, and D, just as the figure shows under commodity department A.
4. There ought to be commodity groups A, B, and C under commodity sections B, C, and D, just as is illustrated under commodity section A in the figure.
5. Likewise, there should be document groups, supply groups, and import/export groups under commodity groups B and C, just as they are illustrated under commodity group A.
6. As for the role of the Party, there should be branches B, C, and D under committees B, C, and D as under committee A.

There are some state-owned enterprises in the West, but there may not be state-owned foreign trade enterprises operating in the United States. Therefore, the Chinese state-owned foreign trade corporations need to be further discussed. Let us compare those China National Import and Export Corporations or their branch companies with the local governmental foreign trade corporations to illustrate some interesting differences. The local governmental foreign trade corporations conduct a great deal of miscellaneous businesses: light industrial products, textile products, hardware, mineral products, foods, local products. The national specialized import/export companies, however, may carry many products, which are categorized into very detailed divisions, merely under one or two headings. There are, for instance, hinges (door hinges, window hinges, commercial hinges, and resident hinges etc.) and pliers (pincers, clippers, etc.) under the category of hardware, but the former is under the division of metal fittings, and the latter is under handtools. Moreover, the local governmental foreign trade corporations usually are controlled by the governments more tightly.

FIGURE 2.3. Second Version of the Typical Organizational Structure for State-Owned Foreign Trade Company

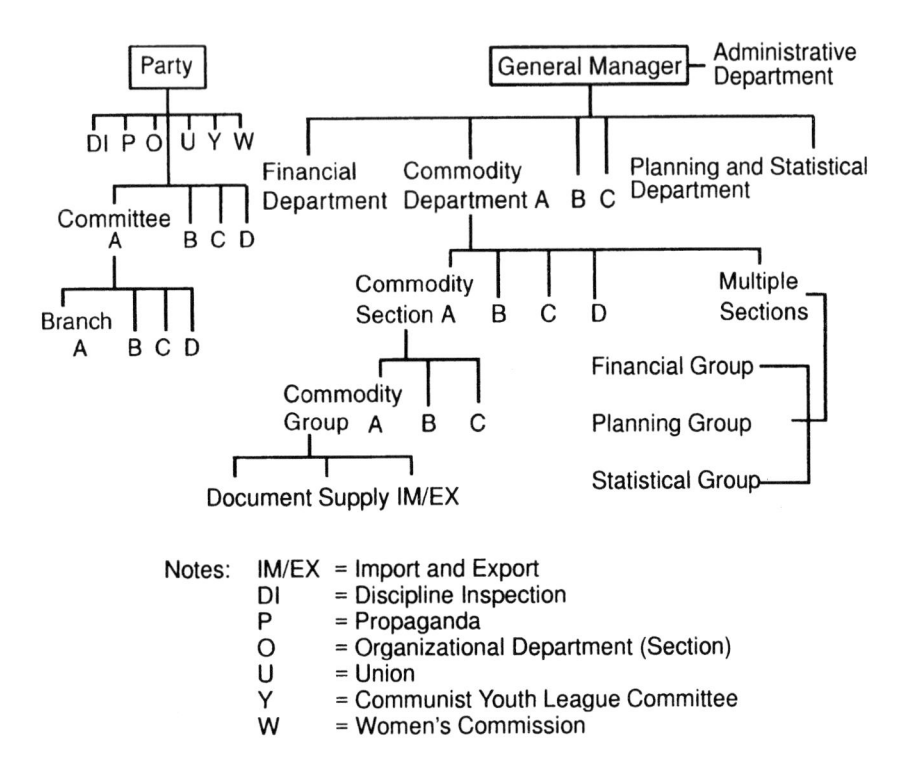

```
                Party                        General Manager ─ Administrative
                                                                Department
         DI P O  U Y W                ┌──────────┬──────────┬──────────┐
                          Financial      Commodity         Planning and Statistical
        Committee         Department     Department A  B C  Department
          A  B C D
                                              │
     ┌──────┬──┬──┐                    ┌──────┼──┬──┐                    ┌─ Multiple
   Branch                            Commodity                           │  Sections
    A   B C D                        Section A  B  C  D
                                              │                     Financial Group ──┐
                                     ┌────┬───┤                                       │
                                   Commodity                        Planning Group ───┤
                                   Group A  B  C                                      │
                                     │                              Statistical Group ┘
                          Document Supply IM/EX
```

Notes: IM/EX = Import and Export
        DI   = Discipline Inspection
        P   = Propaganda
        O   = Organizational Department (Section)
        U   = Union
        Y   = Communist Youth League Committee
        W   = Women's Commission

Or we can say that the local governments frequently get involved in or even interfere with those companies. So if you can influence the local governments' decision making, then you can influence their foreign trade corporations' decision making. To attempt to bring this into perspective, try to imagine if the federal, state, and local governments in the United States had direct and rigid regulatory authority divided into four-digit Standard Industrial Classification (SIC) codes. When we consider that China has a population five times that of the United States, we can begin to imagine the complexities of executing tactical or strategic decision making in the Chinese bureaucracy.

FINANCIAL ORGANIZATIONS

There are six nationwide banks in China: The People's Bank of China, the Bank of China, the People's Construction Bank of China, the Bank of Communications of China, the Industrial and Commercial Bank of China, and the Agricultural Bank of China. There are also three banks of the state-owned overseas organizations, Zhong Xin, Guang Da, and Hua Xia, and about six local banks such as Bank of Shanghai Pudong Development, Bank of Shenzhen Development, Bank of China Investment, etc. In order to better explain most typical Chinese banks, we are going to focus on the six nationwide banks. The readers may basically understand the functions of these six banks through their names. If there is a problem, it may probably be the Bank of China. Many Western people may lose their opportunities to conduct business with China due to a lack of understanding of the Bank of China or the other Chinese banks. We would like to share an example: A Chinese company was going to purchase paper pulp from an American company with a deferred payment letter of credit issued by the Bank of China. But the American company did not understand that the Bank of China is the bank chosen to represent China to deal with foreign countries' banks, so the bank must keep its credit and honor for China to guarantee its payment. The American seller insisted on requiring a deferred payment letter of credit only from a Hong Kong bank, and the business failed. If the owner of the American company had read this book, he might have successfully handled this deal. In fact, to think through the name carefully, the Bank of China, it makes sense for this bank to represent China with foreign countries' banks. Among these six banks, the People's Bank of China is similar to the U.S. Federal Reserve system; the other five banks are professional/commercial banks. These six banks are all state-owned and state-controlled banks. They control the Chinese economic lifeline.

Since the People's Republic of China was founded in 1949, there has not been any private bank in China (at the time of this writing). According to the Central Daily News (December 3 and December 5, 1995), the first private bank in China, the Min-Sheng[6] Bank (民生), opened in early 1996. In January 1994, as the wire-puller (facilitator or go-between), the All-China Association of Industry and Commerce began planning for the establishment of this bank. The State Council and the People's Bank of China officially approved this bank in June 1994. The first meeting of the shareholders, which was held in Beijing in December 3, 1995, approved the Regulations of Min-Sheng Bank, selected its board of directors, and appointed its president and executive vice president for an approval from the People's Bank of China. So far, the bank has collected about 1.38 billion yuans from fifty-nine shareholders; 80 percent of its funds were from private enterprises. To date, this is the last major area to be opened for competition in the new economic field. Nevertheless, to some extent, certain controls still exist. As we have stated, the job qualifications of president and executive vice president of the bank must be checked by the People's Bank of China. And the president, Mr. Tong Zengyin, has just retired from the position of vice president of the People's Bank of China in 1993. The vice executive general manager, Mr. Wei Shenghong, worked for the People's Bank of China for about thirty years. However, the significance of establishing the first private bank in China is very deep and profound. Not only has monopolization of the central state-owned banks been challenged for the first time since 1949, more important, the government is allowing people, particularly the owners of private enterprises, to organize their own banks to challenge the state-owned banks. To state it differently, while challenging the state-owned banks is important, to allow this challenge is even more significant. Because allowing one will pave the way for more. This may begin the next of series of significant commercial changes in China, furthering the movement toward a true market economy.

Foreign banks are allowed to have their branches or offices in China. Recently, some have had their offices in Shanghai and other places. To date, these banks provide limited services that have not yet been well delineated.

Because all of the six nationwide Chinese banks are state-owned, they are very powerful and unique in China. First, there are only two ways for a Chinese enterprise to raise money: financial allocation from the government or a loan from the bank. No matter which way an enterprise acquires capital, the banks are the sole source for obtaining the funds. Second, the only way to save money is to deposit it in the banks. The Chinese people are particular advocates of frugality. If you check the bank accounts of Chinese students in various American universities, you will be very surprised to find that, even with their poor incomes (a few thousand dollars for a whole family per year), most have extremely high savings (from several thousands to tens of thousands of dollars). Many Chinese people desire to save money to be rich; many Americans would like to make money to be rich. There are 1.2 billion people in China who like or prefer to save every cent they can spare. Divide 1.2 billion by six and this equals approximately 200 million people per bank. Imagine how financially sound these banks must be! In short, no matter whether individuals or organizations want to put money "in" or take money "out," the bank is their only option. Inasmuch as individuals', organizations', and governmental money are all in these main state-owned banks, these banks completely control the Chinese economic lifeline. It is not surprising that these banks are so powerful in China.

Moreover, if an organization or individual attains the document of ratification for a financial allocation or a loan, this will not guarantee that the funds will be actually be granted. If you visit China, you can see people building new projects everywhere. Too many people and too many organizations need substantial amounts of funding. This high level of demand has raised not only loan interest rates but also common prices. So in the past ten years, the annual inflation rate in China has often stayed above 20 percent. Therefore, even with a document of ratification from the government, people may not be able to obtain money from the banks. The author, Huang Quanyu, visited China in 1994. There were four presidents and vice presidents of the branch banks who invited him to a banquet, one after another. A friend of his teased him, "You should be proud as a king!" Huang Quanyu asked, "Why?" The friend said, "If one is invited to a restaurant by others, this means he or she is popular. If this person is frequently invited to a restaurant by many persons, this means he or she is more popular. The person who is very frequently invited to a restaurant but always avoids going is the most popular one, such as the leaders of the banks. Now if, the president of the bank who always refuses others' invitations invites you to a restaurant, you are as extremely popular as a King, aren't you?" People invite the leaders of the banks to restaurants with the intent of being granted a loan. Since there is not enough money in the banks to loan for every reasonable and unreasonable business risk, the leaders of the banks often refuse invitations in order to avoid unpleasant situations.

Since China accepted the idea of a market economy beginning in 1992, the banks have become even more powerful. There are at least two important points in this situation.

1. The six state-owned banks were the outcome under the planned economic operation. In other words, a financial monopoly resulted from the planned economy.
2. On the one hand, the market has been opened, and society is being operated by a market-driven economy system. On the other hand, the financial lifeblood is totally controlled by the six banks that were designed under the planned economy.

What a paradox! While monopolization of the market has been broken, the financial monopoly has continued. As a result, the financial monopoly can show its power. Indeed, during the planned economy, the six banks were simply six money machines that only counted money by others' orders. Without market competition, with no winner or loser, when everyone followed government plans, money was not a symbol of power, let alone the bank officials! At that time, a president of the bank might never have a chance to refuse others' invitations for a dinner, and would be very proud if someone invited him or her to a restaurant. Now that the plans have been broken, the market has pushed people and enterprises to find funds. Suddenly, the bank presidents are so popular that they have the chance to refuse others' invitations for dinner. When an enterprise needs to import machines and organize a delegation to inspect machines in a foreign country, a bank leader often would be a member of the delegation. Of course, when a planned economic financial machine was operating in a market system, the financial order was very chaotic, as in 1993. The Minster of the Ministry of Finance, Li Guixian, lost his prominent position. The powerful economic official, Vice Primary Minister Zhu Rongji, who was in charge of economic affairs, took over the position of President of the People's Bank of China. Quite a few leaders and staff members of the six banks were punished in courts of law or with Party disciplinary actions. Zhu Rongji returned the position of President of the People's Bank of China to a professional in 1995 when the financial order was restored, and since then the banks have been adapting better to the change to a market economy.

The six banks have their headquarters in Beijing, with hundreds of branch banks in all provinces, autonomous regions, and municipalities directly under the central government. The banks have thousands of subsidiaries in all the cities and counties; they also have thousands of savings offices in various Xiangs and towns. Because the bank systems are too huge, their business operations are quite slow. In 1995, H.C.K. International needed to issue a letter of credit to a company in the city of Wuxi. Star Bank (a U.S. regional bank headquartered in Ohio), used by H.C.K. International, could not directly wire a letter of credit to the Wuxi Branch of the Bank of China. Then Star Bank wired the letter of credit to the Beijing Headquarters of the Bank of China on September 4, but the Wuxi Branch of the Bank of China did not receive it until September 20. It took more than two weeks to transfer/wire a letter of credit from the Beijing Headquarters of the Bank of China to its Wuxi Branch. This could be a very unusual example, but it is still true that the bank systems are too huge and slow.

There are many credit unions in the countryside and in many cities. They generally collect and loan small sums of money. More important, all credit unions are affiliated with branches of the nationwide banks.

Nonfinancial organizations generally are not allowed to collect funds. It was believed that this would disturb the financial order in China. Besides the case of Shen Taifu illegally collecting funds, another big case of illegally collecting a huge amount of funds has been recently exposed. The general manager of Xinxing Corporation in Wuxi, Deng Bing, was in league with some other persons, and used a very high monthly interest rate of 7 percent to illegally collect about 3.2 billion yuans (approximately $380 million). Their method was to use D's money to pay the interest to A, B, and C, then pay D's interest with F's money. When 1.2 billion yuans (about $140 million) had been squandered, the case was exposed. Around eighty leaders, including a vice mayor of Wuxi city and the Procurator of the Procuratorate of Wuxi, were involved in this case. Deng Ping and two other persons were sentenced with capital punishment. In reality however, many organizations collect funds in private by applying an interest rate higher than the banks. Some of them invest the collective funds to make money from their businesses, and are able to return the funds; some of them just deceive others as Deng Bing did.

The relationships between the governments and the banks in China are markedly special. While the six banks professionally administer their branches and subsidiaries in the various provinces, autonomous regions, cities, and counties, the local governments are involved in the personnel administration of the banks, particularly the appointments and removals of bank leaders. Or we could say, theoretically, that the business of the banks is independent from the local governments. During the period of planned economy, whether or not the business of the banks was independent from the local governments was not so critical because the banks operated as money machines to distribute funds according to governmental plans and financial allocations. The enterprises did not need to loan funds and return money. The enterprises were only held responsible to the governments; hence, the banks were just machines. Now that the market economy has been implemented in China, many enterprises no longer receive financial allocations. Even if they may gain governmental approval for a new project (building a new workshop, importing foreign equipment, etc.), they must borrow money from the banks. So, the banks are no longer passive "machines." For this reason, not only do enterprises want to integrate themselves with the banks, but also the local governments want to influence the banks to loan more funds to local enterprises. Because the local governments are involved in the appointments and removals of the banks' leaders, the relationships between local governments and the banks are extremely delicate and complex even though, by the relative policies, the local governments are not allowed to interfere with the banks' business.

Now that we have described the social and cultural background of the Chinese banks, we need to illustrate their organizational structure (Figure 2.4).

The Structures of Service Organizations 49

FIGURE 2.4. Organizational Structure for Chinese Bank

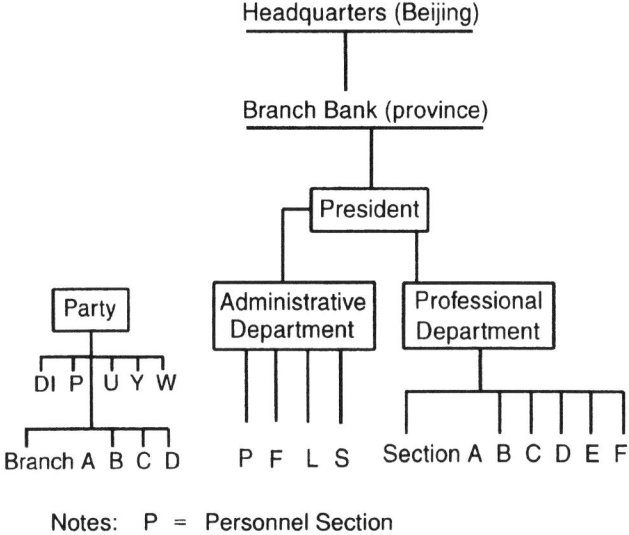

```
                    Headquarters (Beijing)
                            |
                    Branch Bank (province)
                            |
                        ┌───────┐
                        │President│
                        └───────┘
                            |
        ┌───────────────────┼───────────────────┐
        │                   │                   │
   ┌────────┐      ┌──────────────┐    ┌──────────────┐
   │ Party  │      │Administrative│    │ Professional │
   └────────┘      │  Department  │    │  Department  │
                   └──────────────┘    └──────────────┘
   ┌──┬──┬──┐         ┌──┬──┬──┐          ┌──┬──┬──┬──┬──┐
   DI  P  U  Y  W     P  F  L  S    Section A  B  C  D  E  F
   ┌──┬──┬──┐
   Branch A  B  C  D
```

Notes: P = Personnel Section
F = Financial Section
L = Logistical Section
S = Security Section
DI = Discipline Section
P = Propaganda
U = Union
Y = Communist Youth League Committee
W = Women's Committee

Obviously, we need to explain some aspects of this figure.

1. We chose a subsidiary of a bank in a city as an example because we believe that Western people will most often deal with this kind of bank.
2. There may be many kinds of organizational structures for the banks. This is just one example.
3. The professional department is the core of a bank. Usually, the president will be directly in charge of this department. The sections A, B, C, D, E, and F under the professional department could be the loan section, the letter of credit section, the international section, the treasury bills (TB) or government bonds section, and the customer service divi-

sion. There may be some smaller groups under these larger sections (e.g., industrial loan group, agricultural loan group, commercial loan group, and individual loan group under the loan section.)
4. A vice president may directly manage the administrative department, which includes the personnel section, the financial section, the logistical section, and the security section. The financial section could be small. The security section, however, may have an unusually large number of employees. The Armed Police, a kind of army in China, maintain physical security.
5. The secretary of the Party committee could very possibly be the president of the bank. The banks have become more and more important in the Chinese national economy. One way to enforce control of the banks is to have the secretary of the Party committee be the president of the bank.
6. The Party also has its organizational relationships with its higher authority, the Party committee in the province branch bank, which we did not indicate on Figure 2.4.
7. The ratio of Party members to non-Party members may be very high in a bank, compared with ordinary organizations.
8. Branches A, B, C, and D could be Groups A, B, C, and D if a bank is not big, even though the ratio of the Party members is high.
9. Figure 2.4 does not illustrate an organizational department under the Party committee. Some small branch banks may have an organizational section, but there must be an organizational department under the Party committee of a province branch bank.
10. A Women's Committee and Communist Youth League Committee may not exist when there are few employees.

All in all, the Chinese banks comprise a very special system that Western businesspeople need to learn and understand. Many people may have had an experience wherein, because the foreign companies did not understand the Chinese banks, both almost failed to, or simply could not, conduct business. Here is an example similar to the one we gave at the beginning of this section. A German company asked the People's Construction Bank of China to issue an irrevocable and confirmed letter of credit for a deal of more than $500,000. The People's Construction Bank of China said, "We can issue an irrevocable letter of credit, but we have never and will never issue a confirmed letter of credit, which is an insult to ourselves. . . ." When the German company persisted in demanding a confirmed letter of credit, the business almost failed. Finally, Star Bank, which had had a favorable experience in dealing with the Chinese bank, confirmed that the Chinese banks had not issued a confirmed letter of credit to them either, and that they had a good record with the Chinese banks. With the confirmation from Star Bank, the German company and the Chinese factory reached their business agreement. Now, the German company has received its full payment from the People's Construction Bank of China, and the Chinese factory has also received its machines. Hopefully, this section will help our readers to understand the Chinese banks better, and avoid any unnecessary financial losses from some misunderstandings.

DISCUSSION QUESTIONS

1. What controls (both direct and indirect) influence the structures of commercial organizations?
2. Do foreign trade organizations differ in their power structure from other Chinese enterprises? Why or why not?
3. It has been said that foreign trade companies of the state-owned overseas organizations are mysterious. Do you agree? Why or why not?
4. If the foreign trade organizations continue to lose their quasi-monopolistic influences and continue to become more driven by the competition environment, will we see higher or lower profit levels. Why?
5. Why are the Chinese banks so powerful?
6. What is likely to be the climate for foreign banks operating in China in the next decade?

REFERENCE NOTES

1. Its former name was the Ministry of Foreign Trade. Citing it from *The Great Dictionary of Economy and Trade*, on March 8, 1982, the Ministry of Foreign Trade, the Ministry of Economic Relations with Foreign Countries, the Foreign Investment Commission, and the Administrative Commission on Import and Export Affairs were combined into the Ministry of Foreign Economic Relations and Trade.

2. The Ministry of Foreign Trade decided to transfer its foreign trade companies in various provinces and autonomous regions to the local governments. Nevertheless, those enterprises were administered by double leadership from the Ministry of Foreign Trade and the local governments. Yet, the local governments did not have the essential control and authority over those foreign trade companies. In general, the foreign trade companies with a local name and "foreign economic relations and trade" are local governmental foreign trade organizations that are essentially controlled by the local governments. The foreign trade companies with a local name plus a concrete product are the foreign trade companies that are administrated by double leadership from the Ministry of Foreign Economic Relations and Trade and the local governments. For instance, if a company is named Zhejiang Province Foreign Economic Relations and Trade Corporation, this is a Zhejiang provincial foreign trade organization. Zhejiang Metals and Minerals Import and Export Corporation is a foreign trade organization under double leadership from the Ministry of Foreign Economic Relations and Trade or China National Metals and Mineral Import and Export Corporation, and the local government of Zhejiang province.

3. The use of import permission certificates is a means by which the Chinese government plans and controls certain items of import (e.g., grains, steels, tobaccos, etc.).

4. Granting export permission certificates is a means by which the Chinese government plans and controls certain items of export (e.g., rice, crude oil, cottons, etc.).

5. There are two kinds of quotas: initiative (active) quota and passive quota. The initiative (active) quotas could simply mean export permission certificate and/or import permission certificate. In other words, initiative (active) quotas are that the Chinese government plans to import a certain quantity of certain items that China needs but does not need too much. On the other hand, initiative (active) quotas are also that the Chinese government plans to export certain amounts of certain items of which China does not have too much. As for passive quotas, they are the items for which foreign countries control the quantity that is allowed to be imported to their countries. For instance, the United States (some other countries, as well) controls the quantity of textile products to be imported to the United States. The United States plans and negotiates with China about the quantity of textile products to be imported to America. When both have reached an agreement, the Chinese government will allocate the quota of textile products to export to America to its state-owned specialized foreign trade corporations. In short, with

passive quotas, the goods will be allowed to enter foreign countries by these foreign countries' customs. On the contrary, with the active (initiative) quotas, the Chinese customs will release the allocated amount of goods to export to foreign countries.

6. Min-Sheng (民生) means the people's livelihood, which is one of the Three People's Principles (Nationalism, Democracy, and the People's Livelihood) put forward by Dr. Sun Yat-sen (Sun Zhongshan). To translate the Min-Sheng Bank into English, it would be "the bank for the people's livelihood."

Chapter 3

The Structures of Governmental Organizations

The structures of governments is an interesting topic. Before we discuss the structures of governments, we need to briefly address semigovernmental organizations and nongovernmental organizations.

SEMIGOVERNMENTAL ORGANIZATIONS

The semigovernmental organizations we will discuss are officially categorized and listed as the mass organizations in China.

In our opinion, a mass organization could be either a political organization or a nonpolitical organization, but it must not be part of a governmental structure. When we use this definition to measure the organizations that are categorized and listed as mass organizations in China, we discover that most of them are not truly mass organizations but rather semigovernmental organizations. Therefore, we do not label them as mass organizations. Here, "semigovernmental organizations" are organizations that are not entirely, but only partially governmental structures that exercise governmental functions and powers.

When we judge the organizations with the above definition, we think that the following organizations could be listed as semigovernmental organizations:

All-China Federation of Trade Unions
The Communist Youth League of China

All-China Federation of Youth
All-China Students' Federation
The China Young Pioneers
All-China Women's Federation
The China Association for Science and Technology
The China Federation of Literary and Art Circles
The China Welfare Institute
The Red Cross Society of China
The Association of Industry and Commerce
All-China Federation of Returned Overseas Chinese
China Council for Promotion of International Trade

Obviously, many of these are political organizations, but a political organization can be a mass organization. The essential distinction is whether or not the organization is independent from the governmental structure, and whether or not it exercises or at least partially exercises governmental functions and powers. It must be noted however that most of the key leaders and administrators of the above organizations are selected, appointed, and/or removed by the Organizational Department of the Central Committee of the Chinese Communist Party. Likewise, as well we know, the key leaders and administrators of the branch organizations in various provinces and autonomous regions are selected, appointed, and/or removed by the Organizational Departments of the Communist Party Committees of the provinces and autonomous regions. Moreover, all employees of these organizations are paid by these governments. Finally, in many cases, these organizations directly implement governmental decision making, but not only the decisions from their organizational higher level. Of course, their headquarters unconditionally carry out the central government's decision making, too.

The last three organizations, the Association of Industry and Commerce, the All-China Federation of Returned Overseas Chinese, and the China Council for Promotion of International Trade, are all organizations that Western businesspeople may have had an opportunity to deal with, particularly the China Council for Promotion of International Trade. We will briefly introduce this organization.

As we know, most businesspeople of foreign countries, especially the Western countries, are nongovernmental people; on the contrary, most Chinese people who engage in business are government employees. The Chinese business decision makers felt that some foreign businesspeople might feel uncomfortable dealing with Chinese governmental businesspeople; in many cases, a nongovernmental trade organization could foster a more flexible, proper, and advantageous situation in which to associate with foreign nongovernmental businesspeople than in a governmental organization.

Based on this consideration, the China Council for Promotion of International Trade was established as a mass organization in 1952.[1] Its missions are to promote the international trade relationships between the Chinese foreign trade organizations and foreign economic and business circles; to host foreign nongovernmental economic and business delegations; to arrange for Chinese economic and business delegations to visit foreign countries; to organize international fairs in China and in foreign countries; to organize the exchange of technology and information between Chinese and foreign organizations; and to work as an agent for foreign companies to register their brands in China, to handle arbitration of foreign trade, and to engage in propaganda for foreign trades.

The China Council for Promotion of International Trade is headquartered in Beijing and has hundreds of branch organizations in various provinces, autonomous regions, many important cities, and some vital counties.

The president or chairperson of its branch organization could be the director of the foreign trade department of a province (autonomous region), the director of the foreign economic relations and trade committee of a city, a famous returned overseas Chinese person, or a well-known "democratic personage."[2] The purpose of this type of appointment is to balance nongovernmental "color" (i.e., image, influence, or elements) and governmental directions.

NONGOVERNMENTAL ORGANIZATIONS

In a broad sense, nongovernmental organizations include all organizations that are not physically constructed within the governments, such as the National People's Congress, the Chinese People's Political Consultative Conference, and even some commercial organizations. In reality, the Party leads the government, the

National People's Congress, and the Chinese People's Political Consultative Conference. Undeniably, they are politically tied to each other. They are actually not nongovernmental organizations.

In a limited sense, nongovernmental organizations imply those nationwide organizations whose headquarters are located in Beijing which are not physically and tightly constructed within the government.

Considering the concept using this narrow definition, we list the following organizations as nongovernmental organizations:

The Revolutionary Committee of the Kuomintang
The China Democratic League
The China Democratic National Construction Association
The China Association for Promoting Democracy
The Chinese Peasants' and Workers' Democratic Party
The China Zhi Gong Dang
The Jiu San Society
The Taiwan Democratic Self-Government
The Chinese Buddhist Association
The Chinese Islamic Association
The Chinese Taoist Association

Strictly speaking, these are not nongovernmental organizations as well. There are three reasons why we categorize them as nongovernmental organizations as compared to the semigovernmental organizations.

First, many of the members in these organizations may not directly get their salaries from the governments. For example, most of the members of these parties who are not in office are professors, scientists, artists, musicians, writers, and engineers. They get their salaries from their primary professional work and in their work units. Though the payments may come from the government as well, these differ in that all of the employees of the semigovernmental organizations get their salaries directly from the governments for their main organizational works.

Second, some of these organizations, in a sense, may be able to influence governmental decisions, not just implement governmental decisions as the semigovernmental organizations do. There is a fine line between influencing a decision and simply executing a decision.

Third, these organizations may have their own funds.

As nongovernmental organizations, they have their responsible departments in the government. For instance, the governmental department responsible for those parties, which we have previously listed as nongovernmental organizations, is the United Front Work Department. In fact, the United Front Work Department is an organ of the Chinese Communist Party, but since the government and the Party are connected, we are addressing it here as a part of the government. The government organization responsible for religious organizations is the Religious Bureau of the State Council.

These parties have their branch organizations in various provinces, autonomous regions, cities, counties, and thousands of work units. But their members are mainly intellectuals, not workers or peasants.

The religious organizations are not as "strong" as the parties, although they both are merely political decorations.

One point we want to highlight is that our lists of semigovernmental organizations and nongovernmental organizations are not all-inclusive; we listed only the more important ones.

The nongovernmental organizations have very limited ability to influence the government decisions in China. Thus, we will not focus too much on the nongovernmental organizations, but instead, we will concentrate on government structures.

GOVERNMENTAL STRUCTURES

We will illustrate the organizational structures of the Central Committee of the Chinese Communist Party, the Central Government, and the Ministry of Foreign Affairs.[3]

In terms of the Constitution of China, the Chinese Communist Party is the core leadership in China; hence, we will first illustrate the organizational structures of the Central Committee of the Chinese Communist Party (Figure 3.1).

Some organizations (e.g., the Central Advisory Commission, the Rural Policy Research Center, and the Central Commission for Guiding Party Consolidation) that once had important roles in the

FIGURE 3.1. Organizational Structure of Central Committee of the Chinese Communist Party

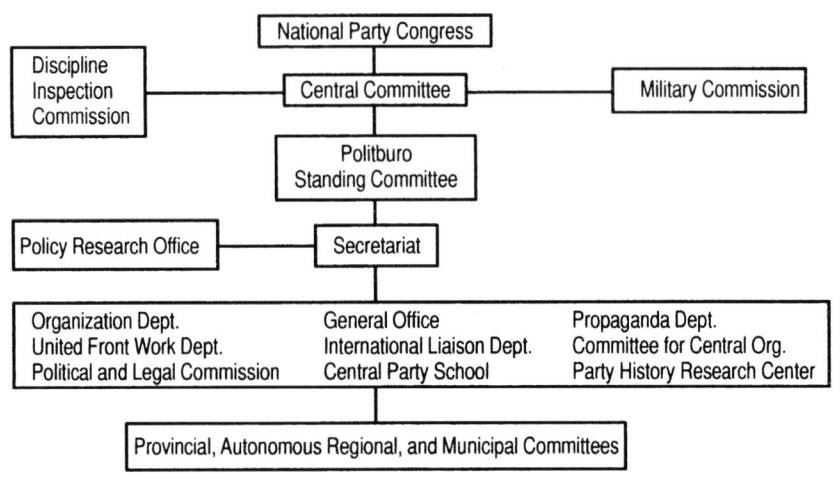

```
                          National Party Congress
 ┌─────────────┐                  │
 │ Discipline  │          ┌───────────────┐          ┌────────────────────┐
 │ Inspection  │──────────│Central Committee│──────────│ Military Commission│
 │ Commission  │          └───────────────┘          └────────────────────┘
 └─────────────┘                  │
                          ┌───────────────┐
                          │   Politburo   │
                          │Standing Committee│
                          └───────────────┘
 ┌─────────────────┐              │
 │Policy Research Office├──────────│   Secretariat  │
 └─────────────────┘      └───────────────┘
                                  │
 ┌──────────────────────────┬──────────────────────┬──────────────────────────┐
 │ Organization Dept.       │ General Office       │ Propaganda Dept.         │
 │ United Front Work Dept.  │ International Liaison Dept. │ Committee for Central Org. │
 │ Political and Legal Commission │ Central Party School │ Party History Research Center │
 └──────────────────────────┴──────────────────────┴──────────────────────────┘
                                  │
           ┌──────────────────────────────────────────────────────┐
           │ Provincial, Autonomous Regional, and Municipal Committees │
           └──────────────────────────────────────────────────────┘
```

Note: Some departments and offices not listed in the chart are the Bureau for Translating the Works of Marx, Engels, Lenin, and Stalin; the Information and Media Agencies; and the Commission for Collecting Party Historical Data.

Chinese Communist Party history have disappeared. The Central Advisory Commission was organized by senior leaders who were old enough to retire but were able to influence the Party decision making with their authority. Because those Advisory Commissions (either central or local) often bothered various levels of the Party committees' decision making, the Advisory Commissions were canceled in the 14th National Party Congress at Deng Xiaoping's suggestion. The pioneering of the Chinese reformation actually stemmed from agricultural reform (e.g., the contracted responsibility system, where lands were contracted to individuals and remuneration was linked to output, that destroyed the system of the peoples' commune in China). For this reason, the Rural Policy Research Center was organized to guide the Chinese reformation. Finally, this center disappeared along with the two General Secretaries of the Party, Hu Yaobang and Zhao Ziyang, who lost their powers one after the other. The corruption in the Chinese Communist Party had bolstered people's confidence enough to push for the Movement of Reformation and Opening, and the mission of the Central Commission for Guiding Party Consolidation was to clean up corruption in the Party. The commission disappeared after the failure of this "cleaning" movement. Mr. Hu Yaobang, the General Secretary of the Party, and some other leaders believed that changing the cadres' and ordinary people's thoughts and concepts was the prerequisite needed to gain support for the Movement of Reforming and Opening in China; thus, the Leading Group for Education of Cadres and the Leading Group for Educational Reform were organized. After Hu Yaobang was forced to leave office, these two organizations disappeared, too.

Also, we must explain some critical organizational relationships that the readers may not be able to understand from the chart.

1. In the Chinese Communist Party history, there have been two highest positions: the Chairman of the Central Committee and the General Secretary of the Secretariat. Mao Zedong was the Chairman of the Central Committee of the CCP for about forty years. Attempting to avoid dictatorship but carry out collective leadership since the 12th National Party Congress, the position of the Chairman of the Central Committee has been canceled, and the General Secretary of the Secretariat has been kept as the highest position in the Chinese Communist Party. As we can see, the General Secretary is the chief of the Secretariat that report to the Politburo and its Standing Committee. If the General Secretary is not a politically powerful man, the Standing Committee of the Politburo could be a powerful leading group.
2. The Chinese troops, the People's Liberation Army, is essentially the armed force of the Party, but not the state troops. Mao Zedong had a very famous saying, "Political power grows out of the barrel of a gun."[4] Therefore, the Central Military Committee of the Party is a tremendously important organization. Deng Xiaoping could have retired from all of his official positions. He elected not to retire as the Chairman of the Central Military Committee; this was his sole and last position, which he retained until 1989.
3. The General Office is very powerful in the handling of daily affairs including the secret service and security, and schedules the daily activities for the senior leaders of the Party, such as the members of the Standing Committee of the Politburo.

4. The Organizational Department selects, tests, appoints, and removes the leaders with ranks above the main leaders of a province, autonomous region, municipal city, and ministry.
5. The United Front Work Department is to work on any legal parties other than the communist party, any legal religious organizations, and any famous individuals for the interests of the communist party. Therefore, any famous overseas Chinese individuals, or even foreign business people may have an opportunity to associate with the United Front Work Department.

From a business viewpoint, if we view the Central Committee of the Chinese Communist Party as "the Board of Directors," then the Central government can be considered an "administrative group" that manages daily administrative affairs. Figure 3.2 shows the organizational structure of the Central Government.

FIGURE 3.2. Organizational Structure of the Chinese Central Government

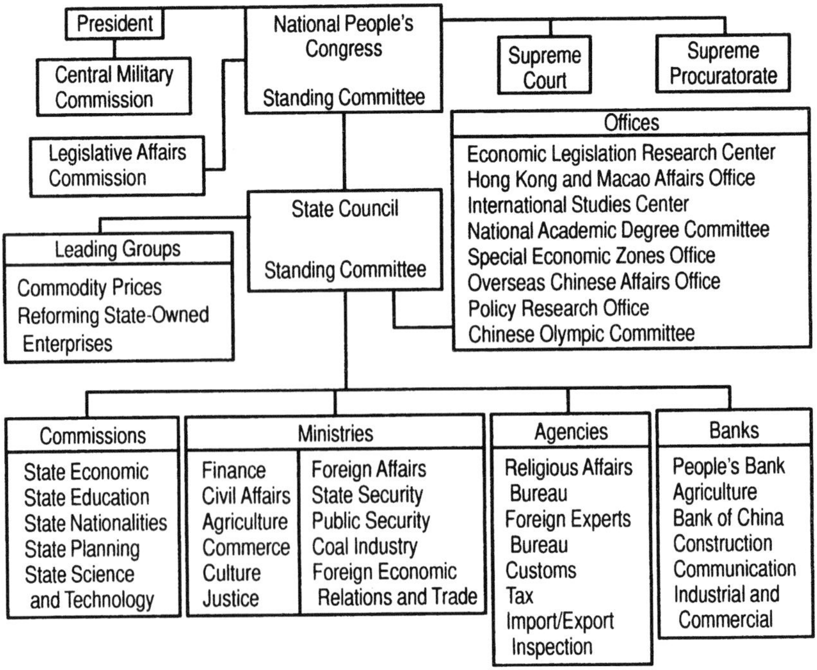

- President
- Central Military Commission
- National People's Congress
  - Standing Committee
- Supreme Court
- Supreme Procuratorate
- Legislative Affairs Commission
- State Council
  - Standing Committee
- Leading Groups
  - Commodity Prices
  - Reforming State-Owned Enterprises

Offices:
- Economic Legislation Research Center
- Hong Kong and Macao Affairs Office
- International Studies Center
- National Academic Degree Committee
- Special Economic Zones Office
- Overseas Chinese Affairs Office
- Policy Research Office
- Chinese Olympic Committee

Commissions	Ministries		Agencies	Banks
State Economic	Finance	Foreign Affairs	Religious Affairs Bureau	People's Bank
State Education	Civil Affairs	State Security	Foreign Experts Bureau	Agriculture
State Nationalities	Agriculture	Public Security	Customs	Bank of China
State Planning	Commerce	Coal Industry	Tax	Construction
State Science and Technology	Culture	Foreign Economic Relations and Trade	Import/Export Inspection	Communication
	Justice			Industrial and Commercial

So many organizations are not shown in the chart because of the limited space. They are listed and categorized as follows:

Commissions:

The State Family Planning Commission, the State Physical Culture and Sport Commission, and the State Restructuring of Economic System Commission

Ministries:

The Ministry of Aeronautics; the Ministry of Agriculture, Animal Husbandry, and Fishery; the Ministry of Astronautics; the Ministry of Chemical Industry; the Ministry of Coal Industry; the Ministry of Communications; the Ministry of Electronics Industry; the Ministry of Foreign Economic Relations and Trade; the Ministry of Forestry; the Ministry of Geology and Mineral Resources; the Ministry of Labor and Personnel; the Ministry of Light Industry; the Ministry of Machine Building Industry; the Ministry of Metallurgical Industry; the Ministry of National Defense; the Ministry of Nuclear Industry; the Ministry of Ordnance Industry; the Ministry of Petroleum Industry; the Ministry of Post and Telecommunications; the Ministry of Public Health; the Ministry of Radio, Cinema, and Television; the Ministry of Railways; the Ministry of Textile Industry; the Ministry of Urban and Rural Construction and Environmental Protection; and the Ministry of Water Resources and Electric Power

Offices:

The Central Green Commission; the Counselors' Office; the Economic, Technological, and Social Development Research Center; the Environmental Protection Commission; the Government Offices' Administration Bureau; the National Antarctic Survey Committee; the State Commission for Guiding the Examination of Economic Management Cadres; and the State Language Work Committee

Agencies:

The Auditing Administration; the China Council for Promotion of International Trade; the China Travel and Tourism Bureau; the China Welfare Fund for Handicapped; the Civil Aviation Administration; the General Administration of Exchange Control; the

New China News Agency; the Nuclear Safety Administration; the State Archives Bureau; the State Building Materials Industry Administration; the State Commodity Prices General Administration; the State Environmental Protection Bureau; the State Industry and Commerce Administration; the State Materials and Equipment Bureau; the State Meteorological Administration; the State Oceanography Bureau; the State Patent Bureau; the State Pharmaceutical Administration; the State Standardization Bureau; the State Statistical Bureau; the State Tobacco Monopoly Administration; the State Weights and Measures Bureau; and the Trade Mark Bureau

Regarding the figure, we need to explain some critical organizational relationships that our readers may not be able to understand.

1. The candidate of the President of the People's Republic of China is nominated by the Party, and then will be elected, or let us say "approved," by the representatives of the National People's Congress.
2. The members of the Central Military Committee are the same as the members of the Central Military Committee of the Party. That is, the Central Military Committee of the Party has been organized first, and then the National People's Congress will appoint it as the Central Military Committee of the state. Theoretically, the Central Military Committee of the state will report to the president. Nevertheless, it will depend on who is the chairman of the Central Military Committee. When Deng Xiaoping was the chairman of the Central Military Committee, he did not need (we think) to report to either Zhao Ziyang, the General Secretary of the Chinese Communist Party, or Yang Shangkun, the President of the People's Republic of China. Usually, the number-one person in the Party, either chairman or general secretary, is the chairman of the Central Military Committee.
3. The candidates for the Prime Minister and Vice Prime Minister are nominated by the President of the state and then will be voted on (approved) by the representatives of the National People's Congress.
4. As we can see from the chart and the list of organizational names, the State Council is the true administrative center. In

other words, the State Council is the core of the central government. The State Council of China and the Department of State of the United States are both translated into the same name in Chinese,(国务院), but, obviously, they have quite different functions.
5. The National People's Congress is a legislative body. The laws, regulations, and governmental policies, however, are formulated based on the Party policies; moreover, personnel appointment and removal are controlled by the Party. Accordingly, the National People's Congress is not a really powerful political organization.
6. The Leading Groups that are under leadership of the State Council could be temporal organizations that are established for certain purposes or goals. For example, the Leading Group of Nationwide "Safety Month" activities was organized in 1986 because of the unusually high number of accidents during those years. Currently, since reforming the state-owned enterprises is a critical task in China, a leading group has been organized by the State Council.
7. The China Council for Promotion of International Trade has been declared a nongovernmental organization, but it is under the leadership of the State Council as an agency.

The Ministry of Foreign Affairs is an important governmental organization that Westerners may often have to deal with. We draw its organizational structure in Figure 3.3.

Our explanations for this figure:

1. The Institutes A, B, and C are the Institute of International Relations, the Institute of International Studies, and the Chinese People's Institute for Foreign Affairs.
2. Vice ministers' responsibilities could be different than indicated in this figure. The key to the difference or change might be the expertise of the vice ministers involved.
3. The Chinese People's Association for Friendship with Foreign Countries has been declared a nongovernmental organization, too. Actually, it is under the leadership of the Minister of Foreign Affairs.

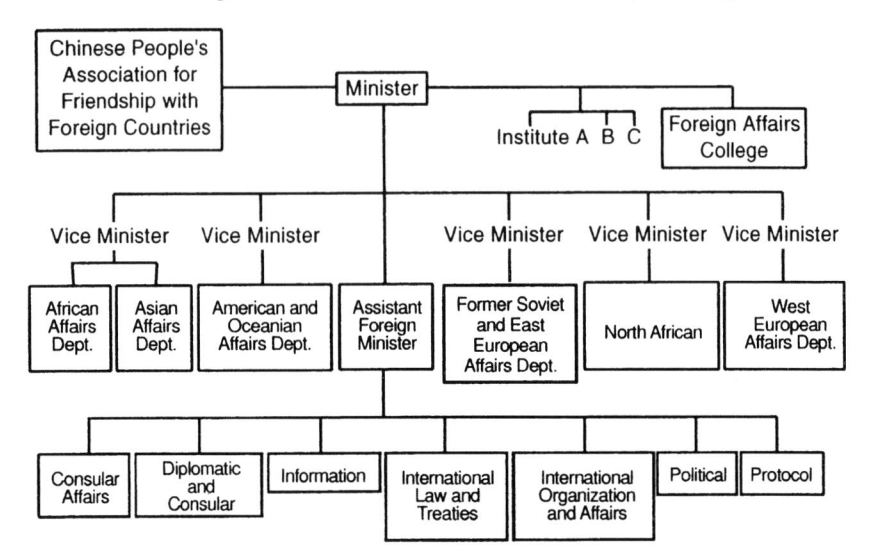

FIGURE 3.3. Organizational Structure of Chinese Ministry of Foreign Affairs

```
                    ┌─────────────┐
                    │  Minister   │
Chinese People's ───┤             ├─── Institute A B C ─── Foreign Affairs College
Association for     └──────┬──────┘
Friendship with            │
Foreign Countries          │
                           │
   ┌──────────┬────────────┼────────────┬──────────────┐
Vice      Vice          Vice          Vice           Vice
Minister  Minister      Minister      Minister       Minister
   │         │             │             │              │
┌──┴──┐   ┌──┴──┐    ┌─────┴─────┬───────┴──┐    ┌──────┴──────┐
African  Asian    American   Assistant  Former Soviet  North    West European
Affairs  Affairs  and        Foreign    and East       African  Affairs Dept.
Dept.    Dept.    Oceanian   Minister   European
                  Affairs               Affairs Dept.
                  Dept.
```

Consular Affairs | Diplomatic and Consular | Information | International Law and Treaties | International Organization and Affairs | Political | Protocol

DISCUSSION QUESTIONS

1. Discuss the historical role of the Chinese Communist Party in business decision making.
2. Discuss the present role of the Chinese Communist Party in business decision making.
3. What are some key characteristics of semi-governmental organizations?
4. What are some key characteristics of nongovernmental organizations?
5. What are some key characteristics of government structures?
6. In the West, the governmental organization is typically thought to be separate from political party structures. In China, the Communist Party cannot really be separated from the government structures. Agree or disagree? Why?

REFERENCE NOTES

1. Huang Yuanwu, Chief Ed. (1992). *The Great Dictionary of Economy and Trade*, (Beijing, P. R. China: China Foreign Economic Relations and Trade Publishing House), 1075.

2. All the legal parties that are not in power and accept the leadership of the Chinese Communist Party are called "democratic parties" in China. The members of these parties are called "democratic personages," and most of them are intellectuals, professors, scientists, artists, musicians, writers, and engineers.

3. When we drew these three charts of organizational structure, we referred to the charts that were published by the National Technical Information Service in 1984. However, quite a few organizations or organizational structures have been changed since they issued those charts. Therefore, we have changed and drawn the charts according to the current reality of the organizational structures.

4. Mao Zedong, Ed., *Chinese-English Dictionary*, The English Department of the Beijing Institute of Foreign Languages (Beijing, P. R. China: Change Publishing House, 1981), 544.

PART II:
THE OPERATION
OF DECISION MAKING

At the very beginning of this book, the life experience of observing mechanics checking cars was addressed. We believe that mechanical engineers should know the structures of machines, physicians must know human structures, and administrators ought to know organizational structures. However, knowing those structures is to understand *what* those structures are; this is not enough. Engineers need to know *how* the structures of machines conduct, physicians must know *how* human structures work, administrators should know *how* organizational structures operate. As we know, decision making is an active and moving process rather than a static spot; therefore, to know the operation of decision making in China is to understand *how* the process is moving, and to learn its characteristics, including the strengths and weaknesses.

Chapter 4

The Processes of Decision Making

DECISION MAKERS CONCERNED

The topic of persons who are involved in decision making in China is complex and interesting. Mao Zedong said, "The Chinese communist party is the core of the leadership of our cause."[1] This is also clearly stated in the Chinese Constitution. However, who really makes the decisions is very complicated. Different organizations dealing in different time frames may make decisions in quite different ways. Decision making by the Party secretary or the professional has often been a source of conflict in the Chinese political-business system.

The Chinese Communist Party seized the Chinese state power through its armed forces in which there has been established a very special position, called "political commissar" in regiment or higher levels, or called "political instructor" in a company or battalion. Who makes the decision has always been a problem between the "political commissar (instructor)" and the different levels of commanders. Mao Zedong repeatedly emphasized, "Our principle is that the Party directs guns, and never allow guns to direct the Party."[2] Nevertheless, since wars were very crude, sometimes people did not even have a chance to consider who should make a decision. This "someone," in most cases, was a military leader who was relying on his or her position of power. In the military sense, the assumption often is that the enemy's actions dictate the next decision. Because of the nature of crude warfare tactical operations, varied levels of commanders have been more powerful than the "political commissars (instructors)." The Chinese Communist Party, however, must control the army. As a result, someone must have two positions (i.e., commander and "political commissar"). Almost by definition, this military commander must be a member of the Party committee or of a Party branch. A commander could even simply be a party secretary. Even so, Mao Zedong was afraid that some of the commanders would become too powerful. So in 1973, he swapped the individual commanders of the eight Military Commands among each other, but not their political commissars.

After the Communist Party controlled China in 1949, construction and infrastructural development replaced wars as the principal task in China. As a result, conflict appeared between the Party secretary and officials (e.g., governor, mayor, and manager, etc.) There are five stages of struggling between a party secretary and/or manager that have fostered the decision-making process in business circles since the 1949 revolutionary political change.

The First Stage (1950 to 1956). When the Chinese Communist Party seized the state power, most enterprises were changed into socialist enterprises. Since the Party did not have any modern industrial administrative experience, learning from the Soviet Union was the only viable choice. Therefore, the "manager/director being in charge" system was borrowed from the Soviet's model. This system had two tenets. First, a manager/director led an administrative committee, and the manager/director had the power to make decisions or veto the decisions of others. Second, the responsibilities of the Party committee (branch) were to supervise the production process and to take care of the political work activities of the employees at the same time.

The Second Stage (1956 to 1966). In 1956 Mao Zedong, in his article "On the Ten Major Relationships," began to criticize China's style of blindly following the Soviet Union's examples. The Central Committee of the Chinese Communist Party had decided to carry out the system that placed the manager/director under the Party committee leadership. The essential result of this system was to locate the manager/director's responsibilities under the control of the Party committee. Every important factor for all affairs had to be discussed and decided by the collective leadership of the Party committee. The manager/director only took care of tactical daily affairs; implementing the decision was the responsibility of the Party committee. The so-called "collective leadership of the Party committee" was an essential leadership style modeled after the Party committee. In this system, the manufacturing administration had been confused with the role of party leadership. Particularly, most secretaries of the Party committee branches were laypersons, but most manufacturing leaders were replaced by the political works system.

The Third Stage (1966 to 1976). This period was widely known in the West as the Cultural Revolution. In the early stages of the Cultural Revolution, China was extremely chaotic because the Red Guards broke down all local Party organizations and all local governments. The functioning of the state was paralyzed, the manager/directors lost their positions, and everyone made autonomous decisions. But no one could really make strategic decisions except Mao Zedong himself. After 1969, the various "Revolutionary Committees" (representatives of the revolutionary army men, representatives of revolutionary cadres, and representatives of the revolutionary masses) gradually gained control of the various levels of power. In many cases, representatives of the revolutionary army men made key decisions. After the former minister of the Ministry of National Defense, Lin Biao, died in an air crash when he was escaping to the Soviet Union in October 1971, representatives of the revolutionary army men gradually lost their power and representatives of the revolutionary cadres (who could be former Party secretaries or former manager/directors) were placed in charge of the Revolutionary Committees. Thus, the last four or five years of the Cultural Revolution resulted in continuing unrest and confusion involving the flow of authority and decision making.

The Fourth Stage (1976 to 1981). After the Cultural Revolution, the Revolutionary Committees were canceled. The system whereby the manager/director was under the Party committee leadership was restored. Thus, decision making was essentially the same as during the Second Stage (1956 to 1966). Compared with the Cultural Revolution, this stabilizing time resulted in economic development to some extent.

The Fifth Stage (1981 to present). Deng Xiaoping was in power again in 1978. In 1979, he suggested a system that placed the manager/directors in charge of decision making. In 1981 some factories began to implement this system. The Central Committee of the

Chinese Communist Party discussed and agreed to accept this system in 1983, and the system was formally confirmed in 1984. The first meeting of the Seventh National People's Congress approved "the Law of Enterprise" to legally confirm the manager/director as a "Legal Person." As a result, the central government fully agreed to implement by 1988 this system that placed the manager/director in charge. Under this law, a manager/director of an enterprise has five areas of authority including the final decision about important issues for enterprise, manufacturing administration, staffing and personnel administration, financial management, etc. The responsibilities of the Party committee (branch) of the enterprise are to supervise the enterprise in the execution of the Party's policies and governmental policies, to control the behavior of members of the Party involved in the enterprise, and to be in charge of the political works of the enterprise. Of course, in some cases, the manager/director and the secretary of the Party may be the same person. But, typically, they are two different people.

This method of power assignment has been generally suitable for the government organizations. For instance, between the director and the secretary of the Party committee of the light industry bureau in a city, between the director and the secretary of the Party committee of the commerce department of a province, or between the minister and the secretary of the Party committee of the Ministry of Foreign Economic Relations and Trade, the formers are the key decision makers. Nevertheless, the secretaries of the Party committees in the localities, i.e., town, county, city, prefecture (subprovincial administrative regions), and province, have a more advantageous position in which to make vital operational decisions than governmental officials such as town/city mayor, county magistrate, prefecture administrator, and governor, with regard to the Constitution of China and the Constitution of the Chinese Communist Party.

However, China, is a society in which authority is emphasized more than power. For example, according to the Constitution of China and the Constitution of the Chinese Communist Party, the General Secretary of CCP, Jiang Zeming, should have the most power in China, but in reality he must listen to Deng Xiaoping who, as a retired official, has no direct constitutional power.

We will discuss this interesting phenomenon of power in Chapter 7, Traditional Culture. This phenomenon poses a key question: Who will be the key decision maker in a Chinese organization? Chapter 5 will suggest that, in reality, the true answer comes from the facts, not from just a written law or regulation.

THE GENERAL MODELS OF DECISION MAKING

Though the organizational structures (e.g., governmental, manufacturing, and service organizations) may be different in China, their models of decision making generally have many similarities. Of course, the organizations we are examining are state-owned and collective–as are nearly all of the main business organizations in China. We can generalize their decision-making styles into two methods: (1) decision maker is pushed by a higher authority to make a decision; and (2) a decision is made without basing it on a decision from a higher authority.

1. *A decision maker is pushed to make a decision by a higher authority.* Since these organizations are state-owned and collective within a hierarchical system where higher authority is mandated, in many cases the organization merely implements decisions from higher authorities. These organizations serve to facilitate decisions from a higher authority. This model is illustrated in Figure 4.1.

From Figure 4.1, we can see that organizations must concretely carry out the decision from the higher authority no matter whether the decision from the higher authority is proper to the situation or not. For example, the very uniqueness of the Western marketing approach of the multilayered distribution network system of Amway was introduced in China. The Chinese central government soon found out that this marketing style brought many problems to China (e.g., some governmental officials gained huge profits by using their special positions in this kind of pyramid selling method). Thus, the central government decided to prohibit this marketing method in 1994. Most local governments analyzed their local situations and identified problems, then formulated plans to implement the decision of the central government. However, people do not always carry out a decision from a higher authority. Although they

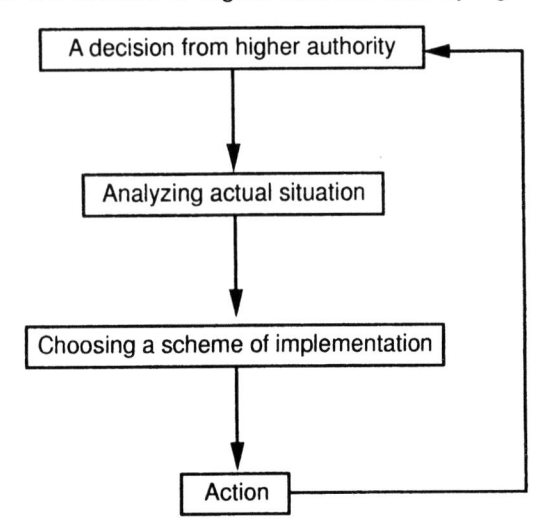

FIGURE 4.1. Structure of Organization Mandated by Higher Authority

```
┌─────────────────────────────────┐
│  A decision from higher authority │◄──┐
└─────────────────────────────────┘   │
                │                      │
                ▼                      │
┌─────────────────────────────────┐   │
│   Analyzing actual situation    │   │
└─────────────────────────────────┘   │
                │                      │
                ▼                      │
┌─────────────────────────────────┐   │
│ Choosing a scheme of implementation │   │
└─────────────────────────────────┘   │
                │                      │
                ▼                      │
         ┌──────────┐                  │
         │  Action  │──────────────────┘
         └──────────┘
```

usually do not openly reject decisions from higher authorities, they do formulate skillful tactics to carry out their own decision while seemingly implementing the exact decision from the higher authority. This is exemplified by a popular saying in China, "[Where] there is a policy from above, there will be a countertactic from below (上有政策,下有对策)." In American culture we often hear the expression, "Where there is a will, there is a way." While this American saying may be more general that the Chinese saying, the result is the same. This model of decision making is illustrated in Figure 4.2.

Before China carried out the policy of opening its door to the outside world in 1978, only the governmental foreign trade companies had the authority to operate an import/export business. Later, joint-venture, foreign enterprises, and some other special factories/firms also gained the right to engage international business. Because governmental foreign trade companies usually cannot offer satisfactory service, many factories/companies would like to sell their goods to joint ventures, foreign enterprises, or the enterprises that do have the right to conduct international exporting, or they simply wish to pay a commission for those enterprises to import/ex-

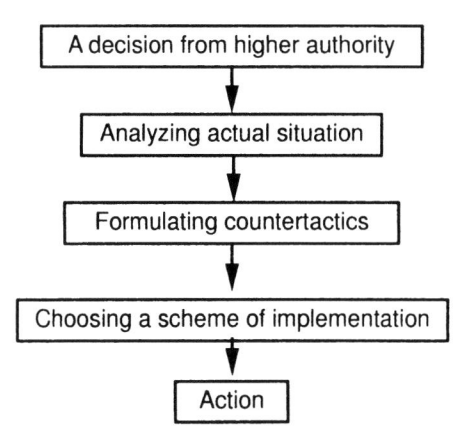

FIGURE 4.2. Countertactic to Mandate by Higher Authority

```
A decision from higher authority
              ↓
    Analyzing actual situation
              ↓
    Formulating countertactics
              ↓
Choosing a scheme of implementation
              ↓
             Action
```

port their goods for them. As a result, the governmental foreign trade companies lose much business. Because of this situation, the central government formulated a policy in mid-1995. This policy stipulated that (excepting the governmental import/export companies) only when the organizations with authority to conduct import/export trade export their own products can they enjoy the priority policy of tax deduction. Thus, the joint ventures, foreign enterprises, or the enterprises that have the right to conduct international trade could continue to buy other's goods for their export businesses, but they could not deduct tax from those kinds of exports. As a result, only the governmental import/export companies had the right to purchase other's products for export and still deduct tax from these exports. Facing this change and challenge, many local governments formulated corresponding local policies to protect their joint ventures, their own enterprises that have the authority to conduct import/export trade, and even the foreign companies located in their areas. For example, one of the local policies was to "organize" a local governmental import/export company; those organizations continue to conduct their export trades just as in the past. The only difference was that when they completed their export paperwork, they used the name of the local governmental import/export company. Therefore, those organizations could export other's products but continue to enjoy the priority policy of tax deduction. Of course, they may need to share something with the local governments.

2. Decision making without basis from a higher authority. During the past decades, China carried out a planned economy. The decision making employed by enterprises was to implement the plans from their higher the authorities, namely as described in the previous model. Since the Chinese government began to officially accept the ideas of a market economy in 1992, some Chinese enterprises have initiated their own decision making. The decision making model illustrated in Figure 4.3 is quite typical.

Decision making not based on a decision from a higher authority could also be related to the consequences from the decision making of lower levels. We have previously discussed "a decision maker is pushed to make a decision by a higher authority." However, one individual's higher authority could be another's lower level. For instance, a city government is the higher authority of its light industry bureau, but the city government is the lower level of the province government. Therefore, one could be another's higher authority while also being someone's lower level, except for the Central Government or the Central Committee of the Chinese Communist Party, which has no higher authority. For this reason, anyone could have a higher authority to make a decision that results in consequences

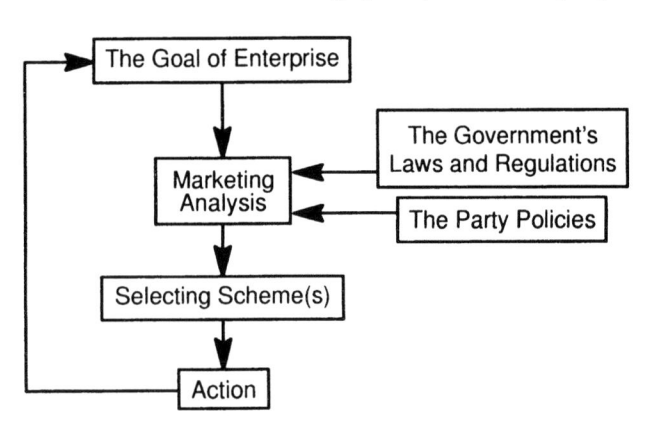

FIGURE 4.3. Decision Making by Independent Company

for the decision making of a lower level. When we consider "the consequences of the decision making of lower levels" as a situation in which one needs to make a decision, we may easily understand this explanation. In fact, this is a reaction of "[Where] there is a policy from above, there will be a countertactic from below (上有政策,下有对策)." For the circle to be completed, "[Where] there is a countertactic from below, there will be a policy from above (下有对策,上有政策)." Let us consider this: Before 1978 only the central government's foreign trade corporations and their branches had the authority to conduct any import/export business. In order to gain foreign currencies and strengthen the local economy, various provincial governments established their own foreign trade companies one after another. From their higher authorities, the counties, cities, and prefectures (subprovincial administrative regions) learned how to establish their own foreign trade companies as well. While the provincial governments formulated some centralized policies to control the foreign trade companies of their counties, cities, and prefectures, the central government decided that certain products could only be imported or exported through the central government's foreign trade corporations and their branches. For example, the authority for grain imports is firmly controlled by the central government's grains, oils, and foods import/export corporations and their branches. The authority for exporting textile products is controlled by quotas[3] that in general only allow for distribution arranged by the central governmental textile and products import/export corporations and their branches.

STEPS OF DECISION MAKING

The steps of decision making in China, defining the project (problem), collecting and analyzing information, formulating alternatives and schemes, choosing alternatives and implementing actions, are about the same as in the West. These steps have been followed by many Western business organizations for many years. Over the past quarter-century, management theory has developed the strategic management process. Many strategic management business textbooks encourage businesses to follow this process as a successful management technique.[4] However, the specifics of the steps and the process of the activities in China do have some differences.

Defining Project(s)

Very interestingly, while a Chinese manager/director once operated in an extremely restricted way in defining a project for the enterprise business direction, he or she had too many choices in defining projects.

A Chinese manager never had the right to decide what strategic direction an enterprise should follow in a planned economy, but he or she would have quite a long list of projects about which to make decisions. Generally speaking, today, many Chinese managers have the authority to decide the direction of their enterprises and businesses in a market economy, but they still have a very long list of projects that require their decision making.

The daily affairs of the manager of a Chinese state-owned or collective enterprise are also different from that of a Western manager. Most Chinese state-owned or collective enterprises own and operate a clinic or hospital, dining hall(s), store(s), housing/apartments/condominiums, nursery or kindergarten, elementary school or high school or even a university, a barbershop, a library, a theater, etc. Walls enclose the above projects to form a small society in which a manager functions almost as a "king" or "queen," or a tribal chief, who has to take care of everything, occasionally even a quarrel between a husband and a wife. When China operated in a strictly planned economy, manufacturing was not considered to be an important decision-making project. In general, the manager's daily affairs may now be placed into four categories: manufacturing (including finance), political issues, personnel (including staffing and human resource management), and daily lives. Manufacturing and personnel may be more easily understood by our readers, but political issues and daily lives may need to be explained by examples. Political issues could mean that a policy from the Communist Party or the government needs to be operationally put into effect. For this reason, if the birth control policy in a Chinese organization appeared to be experiencing such difficulty that it attracted the attention of or criticism from a higher authority, then birth control would become a decision making project for a manager. Whatever the employees and their families need for day-to-day living falls under the realm of daily lives. If an enterprise cannot supply its employees with enough bottled gas for cooking, they may not work hard. So many projects and problems related to decision making surround a manager. Since decision making is situational, one manager (or secretary of the Party) would choose and define projects differently than another manager. Undoubtedly, manufacturing has become the paramount issue for decision making in a growing market economy. Nevertheless the other three areas (political issues, personnel, and daily lives) remain critical for a manager. Noticeably, as we have explained previously, due to so many problems needing to be solved, sometimes managers do not know how to define a project by themselves, and so may simply wait for a decision from a higher authority defining a project for decision making.

In brief, since the market economy has been strongly influencing Chinese economic lives, not only has manufacturing become the number one issue for decision making, but the democratic style of decision making has also been gradually adopted. Also, defining projects for the enterprise such as, "What products should be made?" or "What kinds of business should we engage in?" has been a possibility and a reality; Second-level projects, e.g., "How should we make it?", "When can we make it?", "Where will we make it?", or "Who can make it?" are no longer the only concerns for managers. Peter Drucker, the famous American management professor and noted business author has often written that to be successful a business must ask these basic questions. "What business are we in?", "What products should we make?", and "Who is/are our customer(s)?" Strategic business expert, author, speaker, and consultant Tom Peters often talks about the vital importance of the product-market match. Based on their long influence on business in the West and in Japan, Drucker and Peters have achieved much notability and both have been labeled as "gurus." In short, along with the market economy growing in China, defining high level projects for enterprise direction, which the Western scholars encouraged, has been a reality among Chinese manager/directors.

Collecting and Analyzing Information

The step of collecting and analyzing information is basically similar to each of the other steps when comparing decision making in China and in the West. There are two vital points we want to mention. First, both cultures have the same understanding of the concept of "information." However, Chinese business decision makers view the relevant and new Party policies as extremely critical information. For example, "the stock market would be allowed to experiment," and "foreign exchange currency would be canceled," etc., once became such vital information that quite a few wise businesspeople could have become rich overnight. Now as we are writing this section, the people in the Special Economic Zones (SEZs) are debating and arguing with an economist in Beijing about whether SEZs should continue to be "special." We believe that this should be vital information for investors. It is possible that some new Party policies may gradually close the gap that has greatly widened in per capita income levels between residents of the eastern and southern coastal areas and the far less developed northwest areas of China. This issue is complicated by the wide range of historical factors and predicted future investment levels in various geographical regions. In other words, quite a few businesspeople understand that collecting and analyzing the relevant and new Party policies are extremely vital acts in this step of business decision making because any government's laws and regulations are under the direction of Party policies.

Second, decision makers may not completely rely on, or entirely trust, some information they collect with a survey questionnaire or information received from face-to-face interviews because of the traditional philosophies of the golden mean, saving face, modesty and implication, and other social elements. (Note: these traditional philosophies are discussed in detail in Part III.) For example, if given a survey or interview to evaluate an American boss among the Chinese, particularly when the Chinese think the boss may recognize their evaluations, or if given information collected from a Chinese political seminar, etc., many decision makers in China would not entirely trust such information. Just as in America, you may not completely believe compliments about your food from dinner guests. The author Chen Tong has recently been gathering information about leisure activities in China. When the respondents replied to the questionnaire, most of them reported their incomes to be much higher than they actually were. Why? Because the information would be sent to America. Chen Tong also conducted a survey among the aged Chinese in the greater Cleveland area. Since many of them could neither read Chinese nor English, an interview was necessary to help them fill out the form. The survey attempted to find out whether or not their children gave them money. The results were very different when someone assisted them with an interview. The respondents who filled out the forms by themselves indicated either "yes" or "no." But most subjects said "yes" if people filled the forms out for them in an interview. Thus, the credibility of the results from a survey must be considered.

One way of collecting information in China is to send political workers to visit or to interview people. We do not know how much people trust those political workers or how truly the subjects would converse with those political workers. And we do not know whether those political workers would collect information slanted by their conscious or unconscious biases.

Even using an ethnographic method of observation to collect information, when people know someone is watching them or may be watching them, they may consciously or unconsciously behave and conduct themselves very differently because of face-saving or some other political or social factors.

Dr. Charles E. Watson argued the following points in his recent book, *The Skills of Analysis*.[5] Analysis is an in-depth look at something. Conducting analysis properly is certainly not easy. Some confuse analysis with reporting; this is unfortunate, because analysis is much more than reporting. Analysis requires the manager to find insights beyond the obvious. Careful investigation of interrelationships, interpretations, logical reasoning, and rigorous probing of the information is required to prudently carry out analysis. Based on the above different characteristics of collecting information in China, analyzing information may be subtley different from Western methods; generally speaking, analyzing information is quite similar in China and the West.

Formulating Schemes and Choosing Schemes

There is a very famous Chinese saying, "Blindly choosing stones to cross a river." Deng Xiaoping used this saying to describe the reforming and opening movement in China. Based on many years of experience and lessons, information, and comparisons, he made the decision of reforming and opening. It was absolutely right. We very strongly agree with and support his decision of reforming and opening. Here, we are using this saying without any desire to criticize him; we use it because it is a very proper saying to symbolize many aspects of Chinese decision making.

In "blindly choosing stones to cross a river," a decision, "crossing a river," has been made. The only choice is to decide which stone(s) should be used. To consider "blindly choosing stones" as a step of formulating alternatives and finding an alternative, the correct and proper process is to first define the project–whether or not to cross the river; second, collect and analyze information about the "stones"; then formulating the alternatives–*what*–which includes crossing the river, *how* to cross the river, and *where* will be the best "stones" to use to cross the river, *when* is the best time to cross the river, and *who* ought cross the river. Yet, the alternatives–*what*– should also include not crossing the river but going some other way which may imply *why*, *how*, *where*, *when*, and *who* as well. In other words, we should first probe every stone, then decide if we should cross the river, and how to cross the river. We ought to collect and analyze the information first, then formulate the alternatives that include whether or not to cross the river, and finally choose the best alternative. Making a decision even before collecting and analyzing the information makes formulating alternatives an unnecessary step, or one can only formulate *how*, *where*, *when*, and *who* as lower levels of alternatives, but not *what*.

Many Chinese cadres (managers) have a very popular excuse– "paying tuition" for wrong decision making or an improper process of decision making. Of course, any decision making implies taking some level of risks. Sometimes the risks may be extremely high. However, many Chinese people may not realize that sometimes the cadres do not actually pay "tuition" for their wrong decisions but for the improper process of decision making. The steps of collecting and analyzing information, and formulating alternatives are to help people choose the best alternative and make a logical decision. Since a decision has often been made before collecting and analyzing information, for formulating alternatives and choosing among them, no wonder the "tuition" has been so high.

Sometimes, some leaders may already have had an alternative scheme or even a decision in their minds, in this case the process of formulating and choosing alternatives will just be to confirm their own decision. If not, they will insist on their alternatives. Many people, for example, believe that some leaders had an idea to build the Project of Three Gorges on the Yangtze River before the experts collected and analyzed information and formulated the alternatives. Though we do not have evidence to prove it, we know it is often true that a manager has an idea or even has made a decision before collecting and analyzing information, and formulating the alternatives.

However, in China there have been quite a few official or semi-official organizations, called "Office of Fact-Finding and Research on Policies" or "Institute for Policies Research," which provide information and selected alternatives for various levels of leaders' decision making. Noticeably, the information and selected alternatives may often be provided to the leaders before a decision has been made, or even an idea/concept has been formed. A market economy has given Chinese managers an opportunity to begin their decision making on *which* products they should make, namely *what* their enterprises and business directions should be–not just the *how*, *when*, *where*, and *who* which they used to make their decision in a planned economy (which was usually a decision about tactics and methods).

Formulating and choosing schemes is about the same as selecting alternatives in the West. There are numerous evaluative processes that can be utilized to assist a manager in the decision-making process. Strengths and weaknesses analysis, strategic audits, and weighing possible outcome techniques are all methods of selecting alternatives. Some American textbooks describe these methods (e.g., see Fred R. David, *Strategic Management*, fifth edition and Lester A. Digman, *Strategic Management: Concepts, Processes, Decisions*).[6] There are numerous scholarly books and textbooks available that give more detail about selecting the optimal scheme or alternative. Here, we do not focus on the methods of formulating and choosing schemes that are very similar between China and the West. We only intend to stress a characteristic of decision making in China–that a decision may have been made before formulating and choosing schemes.

Control and Feedback

In most cases, decision making is a cause, not a point. Decision making usually will not be completed when a decision has been made. Decision makers or administrators need to control the action and collect the feedback until they reach their goals and objectives. This may be done by a variety of methods, most of which make use of systematic means of monitoring actual performance and evaluating and comparing outcomes with desired standards.[7] If necessary, some adjustments may be made, or even some crucial corrective action might be taken. Sometimes, the decision making has to be completely stopped or canceled. This is a democratic and scientific method for decision making.

We have stated that many decisions may be made before collecting and analyzing information, formulating alternatives, and choosing alternatives in China. In fact, we can consider that collecting feedback is the second circle of collecting and analyzing information, and controlling is also a second circle of formulating and choosing alternatives. If we accept this understanding, we may discover two possibilities. First, these kinds of decision makers would not realize how important collecting feedback and controlling are in the decision making process. They would simply ignore these chains of democratic and scientific reasoning and make another decision before collecting and analyzing information, formulating schemes, and choosing alternatives. As we can see, without collecting and analyzing information, formulating schemes, and choosing alternatives, control and feedback almost lose their meanings. Second, as a lesson, decision makers may start to realize the significance of collecting and analyzing information from the bad news of the feedback. As a result, they may begin to collect and analyze information before any decision has been made. Of course, after regretting their mistakes, they may still repeat those mistakes by controlling and collecting feedback that will confirm a decision made before they collect and analyze information. The "Struggle against the Bourgeois Rightists," the Great Leap Forward, the Cultural Revolution, etc., are suitable examples. Actually, from getting bad feedback, even the decision makers have realized the importance of collecting and analyzing information, and that mistakes could have been avoided. Unfortunately, many Chinese leaders and administrators may not realize the significance of collecting and analyzing information, and formulating schemes and choosing alternatives before they collect and analyze feedback.

DISCUSSION QUESTIONS

1. "Who really makes a decision?" is a major concern in China. Agree or disagree? Why?
2. Discuss the significant facts of the Cultural Revolution (Third Stage, 1966 to 1976) that impacted the process of decision-making in China.
3. Discuss the continuity of the five stages (since 1949).
4. What are the main concerns of the Fifth Stage? What/when do you project will be the Sixth Stage?
5. What are the pros and cons of decision making not based on a higher authority?
6. The "steps" of the Chinese style of decision making are about the same as in the West. Agree or disagree? Why?
7. What are the inherent political ramifications of developing projects and what impact might they have on getting the task done effectively and efficiently?
8. Could a communications breakdown in collecting and analyzing information be a significant problem? Why or why not?
9. Formulating and choosing schemes is about the same as what many in the West might call "developing and selecting alternatives." Agree or disagree? Why?
10. What's done is done and you can't change the past. Why should a decision maker be concerned about feedback and control?

REFERENCE NOTES

1. Mao Zedong, *Quotation from Chairman Mao Tse-Tung* (New York: Praeger, 1967), 1.
2. Ibid, 55.
3. Regarding quotas, in order to protect certain natural resources or some industries of a country, this country may limit and control a certain amount of

importing/exporting of these very materials or products. The amounts of materials are limited to be exported, called "initiative (active) quotas." The amounts of products are controlled by foreign importing countries, called "passive quotas." For instance, in order to protect the Western countries' own textile industries, they limit certain amount of importing textile and products from other countries.

4. See for example, *Formulation and Implementation of Competitive Strategy*, sixth edition, John A. Pearce II, and Richard B. Robinson, Jr., Chicago, IL: Irwin, 1997.

5. Charles E. Watson, *The Skills of Analysis*, second edition (New York: McGraw-Hill College Custom Series, 1993).

6. Fred R. David, *Strategic Management*, sixth edition (Upper Saddle River, NJ: Prentice-Hall, 1997).

Lester A. Digman, *Strategic Management: Concepts, Processes, Decisions.* (Houston: Dame Publications, 1995).

7. Joseph W. Leonard, "Strategic control: Is it effectively executed?" *Managers Digest*, Volume 2, Number 1, 1987, 7-12.

Chapter 5

Characteristics of Decision Making

PERSONALITIES

There have been countless rumors about the health of Deng Xiaoping in China, Hong Kong, Macao, and Taiwan since 1989. It is worth noting that financial markets, particularly the stock markets in those areas, have been plagued with large fluctuations following these rumors. Many Western people do not understand why the rumors about the health of the retired Mr. Deng could so strongly influence the investment markets not only in China but also in Hong Kong, Macao, and Taiwan. The President of the United States could be a person with limited ability. If this was true and this kind of person was elected, people would still peacefully drink a cup of coffee before they went to work, ball games would still be played, lottery winners would still scream as crazily as they always have. There would not be a major change in America. Of course, the announcement that former President Ronald Reagan had Alzheimer's disease would influence neither the American nor Mexican and Canadian financial markets. China, however, is different. Throughout the ages, China has been a society that believes it must have a powerful ruler. Most Chinese people do not believe in God, but they need a sage or a powerful man. In Chinese history, when there was not a powerful man who could be emperor or feudal prime minister, China would lose control and enter a stage of chaos in which it would lose wars to foreign countries; wars would arise between Chinese warlords, and even peasant uprisings would occur due to famine from crop failures. These are some of the reasons Deng Xiaoping had so great an influence on China.

According to a Chinese newspaper, in 1991 a terrible flood destroyed thousands of peoples lives and caused massive damage to homes in China. Facing this flood, a peasant did not rescue his family and property first, but, instead, saved a statue of Mao Zedong. The newspapers tried to tell people that the peasants still strongly loved the communist party, socialism, and Mao Zedong. In fact, many people regard Mao Zedong as a deity. As Western tourists can see, many taxi drivers still hang a picture of Mao Zedong in their cars in today's China. Why? They hope that the picture of Mao Zedong will drive away evils. Many people, particularly peasants, even worship a picture or statue of Mao Zedong in their shrines built for idols or ancestral tablets.

Many reasons can be listed to explain a society devoted to rule by a sage or a powerful man. Two main points, however, must be addressed. The first is the idea of ruling by benevolence. Western culture, particularly the Christian culture, believes that human nature is evil. Hence, humans must be controlled by the rule of law. Ruling by laws assumes that, even if by chance a scoundrel were elected president, he must follow the law to perform his office. Otherwise, he would lose his position quickly. The Chinese people always assume that they should be ruled by benevolence—ruled by their leaders with perfect role expectations. The Chinese character of "benevolence" is 仁, and includes two parts: 亻 means people, and 二 means two. It actually implies a moral relationship between people. Using this analogy, ruling by benevolence would imply a moral bond between people (those ruled and the ruler). More interestingly, the pronunciation of "benevolence" in Chinese is identical to the Chinese sound of "person" or "people." Thus, in Chinese, the definition of a ruler (person) implies morality and therefore ruling by benevolence. Most Western people respect and worship the law; Chinese people respect and worship their moral leaders. However, there is not any person in the world who is perfect. As a result, the Chinese people have to tolerate their imperfect leaders, and continue to assume their leaders will be benevolent. We can easily point out examples such as Mao Zedong, Zhou Enlai, and Deng Xiaoping on the mainland, Sun Yat-sen, Jiang Jieshi (Chiang Kai-shek), Jiang Jingguo, and Lee Teng-hui in Taiwan, and Goroug Yao Lee, the former prime minister of Singapore. Without laws to control people, manpower, intelligence, morality, and/or personalities, there could arise an invisible authority and a force to control the people's minds. Ruling by law, the president is elected by votes. Ruling by benevolence, a person can only become the leader through struggles. When Mao Zedong died in 1976, Hua Guofeng was appointed as the Chinese leader. But a leader could not be merely appointed by someone in a society that is ruled by benevolence. The leader must build his authority in the people's minds with his manpower, intelligence, morality, and/or personality. Without these special personal strengths, Hua Guofeng was quickly defeated by Deng Xiaping in 1978. Voting, appointing, and electing does not work in a society ruled by benevolence. Only a sage or powerful man will become popular.

The second important factor about benevolence is that most Chinese people do not believe in God. In the West, most people are either Christians or they have grown up under the influence of Christian values. Being saved by God, they believe that they will someday go to heaven. At any time, they can share their misery and happiness with God through prayer. They feel that they can rely on God, and they can be granted help and salvation from God. With spiritual dependence on God, people may not feel a need to be practical in their lives. God always stays with them anywhere and anytime. Most Chinese people are drastically different. They do not believe in God, so the universe is too difficult to be understood. When you raise your head to the stars to look as far as your eyes can reach—that is the mystery of infinity, might you not feel that you are enveloped by an incomprehensible (agnostic) world? Might you not feel inadequate in your intelligence to some extent? Would you feel that you need something or someone to rely on? Moreover, Chinese culture, particularly Confucianism, has made most Chinese people believe in this life and this world. Heaven does not have any practical or realistic significance to them. The best heaven for them is to enjoy their real lives here on earth. When people do not wish for or expect a perfect heaven waiting for them, they will adopt a very realistic attitude toward the world and their lives. For these reasons, Chinese people need a vital and powerful person to rely on and give support for their daily existence. After those powerful people pass away from this realistic world, people choose one or a few as idols to enshrine and worship. Those idols are their spiritual dependence.

In the past twenty years, two men passed away causing two demonstrations in Tian'anmen Square that the government had to quell. In 1976 Zhou Enlai, the Prime Minister, passed away. Many Chinese people seemed to feel the end of world was coming; millions of people ignored the prohibition of the government to lament Mr. Zhou's death so that the government had to crush the movement with force. The most recent demonstration was in 1989, when Mr. Hu Yaobang passed away. Millions of people went to Tian'anmen Square to mourn him. Finally, these demonstrations became a famous movement that was crushed by military forces on June 4, 1989.

The Chinese people do not entirely understand why American people, who believe in God, have so strong an interest in movies and television shows portraying superheroes. Shows about Superman, Superboy, and Supergirl are very popular in America. Chinese people can understand a similar interest in themselves: since Chinese people do not believe in God, they really want someone to be their superhero to protect them and to drive away evils from their domain. In Christian culture, everyone is equal before God, so "everybody is equal before the law" has become a possibility. In Chinese culture, if leaders have been made into idols or even deities, how could everyone possibly be equal before the law?

As we can see, Chinese culture has provided a deep, strong social foundation to support those powerful men. Even in today's China, many Chinese theorists recommend the idea of a New Authority (the concept of New Authority implies that a powerful man will lead the Chinese people to gradually achieve a democratic society with his authority) instead of a "one person, one vote" system for China in the near future. They believe that without votes, China will be all right; however, without a powerful man who embraces the concept of New Authority, China will not eventually achieve democracy, but will soon fall into trouble.

It is very logical that Chinese culture has provided a deep, strong social foundation for powerful men who, no matter what the direction of the national policy decision making or a company's business decision making, will lead in a strong individual fashion.

Typical examples could be "the project of a senior official," "the project from a note," and "the minister's project," etc. In past decades, the Chinese economy has been developing very rapidly. Foreign visitors are impressed to see new buildings being constructed everywhere. Any new or expanded project, such as importing new equipment, building new complexes, establishing new factories, and constructing new roads, must be approved by the government at every level. We can easily imagine that there is a substantial waiting term while a project goes through the various levels of government approval. "The project of a senior official," as its name implies, means that one of the projects from the long waiting list is abnormally approved to be built by the decision from a senior official. Likewise, "the project from a note" means that a note would come from a higher authority, which could be a former boss or an indirect official, to approve new construction. Somebody might bring a note from Beijing to inform a local government that a certain project that is on the waiting list has been approved. The author, Huang Quanyu, has been involved since 1992 in a deal to import millions of dollars of machinery to China. This project has been on the list for approval for several years. One day, the Chinese manager excitedly called Huang Quanyu from China, "Quanyu, I am calling you from Beijing! Good news! Our project has been listed as a minister's project." "What does that mean?" "The minister has approved it, so it is called a minister's project now. Everything will not be so difficult from now on." About four months after the project became a minister's project, a contract for purchasing machines from Germany was signed in 1995. Still, too many projects are waiting for approval: some are very important, and some may not be necessary. If you let some senior official understand how important your project is, he or she may make a decision concerning your project. When your project becomes the senior official's project, you will have special authority to secure funding and to acquire budgets more quickly.

Indeed, in China, relying on decision making from leaders with personality strengths is a result of the wars. Before the Chinese Communist Party seized the state power in 1949, the troops of CCP had experienced more than twenty years of war with countless battles. Most cadres who occupied various leadership positions in state-owned or collective enterprises, governmental organizations, and various levels of government came from the People's Liberation Army, the troops of CCP. As we can imagine, a commander usually did not have time to review alternatives and discuss a decision during a battle. Missing an opportunity during combat might mean the loss of a battle, or even a campaign. Too often, a commander had to make prompt and timely decisions during a war. As a result, too many cadres who were commanders during the wars like to act autocratically during peaceful times. Mao Zedong often felt he was empowered by the Central Committee of the CCP to make decisions. Many secretaries of the Party committees always thought that "I am the Party committee; my decision is a decision from the Party committee." Even some people with actual authority but without official positions could make a personal decision about a collective issue. For example, in 1986 Deng Xiaoping, who was at that time a member of the Central Committee of the CCP, made a decision in which Mr. Hu Yaobang, who was officially the top leader of the Central Committee of the CCP (the General Secretary) had to leave his position. Mr. Deng also made some individual good decisions along with some bad collective decisions. After the event at Tian'anmen Square in 1989, the movement of Reforming and Opening landed in a predicament. He made an inspection tour in southern China in January 1992. During his trip, he not only appraised the movement of Reforming and Opening, but also openly accepted the ideas of a market economy. The Central Committee of the CCP made a decision to continue the movement of Reforming and Opening and accept the ideas of a market economy during April 1992. This was evidence for the Chinese political theorists to recommend their theory of New Authority. This clearly orchestrates that an individual can have a great deal of power in China.

We have previously mentioned the history of decision making conflicts between manager/director and the secretary of a party. No matter who is in power to make a final decision, the Chinese people call this person "first in command," or "number one person." Sometimes, some people are officially named "first in command," but they may have to listen to someone else for the final decision because China is ruled by one powerful person. Or to state it differently, although some secretaries of the Party were officially in power, they might have to listen to their managers, or some managers who were officially in power might have to listen to the secretaries of the Party. It depends on who would be able to build his or her authority in the minds of the people. The Chinese state-owned and collective enterprises are small societies where there are clinics or hospitals, dining hall(s), store(s), housing/apartments/ condominiums, nursery or kindergartens, elementary or high schools or even a university, a barbershop, a library, and a theater, etc. Those official or unofficial number one persons with authority are similar to a mayor, king, queen, or the tribal chief of a small society. They need to take care of everything, from manufacturing to daily lives and security, in these societies. He or she needs to decide who will be promoted among his or her employees. This person needs to solve the problems of production. He or she needs to discuss with the "kings" of neighboring communities sharing the costs of repairing the road that several small societies are using. He or she needs to devise how to increase the number of apartments to meet people's needs in the small society. However, the planned economy was unable to supply enough materials/products to meet the people's needs. This was an opportunity for an able "number one person" to build his or her authority by using his or her abilities, influences, connections, and means to solve the problems for their small societies. Now that the Chinese economic system is moving from a planned economy to a market economy, the social order, laws, and regulations are not perfect for the move. This very situation has also become an opportunity for those able number one persons to use their abilities to conduct business, or make deals to improve their small societies.

When dealing with certain Chinese organizations, you need to understand their mode of decision making. To understand a certain Chinese organization's decision, you must understand the number one person's decision making. In other words, if you understand the number one person's decision making, you can understand the organization's decisions. That is to say, it is very important to research Deng Xiaoping's ideas and thoughts to understand China's decision making. When you need to deal with a certain organization in China, if you were told that the manager's words could not be counted on even if he or she were an official number one person, you must find out whose words could be counted on, who has the authority to make the final decision. To state it differently, in order to understand Taiwan's decision making, you really need to understand Lee Teng-hui's decision making, but not Lian Chan's. While there may be some situations in Western business deals that require an understanding of who and how an actual decision is made, the procedure in the Chinese system is more dependent upon the individuals involved and the hierarchical structure of society. In the West, a decision is more likely to be able to be made by many different individuals, whereas in China dealing with the appropriate person is often critical.

Many people believe that the relationship between the CEO and the board of directors in American organizations is similar to the relationship between the Chinese manager and the Party committee (branch). There are some similarities, but there are some vital differences as well. One difference we want to point out is that the number one person may be very powerful in an American cooperation, but he or she is certainly under the direction of the board. Although in about two-thirds of major U.S. corporations the chair of the board is also the Chief Executive Officer, the board still has the final authority. With boards becoming more participative in strategic decisions and with the average tenure of a CEO decreasing, clearly most U.S. boards of directors have decision-making power. A generation ago, many boards were criticized as being mere rubber stamps for top-level management; today we see less of these rubber stamp boards. Regarding Chinese "boards of directors," we must recognize that a Chinese number one person in a state-owned or collective enterprise is very strong, even though there is a Communist Party committee (branch) to be considered as a "board of directors." Now China is carrying out a system where the manager/director is placed in charge. The first meeting of the 7th National People's Congress approved "the Law of Enterprise" to legally confirm the manager/director as a "legal person" in 1988. Under this law, a manager/director of an enterprise has the authority to make the final decision about important issues for the enterprise, for the manufacturing administration, for financial administration, and for the personnel administration. The responsibilities of the Party committee (branch) in an enterprise are to supervise the enterprise to carry out the Party policies and governmental policies, to control the behavior of the members of the Party in the enterprise, and to be in charge of the political works of the enterprise. Of course, in some cases, the manager/director and the secretary of the Party may be the same person. Likewise, a CEO may also be the chair of the board in an American organization.

BASING DECISIONS ON THE PARTY'S POLICIES AND THE GOVERNMENT'S VIEWPOINTS

We have discussed individual characteristics of Chinese decision making, but when we view the situation as a whole we will find out that the Party's policies are the highest principles by which business decisions are made in China. This is a fundamental fact that must be taken into account fully and must not be overlooked by any Western businessperson.

First we need to illustrate the relationships between the Party and the government. In 1985 to 1986, the General Secretary of the Central Committee of CCP, Mr. Hu Yaobang, tried to implement a legal system and rule by law. The first step of his plan/program was to instruct the Chinese as to the common sense of laws. To understand the workings of laws, people needed to study the available information. An examination about the legal system was believed to be an effective means to ensure that people would undertake study. Thus, every cadre was required to take the examination about laws during 1985 to 1986. People began to argue: "Are the Party policies under the laws and regulations?" or "Are the laws and regulations above the Party policies?" In other words, "Who controls whom? Who directs whom? Who listens to whom?" These ideas were never questioned before. This program, which Mr. Hu Yaobang had really given much thought to, was not completely carried out after he was forced to abdicate. In Chinese reality, the Communist Party has been declared by the Constitution to be the sole legal ruling party in China. Therefore, the Chinese laws and regulations are based on the Party policies that it formulates. That is to say, any Chinese law and regulation must not go against or conflict with party policies. Furthermore, if the Party policies are changed, the relevant Chinese law(s) and regulation(s) must be changed. For example, the Chinese Communist Party accepted the ideas of a market economy instead of a planned economy in 1992. Since the Party policies have been changed, any action to teach, talk, and write about a socialist country must include a market economy. Or a market economy, which formerly was defined as a capitalist symbol, could now also be a symbol or characteristic of a socialist economy and would not violate any Chinese law or regulation. The four adherences[1] have been clearly stated in the Constitution, and one of the four adherences is to adhere to the socialist path. Advocating a market economy will not be against the Constitution now. Judicature has not been independent yet in China; the government is the sole organization to implement the laws and regulations of the country. We have mentioned that the Chinese laws and regulations, which are approved by the National People's Congress, are based on formulated Party policies. Obviously, the relationships between the Communist Party, the National People's Congress, and the government are as follows:

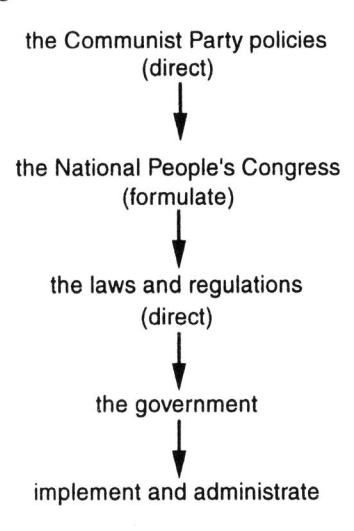

the Communist Party policies
(direct)
↓
the National People's Congress
(formulate)
↓
the laws and regulations
(direct)
↓
the government
↓
implement and administrate

From the above illustration, we can clearly figure out the relationships between the Party and the government.

China is a socialist country whose main properties are state-owned. Accordingly, the various levels of government are the legal representatives of state-owned enterprises and collective enterprises. In this sense, the business decision making of state-owned enterprises or collective enterprises must be based on governmental policies. Also, China is a socialist country in which the Communist Party has been declared by the Constitution to be the sole legal ruling party. The Party policies formulate the laws and regulations that the governments implement to administer the country. After the event in Tian'anmen Square in 1989, many contracts were canceled or temporarily stopped. This could illustrate that business decision making in China must be based on Party policies and governmental viewpoints. Another example, after Lee Teng-hui "privately" visited the United States, Sino-American relationships were cornered. On July 13, 1995, there was a news article in *CND (Chinese News Digest)*:

> The U.S. State Department spokesperson Nicholas Burns said on Thursday that China is expected to make commercial decisions based on economic criteria only, Reuters reported. Burns made a reference to China's recent awarding of a deal to review the possibilities of building luxury Mercedes-Benz. Burns said that the U.S. hoped this decision was not a result of political considerations, which China denied.

There are thousands of instances we can list to expose the undeniable relationships between business and politics. In a sense, business decision making is also strongly influenced by governmental viewpoints in the United States. Determining whether or not to grant MFN (Most Favored Nation) or GSP (Generalized System of Preferences) to certain countries, or to implement economic sanctions against Cuba or some other countries is proof that business is strongly influenced by politics in the United States, too. The differences are that business decision making in China is officially based on the Party policies and the governmental viewpoints, but business decision making in America may be strongly influenced by party (Republican or Democratic) policies and governmental viewpoints. For example, the Federal Reserve (with its director appointed by the president) has the legal power to directly influence interest rates, which directly affects the entire macroeconomic system. In the future, of course, because of changing to a market economy in China, business decision making may gradually rely less on Party policies and governmental viewpoints.

In summary, the Party principles are the core that directs the formulation of the Party policies, which, in turn, direct Chinese laws, regulations, and governmental viewpoints. Hence, the Party principles are supreme to the Party policies, the laws, regulations, and governmental viewpoints. In many cases, we may often find an illustration of Chinese business decision making that is from governmental viewpoints, or the Party policies and principles.

The Party is the core in China, but why is "separation of the Party from the administration" being carried out as an important Party policy? This point may confuse most Westerners, so we need to offer an explanation. Separation of the Party from the administration is a Party policy intended to avoid the conflict between the Party leadership and the administration. From the history of the conflict between the secretary of the Party and the manager/director, we can see the struggle for separation of the Party from administration. On the one hand, adhering to the Party leadership is a principle in China; nevertheless, mixing the Party leadership and administration together has deeply hurt the administration in many situations. Since 1978, China has opened its door more and more to the outside world. This idea of separating the Party from the administration became more acceptable as a Party policy. The purpose of this policy is to create a good environment for administration, but administrative leadership instead of Party leadership is not allowed. Therefore, the system manager/directors' decision making rights are limited in state-owned and collective enterprises and institutions, and governmental departments and organizations. However, Party leadership decisions still reign supreme over various levels of state powers. In other words, the secretary of the Party committee in a city/town, county, province, and state is officially more powerful than the mayor, governor, or Primary Minister.

CHANGEABILITY

The words, "blindly choosing," from the famous Chinese saying, "Blindly choosing stones to cross a river" should be able to vividly describe the "changeability" of decision making in China. Realistically, if you cannot choose a stone, a change of decision must be made. Even if you can choose a stone, whether or not you can choose the second stone still might make the decision questionable. Even if you can select the second stone, it may not mean you can continually find stones that will allow you to cross the river. From this metaphor or image, we should be mentally prepared to understand the changeability of decision making in China.

China is in a great historic era of economic change. The "socialist market economic system" that China is trying is a brand new experience. Not one existing theory can be used to direct China's movement. Any corner of China may reflect countless variability. Accordingly, the changeability of decision making in China is understandable. We will focus on some important causes of the changeability of decision making in China.

The first cause of the changeability is that many Chinese managers may make a decision before collecting and analyzing information as we have mentioned previously. That is to say, collecting and analyzing feedback in the process of controlling a decision might become the process of collecting and analyzing information that should have already been done. In the early stages of transferring to the market system, the economy is very dynamic and changeable. There is variability in decision making anywhere and anytime, and any feedback adds variability to this decision making. For example, the Chinese government approved a technological innovation plan for a Chinese factory with 25 million yuans. The Chinese factory decided to import various machines, including grinders, milling machines with CNC, and inlaying equipment. The factory reached an agreement to buy those machines from an American company. The American company would pay expenses for the Chinese delegation to visit America to inspect these machines. After the inspection, the Chinese delegation found out that the machines they really wanted might be made in other countries. This illustrates that the Chinese delegation should have collected and analyzed information before they made the decision to visit America, but they did not. So, when they collected and analyzed feedback in the process of controlling, they were conducting the process of collecting and analyzing information that they already should have gathered. Obviously, the feedback that the Chinese delegation collected and analyzed would force them to change their decision. This was a lesson for both sides. Of course, you may not be able to collect and analyze some information before you make a decision. H.C.K. International has experienced several such problems. In terms of the Chinese policies, in order to import goods from China, H.C.K. needed to deal with Chinese import/export companies or the companies with the authority to conduct international trade. After repeatedly haggling over prices, then checking the samples that were made with the American customers' blueprints or specifications several times, several months passed. When H.C.K. eventually reached the stage of signing a contract, the Chinese import/export company informed H.C.K. that the manufacturer had raised the prices since the prices of the materials for production had risen. We understand the dilemma of the Chinese import/export companies; they were unable to predict the prices of the materials for production, particularly due to the new market system. The Chinese import/export companies could not quote their prices too high and leave some margin because they might have lost their chances to deal with H.C.K. The Chinese import/export companies were not manufacturers; thus, they could not keep control of the prices. This provided a convenient opportunity to the manufacturers to raise their prices while they bargained and worked with H.C.K. In the West it is likely that such a contract would be predicated as "firm-fixed-price," but in China the situation was different.

Second, the moral standards of ruling by benevolence are changeable. Of course, the legal criteria of rule by law are changeable as well. There are some key differences between both changes. To change any law in a society ruled by laws, leaders must follow complicated legal procedures. These procedures are stated in legal documents, and legislative bodies and/or executive bodies will be involved in making the changes. Likewise, in this kind of society, in order to change any decision that involves the law(s), one has to follow certain complicated legal procedures, too. Nevertheless, to change a decision in a society where "ruling by benevolence" is emphasized will not be so complicated because "being reasonable" is highlighted in a society ruled by law, and "being considerate" is emphasized in a society that prefers ruling by benevolence. If "being considerate" in Chinese implies emphasis on human feeling, change, accommodation, and adaptation to a certain situation, "being reasonable" means following laws, regulations, rules, and policies. In a certain situation, a decision can be changed if human feeling, accommodation, and adaptation are considerable in the eyes of the Chinese, but a decision would not easily be changed if the change would involve laws, regulations, rules, policies, and contracts. A typical instance that the author, Huang Quanyu, experienced was an import/export business deal between China and the United States. Part of the business relationship involved a Chinese manufacturer, an import/export company, and a bank in China. An American firm was interested in purchasing some manufactured goods, and accordingly, a contract was agreed to by both parties. According to the understanding of the letter of credit, the Chinese bank sent the documents to the American bank. The American bank then asked the American company to pay for the goods, at which time the bank in the United States would release all the documents to the U.S. company's agent in Hong Kong for signing, and the Chinese side could issue the documents for the letter of credit collection. The American bank would not release these documents unless the goods were paid for in full. The American company would not pay for the goods unless their Hong Kong agent had them in his possession. Without the documents, the American company's agent in Hong Kong could not take delivery of the goods from the storehouse at the port in Hong Kong, which was charging HK $150 each day for storage. In order to break this catch-22 and avoid more unnecessary costs, Huang Quanyu tried to persuade the controller and general manager of the American company to pay the letter of credit first. This suggestion was based on the fact that the only cost was about $10,000 and the Chinese factory was planning on doing at least $1 million worth of additional business soon. From the Chinese perspective, this is considerate. But in order to be reasonable, the controller and general manager of the American company would rather pay the Hong Kong warehouse charge than cause potential damage to future business.[2]

Third, the Party policies are changeable. There is a saying in China, "The policies of the Communist Party look like the full moon tonight, [but it] may not be so tomorrow." Since the Chinese Communist Party was born in 1921, there have been more than ten major "two-line struggles" (not including numerous minor "struggles"). So-called "two-line struggles" occur when the leaders of the Party fight with each other about their serious differences or totally contrary understandings of the Party principles. As we know, the Party principles direct the Party policies. As a result, any struggle or change of understanding about the Party principles will cause many changes in the Party policies. Moreover, even a minor struggle or change of understanding about the critical concepts may cause many changes in the Party policies. For example, the struggle of understanding a planned economy and a market economy has caused nearly twenty years of changeable Party policies. When a planned economy was the only focus, the orthodox socialist economic system got the upper hand; the Party policies were formulated around this focus. As the market economy issue won respect, a whole set of the Party policies had to be changed and reformulated, e.g., the Party policies about the stock market, the Party policies about market competition, and the Party policies about unemployment, etc. Particularly, during the era of economic system change, there is not any existing theory about the "socialist market economic system" that can be borrowed by the Chinese Communist Party to direct the Chinese economic operation. This has resulted in an understandably difficult situation for the Party. Many Western businesspeople cannot understand that thousands of orders and business opportunities might emerge in this year, and many international agreements or even contracts might suddenly have to be canceled or temporarily stopped in the next year. Actually, this was the Chinese governments experience with the Party policies about economic macro-controlling in a market economy.

Changing the Party policies in China is not as complicated as changing a law in a society ruled by laws. Either the Political Bureau or the Standing Committee of the Political Bureau of the Central Committee of the Chinese Communist Party can decide to change the Party policies. In some cases, the individual with authority such as Mao Zedong or Deng Xiaoping could decide to change the Party policies without any difficulty. This is a point we explain in our fourth argument.

Fourth, the personality of decision making that we have discussed in the last section is an element of the changeability of decision making. During the celebration of the fiftieth birthday of the United Nations, many American people felt that the President of the People's Republic of China, Jiang Zemin, was quite open and friendly when he informally met people and answered reporters' questions, but he was so different and even rigid when he officially read the lecture notes. These Americans might not realize that the lecture notes were decided and approved by the Political Bureau of the Central Committee of the Chinese Communist Party. He must read item by item from the text of his speech. However, when he informally met people and answered the reporters' questions, he would be able to show his flexibility and his personality. Personality with authority may make decision making more changeable. In the 1960s, Mao Zedong decided to treat North Vietnam as "Comrade plus brother." North Vietnam then became one of the three closest friends of China with Albania and North Korea. In the 1970s, Mao Zedong decided to improve China's relationship with the United States, which was engaged in war with North Vietnam. A seed for Vietnam to side against China in the future was planted. In 1979, Deng Xiaoping changed his mind and decided to punish Vietnam, which had been "Comrade plus brother" just a short time before. When Deng Xiaoping's idea that "one country can accommodate two different social systems" had gained attention and considerable fame in the world, there was no reason to fight with the old "Comrade plus brother" just to accommodate an antagonistic (hostile) ideological social system. China and Vietnam reopened their border for normal association and trade. As the examples illustrate, personality in decision making has provided the soil and climate for the changeability of decision making.

The previous analogy of the "changeability" of decision making in China has explained its causes, which are mainly passive elements. In fact, changeability of decision making can be positive. Changeability could cost more, but it could avoid more losses as well. Changeability may imply instability, but it could also imply dynamics, accommodation, and adaptation. America is a society ruled by law. Although there are more lawyers in the United States than engineers in Japan, there are many quite obvious legal loopholes that have not been corrected. The way of counting votes for electing the U.S. President is an example. The candidate for President who wins the highly populated states such as California, Texas, New York, Pennsylvania, Ohio, and Michigan, etc., will win the election. However, the candidate who wins in these big states may not need to win the majority of votes in the whole country because as long as he gets one more vote than the others, say in California, then he would take all of the electoral votes from California. This rule allows a candidate who is voted in by a minority to be the President of the United States. This rule enables candidates to neglect the less-populated states. Why don't the U.S. legislative bodies change this and simply count the majority of the votes? For over 100 years, every four years, American people are involved in this type of election. Why don't they change this rule? By this example, it is evident that changeability of decision making could be bad, but might not always be so. Changeability of decision making truly based on "being considerate" and "being reasonable" could be perfect.

INFLEXIBILITY

The Chinese philosophy of *Yin* and *Yang* dialectics believes that the origin or essence of the universe is created by two poles. The *Yin* and the *Yang* can be interpreted in numerous ways, such as cold and hot, female and male, moon and sun, conservative and liberal, negative and positive. . . . As we can see, most of the characteristics of decision making in China that we list in this chapter can be organized as two poles of the *Yin* and the *Yang* such as changeable and inflexibility, predictable and unpredictable, complexity and simplicity, radical and the golden mean. From this, we may find out how strongly the Chinese philosophy of *Yin* and *Yang* dialectics has influenced the Chinese mode of thinking and their way of behavior. On the other hand, this may remind us to notice the contradictory unity of opposites of the characteristics of decision making in China. In other words, we may need to understand the characteristics of Chinese decision making from two different or contrary perspectives. Accordingly, our readers should not consider that business decision making in China is only changeable. In the following section we will discuss the characteristic of inflexibility in decision making in China.

Many Chinese managers may make a decision before collecting and analyzing information. This indicates that they may entirely ignore the significance of information. If this is true, then they might also neglect the importance of collecting and analyzing feedback. Undoubtedly, when a decision maker neglects the importance of collecting and analyzing feedback, he or she will lose, give up a chance or even miss the last opportunity to change his or her decision. This simply means that he or she will inflexibly adhere to the decision until it has completely failed. Of course, in the case of war, inflexibility might be a guide to victory. The Chinese Marshal Chen Yi had an example, the "Battle of Annihilation at Huang Bridge" in the War of Resistance against Japan. After he arranged every detail of the line of operation for the battle, he played chess with someone. The reports (feedback) from the forward positions came one after another to indicate that the situation was extremely dangerous. His aids tried to persuade commander Chen Yi to withdraw as soon as possible. While he inflexibly ignored all reports (feedback) from the forward positions and sent all of the persons around him to these positions, he continued to play chess with the person who was almost the last one left. Finally, his plan of attacking from within, in coordination with an operation from without, was achieved by his reinforced units. Yes, it was true that commander Chen inflexibly ignored all reports from the forward positions that indicated he should withdraw. But that did not mean he did not collect and analyze information before he made the decision for his line of operation. There are two points in this story that are important. First, the wars that most Chinese soldiers and commanders experienced were not modern wars in which people have enough means and powerful tools to collect and analyze information. This might have been cause for them to neglect collecting and analyzing information when they were managers of enterprises after the wars, and may also have influenced the coming generation of managers to some extent. Second, people may enjoy the examples from the wars that show how inflexibility guided a victory, but they do not notice that those inflexible commanders might also pay attention to collecting and analyzing information.

In brief, if a leader ignores the significance of collecting and analyzing information before a decision has been made, he or she may be highly likely to neglect the importance of collecting and analyzing feedback. Then, inflexibility of decision making will be a logical result.

The politically powerful man could be another cause of the following three possibilities for inflexibility in decision making. First, a powerful man may lack a channel to collect information. We do not have very convincing evidence to prove that Mao Zedong decided to launch the Great Leap Forward before collecting and analyzing information. However, we believe that there was no channel through which he could collect and analyze the feedback about the Great Leap Forward because of his all-powerful authority. For instance, while thousands of people began to starve and die, the various levels of governments reported to Mao Zedong about good harvest news everywhere. The most surprising phony "achievement" was from Huanjiang county of Guangxi Zhuang Autonomous Region that claimed to harvest more than 130,000 *jins* of rice per *mou*. As we know, one *jin* is equal to 1.1023 pounds, and one mou is equal to 0.1647 acre. Three big trucks with three 40-foot containers are not capable of carrying 130,000 *jins* of rice. Mao Zedong grew up on a farm in the countryside; he was intelligent enough to know that this report was as false as if you told him the sun was rising from the West. Telling a truth looks easy, but may not be so in reality. You can easily say to a person, "You are so beautiful!" even if it is not true. But you will have an extremely difficult time telling a person, "You are so ugly!" even if it is true, particularly if this person is very powerful. People only told Mao Zedong that good harvests were everywhere during the Great Leap Forward, but China was strewn with the bodies of the starved, and false boasts, such as producing 130,000 *jins* of rice per *mou* were misleading. Mao Zedong was fooled by the bureaucracy because he lacked a channel to collect and analyze information.

Second, a powerful man with overly strong authority would neglect collective decision making. Hence, majority votes will not have any binding meaning and will just be considered nonsense by any strong dictator. The Cultural Revolution was a typical example. We can find an example of a powerful man neglecting collective decision making from several sages' words. Confucius said, "Ordinary people are only allowed to do what they ought to do, but are not allowed to know why they ought to do so,"[3] and "Only the most intelligent man and the most stupid people would not be changed."[4] These words of Confucius were quite clearly written to advise a wise ruler to merely give the order "what" to his people, but not to share the "why"; also Confucius believed that the most intelligent man would be stubborn.

Let us share a story.

One day the King of Qin state, Qin Xiaogong, discussed how to rule people with his three officials, Gong Sunyang, also named Shang Yang (390-338 BC), who was one of the most well-known sages of the Legalists,[5] Gan Long, and Du Zhi. Qin Xiaogong said, "To honor their forefathers, but always think about the country; this is the attitude a king should have. To propagate the king's prestige in every way, that is the behavior the ministers ought to have. Now I am going to reform the rules to administer the country, and reform the etiquette (protocols) to educate the people. But I worry that people will criticize me."

Gong Sunyang said, "I was told that without decisiveness, an action would not be successful; without a resolution, a cause would not be achieved. You should make a decision to reform the rules as soon as possible, and do not worry about critics. A man with noble behavior would be ridiculed by mediocre persons; and a man with distinctive ideas would be criticized by ordinary people. An old saying is: 'The stupid people often do not understand the thing that has been successful, but an intelligent man is able to predict the thing that will have not yet shown its symptom of a trend. You cannot discuss the origin of a cause with ordinary people, but merely cerebrate the success of the cause of them.' Guo Yan cited from the code: 'The man who expounds a profound philosophy will be different from the mediocre persons. The man with great achievements will not discuss anything with ordinary people.' The rules are to protect the people, the etiquette (protocols) are good for the people. Accordingly, as for a sage, as long as [the reformation] can make the country strong, [we] do not need to keep the old rules; as long as [the reformation] is good for the people, [we] do not need to follow the old etiquette (protocols)."

Gan Long and Du Zhi argued with Gong Sunyang. Finally, Qin Xiaogong, the King of Qin state, agreed with Gong Sunyang, and said, "Good! I also heard that the persons who lived in poor areas and small alleys commented excitedly and strangely on something without experience; and the scholars with poor knowledge liked the futile arguments. The things that stupid people enjoy are just the ones the intelligent man feels upset about; the projects that crazy persons like are just the things the intelligent man worries about. Being restrained by philistine points of view to discuss the important national affairs is no longer for me." Soon thereafter the order for cultivating barren lands was promulgated.[6]

Xunzi, a sage of Confucianism, said, "The sky would not cancel the Winter because people hate snow and coldness. The earth would not shrink its size because people dislike hugeness. A gentleman would not change his mind because of clamor from the mediocre persons."[7]

We can make a conclusion from the above sages' words: If you are an intelligent man, you should make your decision and adhere to your decision, but ignore what others who are mediocre persons, ordinary people, or scholars with poor knowledge may say. Obviously, in most cases, the behavior that ignores others' opinions is not democratic. However, the people who believe the theory of New Authority may enjoy the few cases in which inflexibility foils the disturbances from mediocre persons, ordinary people, or scholars with poor knowledge. For example, after the event at Tian'anmen Square in 1989, many Marxist theorists began to suspect whether the movement of Reforming and Opening should be labeled "capitalist" or "socialist?" Some even tried to prove that the Reforming and Opening movement was guiding China toward a capitalistic path. The Chinese Reforming and Opening Movement was in a very difficult condition. In January 1992, Deng Xiaoping made an inspection tour in southern China. He seriously ordered people to stop arguing as to whether the Reforming and Opening movement should be labeled "capitalism" or "socialism," but firmly continued his decision about reforming and opening. In other words, no matter what kinds of "stones" we can "choose," we must "cross the river." Interestingly enough, many people compared his order to stop arguing whether the movement should be labeled "capitalism" or "socialism" to Qin Xiaogong's words, "the scholars with poor knowledge liked the futile arguments." His inflexibility is credited with rescuing the Reforming and Opening movement. In the opinion of the theorists of New Authority, undoubtedly the Marxist theorists with "poor knowledge" and the mediocre persons strongly oppose the Reforming and Opening movement. But while many ordinary people agree with the Reforming and Opening movement in words, they may oppose it in deeds when the movement affects their actual interests, such as increasing unemployment or skyrocketing prices resulting from competition in a market economy.[8] Hence, there must be an authority to strongly mediate the disturbances from mediocre persons, ordinary people, or scholars with poor knowledge, and indomitably pursue or even push the Reforming and Opening movement in China.

Should we also consider the two sides of the inflexibility of decision making in China with the Chinese *Yin* and *Yang* dialects? While Chinese people are arguing about that, hundreds and thousands of Israeli people–young and old, male and female–were choked with tears when they lost their strong leader, Yitzhak Rabin, who wanted to indomitably pursue the peace program with Palestine. Also, many people from other countries are observing the health of Boris Yeltsin who has been prevailing over all dissenting views to persist the political and economic reformation in Russia, but was hospitalized with heart problems. Do these two examples prove something from a different perspective?

Third, there are some so-called "ironclad cases" that the powerful men have finally decided, and no one can change their decision. Such "ironclad cases" become forbidden zones that no one wants to touch until the powerful man who decided the case loses his authority or passes away. The political "ironclad cases" we can list are the Great Leap Forward, the Cultural Revolution, and the April 5th Movement at Tian'anmen Square, all of which have been changed or reversed after Mao Zedong passed away. The case of the "Struggle against the Bourgeois Rightists" has not been completely reversed yet because Deng Xiaoping, who was once involved in deciding this case, is still alive. In the business circle, there are some "ironclad cases," too. People are very afraid that some officials from a higher authority will make inspection tours before really collecting and analyzing information and then make arbitrary decisions to stop some projects. To stop implementing the projects that have been started would waste money, but continuing the projects against those powerful men could imperil one's position or career. How big a dilemma it is!

Similar cases, in a sense, occur in the United States as well. After the twelve members of the jury decided that O.J. Simpson was innocent, no one could change the ruling, no matter whether he was guilty or not. Here, we are not interested in if O.J. Simpson was guilty or not, we merely want to stress that there are phenomena of ironclad cases in the United States as well. The only difference is that the authorities of the U.S. "ironclad cases" come from the legal-judicial system, but the authority of Chinese "ironclad cases" come from personal will. In a society ruled by law, you can change a decision through certain legal procedures. Though the legal procedure may be very complex, you can follow one step after another to try it. Yet, for some Chinese "ironclad cases," with powerful men's inflexibility, you may not be able to follow a certain complicated procedure to change them. Of course, for some U.S. "ironclad cases," the legal procedure can be too complex to follow or simply impossible to reverse, as well. Whether in China or the West, it is difficult for any decision maker or leader to admit a major mistake and to reverse a key decision.

Usually, the powerful men have very dominant, or even inflexible personalities. For this reason, in the case of choosing the stones to cross the river, flexibility will only be in choosing which "stone." Crossing the river is an inflexible decision. When crossing the river is the right decision, the inflexibility is estimable. On the contrary, if crossing the river is a terrible decision, the inflexibility will cause more troubles. Therefore, putting our hopes on inflexibility, but not scientific and democratic decision making, is like taking the branch for the root (put the incidental before the fundamental). We ought, instead, to probe to the roots of the inflexibility of decision making and build a strong supervising and controlling system to balance decision making from the strong political men. In brief, while we need to be aware of the cultural roots of powerful men, we must build a complete, scientific, and democratic administrative structure.

PREDICTABILITY

Many people from the mainland (China) are very adept at discovering real "news" from the official newspapers, television programs, and radio broadcasts. The press and media are labeled as "the mouthpiece of the Party." Therefore, the way something is presented–formulation, wording, the position or location of where a news story is published, the order of names of leaders, arguments, and stories, etc.–can be the means to provide some essential "news" and meanings that are hidden between the lines. This may be interesting for Western readers, but may not be easily understood. Let us look at some examples.

People can derive meanings from the choice of wording, the formulation, or the way something is presented. From the change in the ways the economic system has been described (the Socialist planned economy to the Socialist planned commodity economy to the Socialist market economy), we can sense that the Party policies have been changing. The Socialist planned economy was an orthodox formulation. After reforming and opening in 1978, the Socialist planned economic system was challenged. The reformers wanted to reform the planned economy, but the market economy, at that time, was considered as the symbol of the capitalist system, which was a restricted zone. They borrowed the theory from Marxism-Leninism in which commodities were acknowledged and allowed to exist for a long time in a Socialist system, in order to mix a market economy into a planned economy, but they named it the Socialist planned commodity economy. Due to bias against a market economy, however, it was limited in operations. The planned economy, which had hindered Chinese development, was still playing a leading role. Once Deng Xiaoping openly affirmed the market economy to be the economic means that could be operated in a Socialist system, the proper wording for the economic system in China became "the Socialist market economy."

Certain news in certain positions and locations can indicate certain meanings. Suppose a news story about some problems of Sino-American relationships is placed as the leading front-page news. The Sino-American relationships would be considered a real "problem" in the Chinese key decision makers' eyes. If the story's location is not very prominent, say on the fourth page of *People's Daily*, the "problems" will not be considered very important. Hence, they would be solved one way or another even though there was some serious argument or conflict between two countries. When the news was written that First Lady Hillary Rodham Clinton would attend the World Women's Conference in Beijing, it was on the front page of some Chinese newspapers. Though it was not very striking, many people knew that human rights activist Harry Wu[9] would be released soon.

We also can determine something from the order of names of Chinese leaders. Chi Haotian, the Chinese Secretary of defense, occupied a higher position than Zhang Wannian, the Chief of General Staff. One day, the new members of the Military Commission of the Central Committee of the Chinese Communist Party was listed in the Chinese newspapers, and the name, "Zhang Wannian" was listed before Chi Haotian. We do not know yet the reasons for this decision, but Zhang Wannian has been confirmed to play a more vital role in the People's Liberation Army than Chi Haotian is doing though both are vice chairmen of the Military Commission of the Central Committee. When people could not find the name of the former mayor of Beijing city, Chen Xitong, in the news of the activities that he should attend as the mayor of Beijing, people had strong reason to suspect that he had either political or health problems though he was a member of the Political Bureau, in a very critical position, and looked very healthy. Later, he lost his position because of corruption. Hu Qili used to be listed as the third member of the Standing Committee of the Political Bureau but lost his position as vice minister of the Ministry of Electronics Industry after the event at Tian'anmen Square. If his name begins to appear in the Chinese newspapers, then you can be assured that some decisions will have been made. Similarly, the U.S. Central Intelligence Agency (CIA) viewed the Soviet Union's official press photos to determine if there had been a structural shake-up in the top central leadership.

The arguments in the Chinese newspapers can also indicate the degree of importance. When some person positively argues something in newspapers that is not allowed to be discussed openly, this hints that something will change or will happen soon. After the Tian'anmen Square event in 1989, almost all the articles in the Chinese newspapers discussed anticapitalism and anti-peaceful-evolution from the West. However, occasionally a couple of essays discussing adherence to the reforming and opening, by a commentator named "Huang Puping," appeared in the newspaper, *Liberation Daily*, which was published in Shanghai where Deng Xiaoping visited quite often. That was viewed as very atypical. As a result of these unusual articles, many politically sensitive people believed that something had happened. There was a similar case before Mao Zedong launched the Cultural Revolution, when he arranged for Yao Wenyuan to publish a long article in Shanghai's newspaper attacking his political opponents in Beijing. After several arguments, nothing happened, but the sensitive people knew something would happen soon. One day, an article by Fang Shen appeared on the front page of the *People's Daily*, which was the largest circulation newspaper with the highest authority from the Central Committee of the Chinese Communist Party. The article openly suggested that China should learn beneficial things such as science, technology and modern administration from the Western capitalist countries. This was like a bomb for some people, but sensitive persons knew something had happened politically to influence the newspaper. The true story was that Deng Xiaoping found the essays by "Huang Puping" published in *Liberation Daily* were not strong enough to change the situation in China at that time. Then, he went to visit the Special Economic Zones[10] and the coastal cities in southern China in January 1992. During his trip, he appraised the movement of Reforming and Opening, attacked the "Left" conservative officials (the so-called orthodox Marxists and Leninists), and openly confirmed the ideas of a market economy. Since then, the situation in China has changed entirely.

While we are writing this chapter, Mr. Li Youwei, the secretary of the Party Committee of Shenzhen city has published articles in Shenzhen's newspapers to argue with the well-known theorist Hu Angang in Beijing as to whether the Special Economic Zones should still be "special." Many people believe that this is a sign of change in the Party policies. They predict that there may be some changes that will lessen the huge economic gap that has been continually expanding between the coastal areas and the interior of China.

From the stories, pictures, and advertisements from the newspapers, journals, radio, and TV, we can detect any essential changes in the Party policies. Some American scholars are surprised about our unique capability to read and discover so many subtleties from between the lines. Indeed, this is a means of protection, a tool to survive and make money for your business. Because when you can predict the governmental viewpoints from the Party policies, then you can predict your business partners' or business opponents' decision making from the governmental viewpoints. For example, one day Mr. Terrence W. Hosty, Vice President of Investments for PaineWebber, called H.C.K. International, a consulting company that the author Huang Quanyu owns, to discuss investments in China. After a quick review of the information from Mr. Hosty, Huang Quanyu gave this advice: Please consider as a project the cellular telephone system because of its growing and extremely huge market potential in China. If it is a 100 percent foreign investment project, it could be approved by the government. And forget the projects about commercial complexes. (Why the reasons for the project of a cellular telephone system? Our readers can read the first section, "Saving Face," of Chapter 7, "Traditional Culture," in Part III, "The Elements that Impact Chinese Decision Making.") Huang Quanyu explained to him, "As for the projects of commercial complexes, we should not waste our time, energy, and money on them. First, China is repeatedly emphasizing macrocontrol of investments. Therefore, even though the investment information of commercial complexes indicates that the Chinese side would invest at least 50 percent, it will be very difficult to get funds or an approval from the government. Second, the former mayor of Beijing city, Chen Xitong, got into trouble from the projects of commercial complexes in Beijing. The central government will use this excuse to order chaotic real estate markets in the whole country, particularly in the big cities. Third, several days ago there was an article in the *People's Daily* that criticized the too large amount of money being put into the commercial complexes in which the supply has been exceeding the demand, but economic apartments are in short supply for ordinary residents who have enough money. I think that when they made the decision about these commercial complexes, the situation was different from now. Even now, if we decide to deal with them, they will change their decisions because of a different situation. Based on the above three reasons, we should simply forget this deal or at least wait for a while."

This ability to find forthcoming changes based on the subtleties of the Chinese newspapers does have a parallel business potential advantage in the West. American business schools typically teach their seniors and MBA students about the importance of environmental scanning. Put in simple terms, environmental scanning is keeping your eyes and ears open and tuned in to foresee changes in the external environment that might pose opportunities or threats for a business organization. Executives regularly read publications such as *The Wall Street Journal, Business Week,* and various trade journals specific to their company's industry. In so doing and through other activities such as informally talking with customers, suppliers, competitors, and other stakeholders, the executives are able to better keep up with potential changes that may impact their industry. Companies that could foresee major events such as the breakup up the Soviet Union or more specific consumer demand phenomena such as a rapid increase in the popularity of fax machines have a comparative advantage over their competitors. Often in a free and competitive marketplace, anticipating product demand changes a short time before the competition can result in increased sales followed by enhanced profitability. In the West, the government is one of the top ten or so major stakeholders for a typical medium or large company. In China, the government is often the number one stakeholder for any sizes of enterprise.

In summary, people can often predict business decision making in China based on the current or updated Party policies and the governmental viewpoints.

Besides predicting the Chinese business decision making from an analysis of the updated Party policies and governmental view-point, there are several more ways or possibilities of predicting business decision making in China.

First, the inflexibility of decision making from powerful men is a method of predicting business decision making in China. Many business projects, particularly the large long-term ones, may not operate smoothly. Some temporary difficulties or problems may impede our prediction. Nevertheless, as we know, most business decisions are made by the powerful men; as long as they are still the "number one persons," or in power, sooner or later they will continue enforcing their decisions. In our experience, some projects might stop being implemented for one or two years, and then be continued. Eighteen years have passed since 1978, when Deng Xiaoping decided China would "cross the river." The Chinese people have experienced many trials and hardships, even smelling blood on the wind and the rain. As long as Deng Xiaoping is alive, the decision for "crossing the river" will not be changed. After the event at Tian'anmen Square, he met with the officers of the army and strongly emphasized that no matter what, any single word of the general principles about reforming and opening must not be changed. The Reforming and Opening movement must be adhered to without any wavering whatsoever.

Second, because the general direction of China is unchangeable, many business decisions are predictable. The general direction, such as developing the economy, reforming and opening, supporting the market economy, etc., namely the historical tendencies, will remain unchanged. During the last eighteen years, particularly after the event at Tian'anmen Square, some people tried to change the general direction in China. Using the theory of class struggle as an argument against the developing free market economy, they intended to close the door to the outside world and go back to the planned economy. They failed. Therefore, some relapses may happen to some extent, but the general direction of China, and its major business decisions remain unchangeable and predictable.

Third, the "ironclad cases" will make some business decisions predictable before the powerful men who are involved in the decision making leave their positions, lose their power, or pass away. For instance, the Project of Three Gorges on the Yangtze River, which is to build the biggest dam on the Yangtze, could be viewed as an "ironclad case," whether or not it should be or will be changed. How should it be changed? When? These are unpredictable! Nevertheless, so far the project is unchangeable, and its major business decision makings, in a sense, are predictable, such as pooling resources, inviting bids, seeking technical cooperation, importing equipment, hiring experts, and even joint administration.

UNPREDICTABILITY

On the one hand, business decision making in China is predictable. On the other hand, it is also unpredictable. Let us discuss the reasons why.

First, there is not any theory about Socialist market economy to direct the Chinese economic experiment and operation. All former socialist countries in Eastern Europe are completely transferring from a planned economy to a market economy. Therefore, their economic operations are not reformed, but transferred. Though their economic transfer has specific characteristics that cannot entirely use the capitalist economic theory as a guide, they can basically use the capitalist market economic theory to direct their operations because they have abandoned a socialist economy. Yet the situation in China is completely different. China still keeps the Socialist system, and is adapting the market economic theory to fit it. What China is undergoing is not only an economic transfer but a remarkable social and economic reformation as well. Obviously, the transfer and reformation in China is a process of experiment. Accordingly, during this process of probing, many business decisions may be changeable and unpredictable. For example, China must decide whether or not the domestic retail area, energy, railway, telecommunications, and the money market should be opened to foreign countries and foreign corporations. Should such markets be entirely open? Should some special regulations exist? All these are questions that, on the one hand, may be gradually clarified during the process of probing; on the other hand, at certain times they are unpredictable.

Second, business decision making can be influenced—sometimes strongly influenced—by political elements in China. So, from a business perspective, you may have an extremely difficult time predicting business decision making in China. There is an interesting Chinese saying to distinguish the differences between political pursuit and business perspective: "Some people are willing to engage in a deal in which they may lose their heads (lives), but nobody accepts a deal to lose money." The essence of business is to make money; hence, no businesspeople want their business to lose money. The typical political goal is to win. A political win can be very complicated and subtle. In some cases, a political win could merely imply a good feeling, or saving face, which may mean nothing or may even mean financial losses from the business perspective. As in the current wars in Bosnia, who wins? Who loses? Wins what? Only politicians know this! And who loses what? Obviously, people are losing lives, families, friendships, peace, materials, and economic development. Sometimes, in order to contain the United States,

China may award huge contracts/orders to European countries or Japan. Likewise, sometimes in order to tie up the European countries, China may give many orders to the United States. In those cases, contracting the orders may not be to make money in the short term, but only a means to reach a certain political goal. For this reason, it is difficult to predict business decisions that have been mixed with an array of political elements. Recently, in order to "punish" the United States for granting a visa to the Taiwan President, Lee Teng-hui, to visit America, China considered building Germany's luxury Mercedes-Benz but would not consider building American automobiles. This is an example of reaching a political goal with a business decision. When politics is the end but business is only a means, how can you predict business decision making? As in chess when a player needs to protect his commander by moving other pieces, an opponent may have difficulty knowing which piece will be moved and where it will be moved.

Third, the personality factor may enable decision making in China to become unpredictable. The so-called "powerful man" encompasses at least three characteristics. One is his indomitable personality; another is his superb skills (stratagems). Finally, his power may often be beyond the control of others. The first characteristic is what we have addressed in the last section: the inflexibility of decision making by powerful men provide some possibility for predicting their decisions. However, the second and the third characteristics may often make decisions unpredictable. Mao Zedong successively chose and appointed three of his successors, Liu Shaoqi, Lin Biao, and Hua Guofeng. Nevertheless, he abolished (abandoned) his successors one after the other. Liu Shaoqi was the president of the People's Republic of China and lost his power at the beginning of the Cultural Revolution. Then the vice president of the Chinese Communist Party, Lin Biao, was named in the Constitution of the Party to be Mao Zedong's successor in 1969. Lin Biao's plane crashed on his way to escaping to the Soviet Union because he had lost the trust of Mao Zedong, who decided to punish him. Before Mao Zedong died, he appointed Hua Guofeng to be his successor. Interestingly enough, Deng Xiaoping also successively chose and appointed three of his successors, Hu Yaobang, Zhao Ziyang, and Jiang Zemin. Deng Xiaoping relieved Hu Yaobang of his position in

1986, and recalled Zhao Ziyang in 1989. Before he officially retired from all his official positions, he chose and appointed Jiang Zemin to be the top leader of China. No one could predict these two powerful men's decisions about their successors. As for business decision making, powerful men's superb stratagems and their incontestable power can make their decisions unpredictable, too. For example, Shen Taifu organized a small electrical machinery company. He advertised that he had invented a very unique and brand new electrical machine that could earn a considerable amount of money, but he needed startup funds and promised a very high interest rate. He bribed some of the officials concerned (e.g., one from the State Scientific and Technological Commission) to prove what he stated in his advertisement. He collected some money, and really paid back a very high interest rate as he had promised. Then, he began to collect a huge amount of money and expanded his nationwide branch companies. Nevertheless, he was only interested in collecting funds, and did not focus on the production of the electrical machines. He spent A's and B's money, but used C's money to pay the interests of A and B; then, he collected D's money to pay C's interest. Just like a rolling snowball, his collections became more and more huge, but he sunk deeper and deeper into debt. He was finally sentenced to die because of his illegal money collecting, which was his unexpected business decision as well. Yet, an unusual business decision may not be bad. Successful businesspeople usually do something others would not attempt or could not even imagine. In the West this is often thought of as an entrepreneurial spirit. For instance, a very successful businessman, Mou Qizhong, who was the President of the private Nan De Group Corporation, and believed to be one of the richest men in China, conducted the largest deal of exchanging goods with Russia. When he made this business decision, nobody understood him. He believed he was right for four reasons: (1) Russian Tu-154 passenger planes remained in stock for a long time; (2) Russia needed light industrial goods very badly; (3) a Chinese airline really needed passenger planes but was short of cash; and (4) the Chinese light industrial products were being overstocked. He prevailed over all dissenting views to successfully make a $430 million deal. Some speculated that he was going to send a satellite into space; nobody knows what was in his mind for business decision making.

Fourth, decision making with changeable characteristics could stifle predictions. When a decision has been made before collecting and analyzing information, the decision maker might continue to ignore the significance of collecting and analyzing feedback. On the other hand, any feedback could be an unconditional sign that the decision maker must change his decision. We have previously mentioned that a Chinese factory decided to import grinders, a milling machine with computer numerical control (CNC), and inlaying equipment through an American company. When the Chinese delegation came to the United States, the feedback was like an unconditional order that they must go to Germany and Japan to meet their needs. After four months, the Chinese factory had to inform the American company that they had to change their business decision. The American company was quite upset; they felt that they did not know how to predict business decision making in China. Suppose we consider the business decision making—"import equipment"—to be "crossing the river"; then choosing the stones would be selecting what kinds of machines to import from what companies in which countries. The latter would also be critical business choices for those business partners or opponents to predict.

In short, without an existing theory of the Socialist market economy, the Party policies and government viewpoints that guide business decision making are full of variability. Also, political elements are mixed into business decision making and make predicting difficult. Moreover, business decision making becomes more difficult to predict when one considers the personality and changeability factors.

COMPLEXITIES

In a Chinese company, the number one person usually makes the final decision, but he or she will be unable to be involved in every step of every business decision. For some final decisions, he or she may just sign a signature. Because the number one person of a Chinese company needs to take care of too many things, so he or she will only be able to be completely involved in every step of the most critical business decisions. Hence, other people will handle most cases, and then let the number one person make the final decision. Before the number one person considers the case, no one can really be truly involved in the decision. For instance, you give a sample of a map clamp to a Chinese manufacturer and tell them, "Please make a sample like this one, and quote us the price. If the quality is good and the quote is acceptable, my customers need eight to ten containers each year." Suppose the number one person of the manufacturer has not been involved in the final decision making yet. The other persons concerned may think: "The quantity of ten containers each year is not very big, but it is all right. So-called 'good' quality and 'acceptable' quotes are subtle. If we put our money, time, energy, and labors to make samples, and the quality is not considered to be 'good,' or the quote is not 'acceptable,' others would view my decision as bad. Furthermore, the buyer is not the final customer; his purchase decision will be based on his customers' decisions. If after several months we have made quality samples, we run the risk that the market situation has changed. Even though the quality of samples is good, the buyer can say that the quote is unreasonable." To have an order for ten containers of map clamp is quite attractive, but the risks are present and must be considered. To make samples, several factors of production will be involved, namely labor, materials, machines, and tooling. Therefore, the financial department, supply department, manufacturing department, designing and research department, and the workshop will all be involved in this project. Since the number one person has not been involved in the final decision, the situation is that while everybody may be involved, no one is really involved. This ambiguity presents some potential conflicts for the manufacturer.

We would like to share some other very interesting experiences to support our above words. The signatures of officials on a document, report, letter, or note could have extremely subtle meanings. If an official signs his or her name by him or herself, this signifies that the matter is of vital importance, and you must treat and handle it very carefully. If a secretary signs for the official, even if the signature is very similar to the officials', you can still recognize it as forged. This means the project is less significant than those with the official's own signature, but still very vital, because the secretary would not dare to sign it without official acknowledgment. Suppose the signature or seal is from the office of the official; this would indicate that the matter is not so important. If this is a public affair, you can handle it according to regular principles. However, if this is a private affair, that indicates to you: It is not convenient for the official to deal with this matter, you can handle it in the concrete situation—can do it, do it; cannot, then you need to find an excuse for not implementing it. The official can also just draw a circle on his or her name as well.[11] This is more delicate and meaningful. Suppose an official does not sign his or her name but just draws a circle on his or her name. This could just mean: "I have read it." This could also mean that I would agree with whatever the number one person's idea is, or follow the majority idea. Sometimes this might hint that he or she had a different idea but did not want to express it. Sometimes this could imply that the official did not have a definitive opinion, but you can, according to your understanding, do it. If you were right, the official might say, "That is what I wanted you to do." If you were wrong, the official could tell you, "That is not what I wanted you to do." Sometimes these kinds of results were just what the officials expected.[12]

When the number one person does not become involved in decision making, the situation is one in which "while everybody may be involved, no one can really be involved" and may be more complex. Many American companies might have experienced the above instance of making samples. An American company told us that they had spent almost one year working on a project. After many samples and much quoting, eventually the quality of the samples and the quotations were acceptable. When the American company placed an order, the Chinese manufacturer—namely the number one person needed to sign a contract—did not agree with the quote because, through another channel, he obtained some informal but reliable information that the policy of returning 17 percent of the exporting tax would be reduced or canceled. Obviously, the decisions in which the number one person is not involved in the early stages will become more complicated.

Nevertheless, the decisions that the number one person is involved in are also complex because of influence from the following two causes:

1. Business decision making is influenced and/or directed by political elements, e.g., the Party policies and the government viewpoints. The relationships between business decision making, and the Party policies and governmental viewpoints have been discussed previously. We only want to mention that the number one person may be powerful, but since he or she knows more about the Party policies and the governmental viewpoints than others, he or she must consider or view things from different perspectives that others might not consider nor need to consider. Consequently, the number one person's business decision making may be more complicated.
2. There is not a formal channel or procedure to influence business decision making besides the Party policies, the governmental viewpoints, and the economic laws of the market system. As we know, sometimes the pressure from foreign countries, governments, companies, managers/experts, investors, and people may influence the Party policies and the governmental viewpoints to influence business decision making in China to some extent (e.g., protecting property rights, and opening more domestic markets). Nevertheless, this channel is slow, indirect, and complex. Though the economic laws of the market system have been more and more effective to influence business decision making in China, various causes are still making this formal channel informal. For instance, if the number one person is too powerful, the other people do not need to, or cannot really be, involved in decision making. Also, the reward system scares people from taking risks. An example: Whether or not the number three person decides to produce pilot samples from a foreign company, he or she would have the same salary, but must take all the risks in which his or her position could be jeopardized if something goes wrong. If this person, however, does not decide to produce pilot samples from a foreign company, he or she would not lose anything. Due to the influence of Party policies and governmental viewpoints, starting ventures become too difficult and too complicated, and since the market system's economic laws have not effectively influenced business decision making, one informal way to influence is to bribe people. This could be one of the reasons why bribes

and/or gift-giving are so popular in China. Yet, no matter whether formal or informal, those ways are all complex. In fact, large firms in America may have similar problems. In 1993, a gentleman from Shanghai, Mr. Jiang visited the United States with his multimillion dollar plan: he wanted to buy an obsolete/used automobile production line from an American automobile firm. He called the automobile firms, but the operators did not even know where they should direct his call. After numerous calls, he eventually reached the Asian division of an automobile firm. The woman at the office said, "Well, we sell cars. I have no idea about your question. You can leave your phone number. When so-and-so finishes his phone call, he will call you back." Then nothing happened. Mr. Jiang had to return to China with his ambitious plan. While we can criticize him because he made a decision before collecting and analyzing information, perhaps we should instead blame the fact that those American corporations were so big and so complicated that nobody could provide information to him? Sometimes, dealing with some big American corporations, a person might feel that nobody can say, "Yes!" but everybody can say, "No!" Many Chinese businesspeople complain about the large American corporations, with statements such as "If you cannot reach a high level of administration in those big corporations in America, you should simply give up your idea to deal with them. You just cannot move them; they are too complicated . . ."

Decision making in China is extremely complex. Two kinds of people have a great deal of influence on decision making.

One is the secretary. The secretaries of higher level officials can be more important. Chinese secretaries could be considered a stratum of power. The foreign countries' secretaries may just type, deliver, schedule, and host visitors. But the Chinese secretaries are part of a chain of command that links the higher authority and the lower level. According to the policies of the Central Committee of the Party, a leader with the rank of vice minister[13] or higher could have a private secretary, or a "secretary with a specific duty for a leader," or a "confidential secretary." The leader with the rank of vice minister or minister may only have one secretary. The duty of a secretary is to handle the documents that the leader needs to read or sign, take care of the leader's work, life, health, and sometimes even family affairs. The leader with the rank of Commissioner of State or Member of the Secretariat of the Central Committee of the Chinese Communist Party usually has two special secretaries. One, called a "small secretary" or a "confidential secretary," treats the daily work. Another who is called the "big secretary" or "written secretary" is in charge of writing speeches, proposals, and documents. The key leaders of the country and the Party have their special offices. Generally, people add the leader's last name to these offices, such as the "Mao Office," or the "Deng Office." The formality of selecting a secretary is very strict, and investigating back several generations is a common practice. Then the qualified candidate needs to be interviewed by the leader for approval. The secretary manages the leader's car, driver, and orderlies. Secretaries are the extensions of a leader's brain and four limbs. When a leader wants to do something, he or she just needs to tell the secretaries; then they handle it. A leader may just indicate the main points of what he or she wants to say, and the secretary will write a paper for the leader to read or publish in a newspaper. A leader may have some ideas that are not completely developed, but the secretaries do some research or investigation, and then submit a proposal or scheme for the leader who will make the decision. If a leader needs something that is difficult to gain in the market, the secretaries just need to make a couple of phone calls to have the item delivered to the leader's home. As a result, without secretaries, some leaders could not even move a single step. Some people believe that the state power in China is mainly controlled and operated by the secretaries. Hence, Mao Zedong and Hu Yangbang repeatedly advised that the leaders should not rely on their secretaries too much and should conduct things by themselves. The people who are secretaries could certainly be promoted to leadership. When leaders select their successors, they usually consider their secretaries because the good secretaries are obedient. After these secretaries become leaders, they would still listen to their former leaders. The leaders' power could be extended and expanded. For these reasons, in order to become a leader, the best way is to be a secretary first. Many senior leaders' children choose to be secretaries. They may even recommend each others' children to be their secretaries. To be a secretary may be viewed to involve enrolling in an institution of Chinese political power in which one could learn about the structure, the system, and the way of operation of Chinese political power, and where one could learn the principles of connections, the skills of survival, and the philosophy of struggle. If you have the capability to be a secretary, you should be able to be an official. Many officials have secretarial experience. The leaders who previously were secretaries could carry out their offices smoothly and could have harmonious relationships with others, would not only be safe in their power but also would be promoted. The officials who do not have secretarial experience may maintain and exhibit their obvious personalities thus their official career may be difficult.[14] Such conditions may not be suitable for the business situation of a small company. Nevertheless, some information is quite true, so we share this with the readers to facilitate understanding the complexity of business decision making in China.

Other people who influence decision makers are the family (wife or husband, and children), relatives, and friends. Who are closest to the number one person who usually makes the final decision? Of course, they are his or her colleagues and the direct family members. Nevertheless, the colleagues may have their conflicts of interest with the number one person. For various reasons they may not be able to influence decision making directly, or they may have to do official business according to official principles—namely discuss business decision making formally and openly. However, the family (wife or husband, and children), relatives, and friends of the number one person usually do not have these conflicts of interest with him or her, but have common interests. Suppose they make some mistakes or give some wrong suggestions, these actions and behaviors would not damage or hurt the positions, careers, or futures that the colleagues worry about. Moreover, since they usually have common interests, they could easily have a common language. Finally, when the number one person has an informal relationship with these people, he or she may be more easily influenced in a relaxed atmosphere. For example, people believe that many have been trying to influence Deng Xiaoping through his family.

SIMPLICITY

While business decision making in China is very complicated, it could be very simple as well. Any decision that involves a certain amount of budget, or hiring personnel, or change of structure, products, or policy in an American public company must be approved by the board. As long as the board is involved, any decision may become very complex. For one matter, you usually have to wait for a regular meeting of the board and that might mean there would be a long wait for decision making. For another, members of the board with different backgrounds and interests may have very conflicting ideas and serious arguments about any decision making. That is to say, you may have to wait a very long time for a result that might warn you to change some points of your proposal for the next round of argument. Another complexity could be that if a member of the board, for some reason, is absent, voting is impossible. People have found out that a decision to maintain the status quo is more easily approved by the board; a suggestion to change the status quo is more difficult to have approved. The level of change is inversely proportional to that of the possibility of approval. Sometimes, even though some changes or decisions are very important, as people realize the extent that the board will be involved in the decision, they may simply give up. On the reverse side of the coin, a private company or a family-owned company in America could make a decision very simple. The state-owned enterprises, or collective companies, in China have shown their ownership to be similar to a public organization in America to some extent; particularly many state-owned enterprises are now being allowed to buy and own their shares of stocks. Nevertheless, in a sense, the state-owned enterprises, or collective companies in China have shown their decision-making to be similar to a private or family-owned company in America, too. This is why business decision making in China is both complex and simple.

We can generalize at least two reasons why business decision making in China could be very simple.

First, the personality of a powerful man can make a business decision very simple. Many American businesspeople really like to deal with the person who can make a decision immediately. Often a public American company is not able to make a decision for more than a month. Of course, simplicity may not be good; simplicity only tends to save time and work that could be necessary and/or unnecessary.

Second, since many business decisions in China are influenced by political elements, those business decisions could sometimes become very simple. We have mentioned previously that as political elements were mixed into business, business decisions could become very complicated. Do we contradict ourselves? No, we believe that political elements can make business decision making either complex or simple. When politics are the end but business decision making is just a means, whether or not business decision making is complicated depends on how people use business decision making to reach political goals. To state it differently, the purpose will decide if the tool should be complex or simple. For these reasons, when, according to the general business or economic laws, such as higher quality with lower price, good service and supplying on time, etc., you should have an order from China but you do not, then the business decision making in China has become complicated by politics. On the contrary, in terms of the general business or economic laws that we mentioned, you should not receive an order from China but you unexpectedly gain it, this indicates that the business decision making in China has been simplified by political influence. Of course, you deserve what you get from business decision making. It is normal. The essence of business is to make money. When people do not care about the purpose of business, but only pay attention to using business as a tool to reach a political goal, business decision making can be very simple or very complicated.

RADICAL DECISION MAKING

Obviously, since business decision making is influenced or even directed by political considerations, business decision making can be illogical or radical. We can list many examples. The name "Great Leap Forward," suggests this. One of the goals of the Great Leap Forward in China was to reach the output of steel making in England in five years, and of America in fifteen. In order to achieve these goals, everyone had to join the steel-making movement.

People broke their pots or brought whatever iron they could find from their homes to manufacture steel in their tiny "steel-smelting furnaces," an indigenous method of steel making. In 1957, China made about 10.7 million tons of steel including approximately 3 million tons from the "steel-smelting furnaces" by breaking pots and locks. Breaking good pots and smelting working locks to make inferior steel ingots, they then resmelted the poor steel ingots into various steel products, and remade pots and locks. Chinese people, who are not stupid, were conducting and implementing radical and stupid business decision making because of political decision making. During the Cultural Revolution, engineers and scientists were sent to conduct physical labor, and without administering examinations, some workers, peasants, and soldiers were selected and sent to universities to become "engineers" and "scientists." Consequently, the disorder caused by this production caused an economic disorder. Yet the radical decision making was not corrected because it was based on a radical political slogan: "We would rather keep Socialist impoverishment than have Capitalist development." Regarding the Land Reform Movement, the Movement for Agricultural Cooperation, and the Movement of Joint State-Private Ownership of Individual Enterprise, these could also be viewed as radical business decisions that were guided by politics in China.

Lack of market economic experience can be another cause for radical business decision making in China. We can understand this situation with a metaphor. Suddenly opening a floodgate of a reservoir that has been blocked by flood waters for a long time will cause the water to ferociously smash whatever it wants. After the Chinese Communist Party and the government accepted the ideas of a market economy in 1992, two cities, Shanghai and Shenzhen,[15] were allowed to experiment and to open a stock market. In the summer of 1992, when people knew that they could buy stocks in Shenzhen, millions of them rushed to Shenzhen from everywhere in China. Shenzhen was suddenly flooded with untrained potential stockholders. In order to buy an application form to purchase stocks, these potential new stockholders had to wait in long lines and sleep in the streets. Many of them had to pay about 1,000 yuans, which was about several months' salary for a common worker at that time, just for an application form for purchasing stocks from the black market sources. When they even could not buy an application form, they fought with each other, and fought with policemen. Some died, and many were wounded in this unexpected riot and tragedy. Obviously, without market economy knowledge and experience, people are likely to make radical business decisions. When people "select stones" to cross the "market economic" river, they may often seize and manufacture a popular product like a swarm of bees when they believe a good "stone" has been selected. For example, when the supply of color televisions fell short of the demand in the Chinese markets, everyone wanted to manufacture color TVs. As a result, so many production lines of color TVs were imported from foreign countries that the supply of color TVs rapidly exceeded the demand. Air conditioners, refrigerators, golf courses, and commercial complexes, etc., are also being overproduced by "swarms of bees." However, although many of these items are still being constructed or produced, the supplies have already exceeded the demands in the markets. Of course, it is radical that either nobody makes something or everyone makes it. It can be concluded that the capitalistic economic principles of supply and demand tend to fluctuate with overzealous swings in China, and have resulted in radical business decision making.

In fact, as the biggest and strongest socialist country in the world, China's economic style, in which public ownership still plays a leading role, can be considered a radical phenomena compared with private ownership, which is the current world trend since almost all socialist countries have switched to private ownership markets. For this reason, business decisions made from an economic style where public ownership is the dominating factor are probably radical to some extent, if only because only a certain percentage of the stocks (usually a small part) of a state-owned enterprise could be sold to individuals. Because of legal restrictions, some state-owned enterprises could not initiate a joint venture with foreign organizations unless the state-owned enterprise could hold 51 percent or more of the stocks.

In summary, political influence, personalities, and lack of market economic knowledge could make Chinese business decision making radical.

THE GOLDEN MEAN

While business decision making in China could be radical, just as the other side of anything–two sides of a coin, or the *yin* and the *yang*–it could be the golden mean (go-between). The golden mean implies something that does not deviate substantially from the average. In other words, radical views (e.g, very liberal or very conservative) are avoided.

The people revered four books in ancient China–*The Analects of Confucius*, *The Book of Mencius*, *The Doctrine of the Mean*, and *The Great Learning*, sometimes referred to as the "Bible of ancient China." As we can see, the "mean" of *The Doctrine of the Mean* in this case refers to "the golden mean" or "average," or "go-between." The golden mean is a critical characteristic of traditional Chinese philosophy. *The Doctrine of the Mean* cited Confucius' words: "I know why the principles could not be carried out–because the talented people over-implemented them, but foolish people are unable to achieve the standard. I know why the principles could not be understood by the people–because gentlemen have too high a request, but non-gentlemen have too low a request."[16] Therefore, not too high and not too low, not too fast and not too slow, and not too left and not too right, namely average could be the golden mean. Under the influence of this doctrine, Chinese people have become great masters of staying fairly close to the average. One typical example is the current Chinese economic pattern–the Socialist market economy. The essence of socialism is that social properties are publicly owned. The concept of "public ownership" is different from the American concept by which some of the public can own certain property by purchasing stocks on the open markets. The concept of "public ownership" in China means *everyone equally* owns the properties, not just those who could purchase shares. Why are "everyone" and "equally" emphasized? First, some of the public owning something still implies a private ownership, but everyone owning something means a public ownership. Second, suppose everyone owns something, but to varying degrees. Then some may own a lot while others may own very little. Therefore, this inequality is still similar to the situation in which some of the public own something but others do not. The only difference is that some own nothing or very little. Accordingly, it must be emphasized that public ownership means that everyone owns something equally. Yet in reality, everyone equally owning something is impossible. The Socialist concept of public ownership that theoretically states that everyone equally owns social properties is achieved by state-ownership. Generally speaking, however, the competitive law of market economy is that some gain more, others less; some win, and some lose. The conflicts between Socialist public ownership and the competitive law of market economy are the dilemma between everyone equally owning their portion of the social properties; thus, some win, and some lose. Now with the philosophy of the doctrine of the mean, the Chinese people are trying to choose stones to cross the river by mixing the Socialist public ownership with a market economy.

One obvious consequence from the influence of this doctrine is that the Chinese business world may not really want to take any risks, and thus try to be conservative. Many Western businesspeople believe that you take a low risk to make little money, a high risk to make more money (i.e., the greater the risk, the greater the return). However, when a business decision needs to be made, the first issue many Chinese people think of is how not to lose. They believe that only without losing do you have a chance to gain. If you have lost, then you have nothing to gain. Some Westerners think that without putting something at stake (investment), you do not need to mention losing or winning. Nevertheless, many Chinese people think that without putting something at stake, you will, at least, not lose. To summarize, conservative business decision making is derived from the philosophy of the doctrine of the mean.

We have previously discussed how and why radical business decision making may result from political considerations. Meanwhile, political considerations may lead to go-between business decisions, as well. As we know, all Eastern European countries entirely adopted private ownership when they gave up their Socialist systems. China, however, is accepting a mixed social economic pattern—the Socialist market economy—because of one of its Four Adherences is to maintain the Socialist path. As another example, when the members of the Security Council of the United Nations tried to vote for economic sanctions to Iraq or Iran in recent years,

China usually abstained from voting. This could be viewed as a "go-between" way when compared to casting a dissenting vote.

In a sense, the doctrine of the means is used to restrain ourselves and our characteristics while leaving some room or margin for maneuvering. Therefore, a business decision made with the doctrine of the golden mean can be a very advantageous situation in which taking a step forward might place you on the offensive, or taking a step backward might place you on the defensive. In other words, since business decision making leaves some room or margin for maneuvering, the decision maker(s) could lead a decision in any direction—even a radical direction—at anytime.

TIMING (FAST AND SLOW)

The timing of business decision making in China is quiet interesting but often puzzling to Western businesspeople.

An American company intended to import several types of products from China through H.C.K. International. In order to have a better source with lower prices but higher quality, H.C.K. International contacted several Chinese manufacturers. Nevertheless, the samples were not cheap, partially because the sizes of the samples were so big that they were not easily shipped, and H.C.K. did not know who would be a better source. Hence, the samples could not be shipped to every manufacturer, but the manufacturers could order the samples through H.C.K. One of the manufacturers responded very quickly that they needed the blueprints and the samples, and that they would pay for the samples and the mailing costs. After about four months, this manufacturer had made the samples in terms of the blueprints. Receiving and checking the samples from the manufacturer, some problems with the blueprints that had not been found and solved were discovered. H.C.K. felt that this manufacturer really needed the samples from the American company, so H.C.K. bought the samples and mailed them to the factory. After about two months, the Chinese factory had remade the samples again, and after another four months, the payments for the samples and the mailing were still not confirmed. H.C.K. did not really care about the costs of buying and mailing the samples; the purpose of mentioning this story is to expose why the Chinese manufacturer could have made the samples twice but could never afford the costs for shipping and for the samples from the American company. In the Western businesspeople's eyes, making a sample is more much difficult than buying a sample. In Chinese reality, the costs of making a sample were actually much higher than buying the sample. But why did the Chinese manufacturer make the samples so fast and pay the costs of buying and mailing the samples so slowly? The answer is that when decision making is under the decision maker's control, it can be very fast. If it is beyond the decision maker's control, the decision making could be very slow. At that time, the Chinese RMB[17] could not quickly exchange any foreign currencies in China. The foreign currencies were rigorously controlled by a government department, the "Foreign Currencies Administration Bureau," and the China Bank. When an organization needs foreign currencies, even just a few U.S. dollars, the organization must submit its report and proposal to apply for the foreign currencies from the Foreign Currencies Administration Bureau. After going through much red tape, if the proposal were approved, you could bring a government document that is particularly formulated for this approval and Chinese RMB to the China Bank to exchange for the foreign currencies you need. If you are not sure whether or not your proposal will be approved, then you need to find a connection, an official or a staff of the Foreign Currencies Administration Bureau, a friend who knows someone at the Foreign Currencies Administration Bureau, or even your boss's boss who could have some influence at the Foreign Currencies Administration Bureau. This was why the Chinese manufacturer made the samples so fast and paid the costs of buying and mailing the samples so slowly. In brief, when decision making, no matter how difficult, how important, and how much money may be involved, is under the decision maker's control, it can be very fast. If decision making, no matter how simple, how insignificant, and how little money may be involved, is beyond the decision maker's control, the process could be extremely slow. Moreover, without a formal procedure for decision making and a controlled system, a powerful man can make a decision quite quickly, but when authority, responsibility, and position are not identified clearly, then decision making may take a long time.

Suppose Taiwan declares itself to be independent. Now, undoubtedly, Deng Xiaoping can immediately decide to ask the Chinese Communist Party and the government to send troops to attack Taiwan. Such a vital decision as the military attacking Taiwan could be immediate compared to some minor business decision making. The number one person of a Chinese company can decide many important issues at a banquet table or talking with you on the phone or at his or her home. However, when his or her power, responsibility, and position are not clear, decision making would be very slow. For instance, a Chinese manufacturer needs to send a person to bring some products in seeking to develop market(s) in America. It seems that the number one person of the company should be able to make a decision in terms of his or her power, responsibility, and position—but actually he or she cannot. Whether or not an employee of a Chinese company is eligible to be sent to conduct business independently in a foreign country is generally based on decisive factors such as speaking ability, technology, experience, language skill, and political reliability. However, the manger of a Chinese company can only evaluate this person's ability, technology, experience, and language skill, but checking on political reliability will not be the manager's responsibility, or will be beyond his or her power. This is the responsibility of a special department of the government. In fact, even the manager's own political reliability needs to be checked by this department when he or she wants to visit a foreign country. Also, because of power, responsibility, and position, the manager could only decide this business trip's budget in Chinese RMB, whether or not foreign currency could be approved by the Foreign Currencies Administration Bureau, will beyond his or her power, responsibility, and position. In summary, if the power, responsibility, and position of making a decision are not clear, decision making could be very slow.

We have addressed in the last section that often decision making is merely implementing a decision made by a higher authority. In this case, decision making would also be very fast.

Of course, as political considerations have an impact on business decision making, the timing could be either crazily fast or tremendously slow. That is to say, in some cases, the timing of business decision making will be based on political needs, not economic laws. For example, before President Bill Clinton decided whether or not extend the status of Most Favored Nation (MFN) of China in 1994, because of the Chinese human rights situation, China quickly organized a huge business delegation with billions of U.S. dollars of orders to visit the United States in May. At that time, whether or not the Chinese status of the Most Favored Nation could be extended would be determined by the U.S. Congress and President Bill Clinton. On the other hand, because of the U.S. visit of Lee Teng-hui, President of Taiwan, many Sino-American business decisions were delayed. Particularly, the negotiation about three openings, the opening of navigation and air traffic, the opening of postal communication, and the opening of trade association between the mainland and Taiwan, were put off again. Interestingly enough, now people cannot distinguish if the "three openings" between the mainland and Taiwan was a political decision or a business decision.

All in all, the timing of business decision making in China seems to puzzle Western businesspeople. Actually, the readers can get a basic idea about the timing of business decision making in China from understanding decision makers' power, responsibility, and position, the procedure of decision making, and the amount of political involvement.

POOR CONTINUITY

Western businesspeople who dislike certain Chinese business decisions will expect those decisions to have poor continuity. Western businesspeople who are basically enjoying their present business situation and cooperation with China will worry about Chinese business decision making with poor continuity. In general, people, particularly investors, worry about the poor continuity of business decision making in China. There are quite a few reasons why business decision making has poor continuity in China.

First, while the Chinese cadres are enjoying a tenure system, generally speaking, their appointments to certain positions and/or their movements to some other positions are often not regular. To state it differently, the Chinese cadres have a lifetime security for their payments and welfare, but their positions are changeable. In a sense, their situations are similar to the ambassadors and the President of the United States. Their positions can be changed, but their official ranks or profits would be maintained. The point is that their terms of offices are usually irregular. An American businessman enjoys his business relationships with his Chinese business partners. However, he worries most that Mr. X, the manager of the Chinese company that supplies goods to him, will be moved to another position. The author, Huang Quanyu, told the American businessman that Mr. X also worried about his American business partner for the same reason. The appointments and movements of Chinese cadres are mainly dependent on political considerations first and then economic considerations. The appointments or movements of American administrators are generally based on economic considerations first and then political ones, as a distant second. Though American managers of public companies might keep their positions according to their contracts, a severely depressed economic situation could force people to lose their positions, sometimes even the owners.

When a number one person of a Chinese company is in power, he or she makes the most critical business decisions. In order to better carry out his or her business decisions, the number one person might foster and arrange his or her trusted followers in various important positions. When this number one person is moved to another company, the new number one person would probably do the same thing–appoint his or her trusted followers to the important positions and remove the old number one person's people from the vital offices. This illustrates an old Chinese saying, "Different Emperors appoint different subjects." In many cases, a new leader would like to make his or her own new business decisions, which could differ greatly from the old one. Hence, business decision making in China might often show poor continuity. In fact, we can find similar situations in America. The American people elect their president every four years. A new president will select and appoint his new officials for the federal government, and may make new policies. For instance, President Lyndon Johnson sent massive numbers of troops to Vietnam, but President Richard Nixon withdrew those troops, and President Bill Clinton established a diplomatic relationship with Vietnam. Undoubtedly, Mr. Clinton's policies about Medicare will be different from someone else's. While the United States has changed its policies regarding Vietnam, the Chinese government, on the contrary, has never changed its idea about the Vietnam War. In a sense, because a new leader is elected every four years, the American government may show poorer continuity of decision making than the Chinese government does.

An American corporate example can help illustrate the problems that poor continuity bring to some of the company's stakeholders. In the 1950s and 1960s, Chrysler was a good example of a U.S. automobile manufacturing company. Reasonable sales and profitability kept not only the stockholders, the United Auto Workers (UAW), management, and parts suppliers happy, but also the consumers and the U.S. national economy seemed to benefit from the auto industry's economic growth and successes. In the early 1970s, problems began to surface, and by the mid 1970s, Chrysler was in significant financial decline. Since the company was slow to foresee the changing consumer demands for smaller and more efficient cars, such as the one the Japanese companies were beginning to sell in substantial numbers in North America, Chrysler soon found itself being discussed as a possible bankruptcy case in *Business Week* and *The Wall Street Journal* and soon thereafter in major newspapers and by the network television newscasters. Finally, after magnifying reports of gloom, Chrysler's corporate board of directors ousted the CEO and hired Lee Iacocca (a Ford Motors top executive) in 1978. Through his prompt and drastic retrenchment strategy, the giant automaker ordered deep cuts, including the firing of 33 of the 35 highest-ranking managers, eliminating nearly 8,500 financial staff positions, reducing the white-collar staff from 40,000 to 21,000, and halving the blue-collar workers (mostly labor union members) from 160,000 to 80,000. Along with drastic compensation cuts, the closing or consolidation of 20 plants, parts used in production from 75,000 to 40,000, and so on, Chrysler cut its breakeven point to half within a period of three years.[18] The point is that while this extremely disruptive behavior not only kept Chrysler afloat but actually turned the company around, it had a massive impact not only on the company directly (lost jobs for over 100,000 employees), but a mushrooming negative impact on tens of thousands of other people (working for suppliers, local and regional communities, and others).

A second reason why there is poor continuity in business decision making in China is that business decisions are directed by Party policies. The variety of Party policies does cause poor continuity of business decision making. What should the Socialist market economy be? Nobody in the world knows! It is an invention or experiment of the Chinese Communist Party. Nevertheless, this invention is an idea or concept that needs to be proven by the Chinese Communist Party. Therefore, the Chinese Communist Party does not have any existing theory to direct or lead its experiments. As a result, the Party policies are changeable, and business decision making that is guided and led by the changeable Party policies shows poor continuity. For instance, in order to attract as many foreign investments to China as possible, the Chinese government formulated a whole set of priority policies for foreign investment. First, "the income tax law of Chinese-foreign joint ventures income tax" and "the income tax law of foreign enterprises" were formulated to attract foreign investments in the 1980s. A new income tax law, "The Income Tax Law of the People's Republic of China on Foreign Investing Enterprises and Foreign Enterprises," was formulated, and it was approved at the Fourth Meeting of the 7th National People's Congress on April 9, 1991.[19] There were at least two changes in the new law that we need to mention: (1) the Chinese decision makers believed that the tax rates were too high in the old law so that it was not favorable for attracting more foreign investments; (2) in terms of the old law, all of the joint ventures would be exempt from taxation for two years from the first year they began to earn a profit, and reduced to 50 percent of the tax due in the following three years. Also, foreign enterprises that engaged in agriculture, forestry, animal husbandry, and some other low-profit businesses could be exempt from taxation for one year from the first year they began to gain profits, and taxation would be reduced to 50 percent for the following two years. The new law allowed foreign enterprises that engaged in production businesses for a ten-year period of business (not service businesses, e.g., tourist trade, consulting services) to be exempt from taxation for two years from the first year they began to earn a profit, which will be reduced to 50 percent in the following three years. Moreover, foreign enterprises that engaged in agriculture, forestry, animal husbandry, and some other low-profit businesses could enjoy these priority tax policies.

While China has been successfully attracting foreign investments with these priority tax laws and policies, the Chinese state-owned enterprises are encountering a difficult situation. Reforming the state-owned enterprises is the most important and most difficult issue for the experiment of the Socialist market economy. In other words, briefly pointing out the greatest problem of any Socialist economy, the state-owned enterprises, which are the main producers, are not dynamic. Currently, the Chinese Communist Party and the government are trying to stimulate the state-owned enterprises with the competitive machinery of a market economy. Without competition from foreign enterprises, the Chinese state-owned enterprises have already been very difficult to reform. The Chinese state-owned enterprises have been facing the difficult situation of competing with foreign enterprises who tend to have superiority of science and technology, capital, foreign markets (most Chinese state-owned enterprises do not have the authority to directly engage in import/export trade), and tax priority laws and policies, etc. While we were writing this section, we found two sensitive and critical articles in the *People's Daily*. One was on the second page, November 27, 1995; the other was on the front page, November 29, 1995. The two articles suggested the canceling of the priority tax laws for foreign enterprises. Since the articles discussed the importance of a fair competitive environment, we can predict that the law and the policies of income tax for the foreign enterprises might be changed in the near future.

In summary, since the Chinese Communist Party does not have an existing theory to direct its experiments, business decision making that is guided by the changeable Party policies will show poor continuity.

Third, ruling by benevolence does not have as good a continuity as ruling by law. We have previously mentioned that, owing to the election process, the American government may show poorer continuity of decision making than the Chinese government. Indeed, rule by law could allow business decision making to have better continuity. The criterion of "benevolence" is different for every number one person. The Chinese decision makers once debated the relationships between accumulation and consumption. One group believed that to allow people to consume more was a "benevolence." The other group reasoned that accumulating more funds for state development, including a strong defense capability, is a "benevolence" for the people. Additionally, the same issue may influence a common Chinese enterprise. Allowing employees to consume more is a "benevolence." Likewise, accumulating more funds to reinforce the enterprise–including importing advanced machinery–is a "benevolence." Different number one persons may have different beliefs. Suppose a number one person accepts the former idea about "benevolence," he or she may spend more funds to build apartments for the employees. Or a different number one person may adopt the latter idea about "benevolence"; then he or she would improve the machinery and equipment. Joint ventures or independence, focusing on international markets or domestic markets, importing foreign equipment or purchasing Chinese, paying more state tax or employees' bonus–so many issues concern the different views about "benevolence." When a new number one person has a different idea about "benevolence" from the former one, then business decision making will show poor continuity. Indeed, the current debate between the White House and the Congress about Medicare in America has shown different understandings about "benevolence." Of course, if Bob Dole had been elected to be the number one person in the White House he would certainly have a different idea about "Medicare" than would Bill Clinton, resulting in poor continuity of policies, but he must play a legal game in a society ruled by law, which differs from the poor continuity of business decision making in China.

Fourth, short-term administrations will reflect the poor continuity characteristics of business decision making. Because the term of office for a number one person in a Chinese company is usually irregular, quite a few of them may be eager for quick success and instant benefits when they make a business decision. For example, there are no American companies that make paper-cutting knives because of high labor costs. This means the huge American market has to import paper knives from foreign countries. The Chinese paper knives manufacturer has at least three choices. (1) Manufacture paper knives for the American market for 38 percent profit. But in order to do this, the Chinese company must import at least one million U.S. dollars worth of equipment. (2) Do not spend any money to renew old equipment; just use the old machines and work around-the-clock in three shifts with more overtime payments to continue the Chinese domestic market for a net profit level of about 8 percent. (3) Spend more funds to build more apartments for employees and offer better welfare to employees and their families. If the number one person of this Chinese company chooses the first choice, then he or she must stand the risk of importing millions of dollars of equipment and risk any change in the future American market against his or her long-term administration. Furthermore, this number one person not only needs to do numerous work activities, but also may suffer countless complaints. When everything is ready, he or she may be moved to another company, and the successor will sit idle and enjoy the fruits of his or her endeavors. Or to say it unkindly, the successor will "reap the spoils of victory from him or her without lifting a finger." Suppose this number one person selects the second choice. Although this does not cause a significant improvement to the company, he or she would at least not lose during his or her office by accepting a substantial economic loss from the purchase of the machines. If this number one person picks the third option for his or her short-term administration, he or she may make everyone happy for a while, but eventually the company must stand a loss from market competition—particularly when someone else has cornered the American market. A short-term administration could conflict with its replacement. Moreover, the behavior of a short-term administration will be different from the behavior of a long-term administration, as well. Therefore, a short-term administration will certainly result in poor continuity.

Finally, as we know, decision making is not a point but is a cause: defining a project leads to collecting and analyzing information, which leads to formulating alternatives and choosing an alternative. Once an alternative is chosen, action takes place, which leads to collecting and analyzing the feedback that finally causes controlling. Indeed, in many cases, controlling could be viewed as the second circle if collecting and analyzing feedback were considered as collecting and analyzing information. We have said that many Chinese decision makers might make a decision before collecting and analyzing information. When the result(s) from analyzing feedback are strongly against the decision, some necessary adjustments or even crucial changes need to be made. Sometimes, the decision making has to be completely stopped or canceled. Accordingly, making a decision before collecting and analyzing information would usually result in poor continuity for decision making.

DISCUSSION QUESTIONS

1. Some Americans idolize entertainers such as music stars, movie actors, or athletes. Is this similar to the peasant who rescued a statue of Mao Zedong during the 1991 flood?
2. Explain ruling by benevolence; how does this differ from what we normally experience in the West?
3. Discuss the role and power of secretaries of the Party in Chinese decision making. Illustrate how this can either hinder or enhance the ease of decision making by the manager/director.
4. All companies in all countries face changes that challenge decision making. But because China is now going through a very major change to a market economic system, decision making now faces both opportunities and dilemmas that few Western managers face. Agree or disagree? Why?
5. Compare and contrast ruling by law and ruling by benevolence.
6. What are some of the potential negative consequences of not analyzing collected information before making a decision?
7. Since the Chinese are very sensitive and adept at discovering real "news" (as pointed out in the opening paragraph of the "Predictable" section), they should be able to apply this skill to gathering information about competitors. Since in the West, gathering information about competitors is often helpful for successful decision making, Chinese business should have an advantage. Agree or disagree? Why?
8. While political situations and decisions can certainly influence business decision making in the West, in China the political factors have an even greater influence on business. Agree or disagree? Why?
9. Compare and contrast the role of the secretaries of high-level Chinese officials with the administrative role of secretaries

and administrative assistants in the United States? In general, which (China or United States) has more power to influence decision making?
10. Is the role of the family (as an effect on business decision making) about the same in China as in the United States? Why or why not?
11. Generalize two reasons why business decision making in China could be very simple.
12. While national decisions in China since 1949 have sometimes been radical (e.g., "Great Leap Forward"), radical decision making does not filter down to the individual business level. Agree or disagree? Why?
13. Explain the concept of the golden mean? Discuss its implications for decision making.
14. In U.S. business, timing can be everything (i.e., a quick-to-market decision can make the difference between success and failure). Discuss the ramifications of timing in Chinese decision making.
15. Discuss the timing influences on a Chinese business enterprise of a major political change such as a change in MFN by the United States.
16. Compare the potential problems of "poor continuity" for doing international business (from both a Chinese and a Western viewpoint).
17. Discuss the significance of taxation issues for Western companies entering into joint venture agreements in China.

REFERENCE NOTES

1. The Four Adherences are to adhere to (1) the Communist Party Leadership, (2) Marxism and Mao Zedong Thought, (3) Proletarian Dictatorship, and (4) the Socialist Path.
2. Huang Quanyu, Richard Andrulis, and Chen Tong, *A Guide to Successful Business Relations with the Chinese: Opening the Great Wall's Gate* (Binghamton, NY: The Haworth Press, 1994), 154.
3. Confucius, "The Analects of Confucius," in *Concise Edition of the Chinese Philosophy,* 43.
4. Ibid, 57.
5. The school of thought was in the Spring and Autumn and Warring States Periods, 770-221 BC that advocated to rule a country by laws.

6. Shang Yang, "The Book about Shang Yang," in *Concise Edition of the Chinese Philosophy*, 114-115.

7. Xunzi, "Xunzi," in *Concise Edition of the Chinese Philosophy*, 378.

8. In a planned economic China, no matter how poorly an enterprise was conducted, it would not become bankrupt; no matter how lazy an employee was, he or she would not lose his or her job. Moreover, the government controlled the low commodity prices while people made low wages.

9. He is a Chinese American. When the Sino-American relationships were encountering difficulties after Lee Teng-hui, the President of Taiwan, visited the United States, Wu, with an American passport, tried to enter China to collect some information about Chinese prisoners and was arrested at the Chinese border. The Congress and many American people pressured the U.S. government to solve the problem—asking China to release Harry Wu. Under the influence of the U.S. government, he was released in spite of being sentenced to fifteen years imprisonment.

10. There are five Special Economic Zones, Shenzhen, Shantou, Zhuhai, Xiamen, and Hanan. Actually, there are six in China. Although the Pudong District in Shanghai is not called a Special Economic Zone, it is actually a more special one granted many favorable policies that other areas do not have. These are special areas to experiment in the market/commercial economy. While some people believe they are the capitalist green-bed in China, their official description is "the window to the outside world."

11. For some critical documents, the names of officials who have read it may be printed at the end of the document for indicating who has read it, and/or for expressing their comments.

12. Jiang Zhifeng, *The Bridge Game in Beijing*, (San Francisco: Pacific News Service Co., 1990), 40.

13. The rank of vice governor of a province or an associate army commander are equal to a vice minister.

14. Jiang Zhifeng, 143-145.

15. Shenzhen City is one of five Special Economic Zones in China, and separated from Hong Kong only by a bridge.

16. Zisi, "The Doctrine of the Mean," in *The Concise Edition of Chinese Philosophy*, 595.

17. RMB are the first Chinese phonetics from the three words (syllable): Ren (people), Min (people), and Bi (currency).

18. Lee Iacocca, "The Rescue and Resuscitation of Chrysler." *Journal of Business Strategy*. Volume 4 (Winter 1983), pp. 67-69; and Lee Iacocca, *Iacocca: An Autobiography*. (Toronto, Canada: Bantam, 1984).

19. Yang Canying, Administration of Foreign Enterprises, (Tianjin, P.R. China: Nankai University Publishing House, 1993), 54.

Chapter 6

Tactics of Decision Making

Some of the original organizational decision making of human beings came from war–besieging, hunting, or fighting between tribes. Actually, fighting with the natural world, fighting with animals, or fighting among other humans could all be viewed as wars. The only difference was a different fighting object. For instance, the concept "warfare" could be used to mean: wage "warfare" with flood (or drought), air "warfare," diplomatic "warfare," ground "warfare," economic "warfare," offensive "warfare," trade "warfare," or business "warfare."

The author of *The Way of Strategy*, William A. Levinson, simply states, "Business is war" in the introduction of his book. He believed that "Business, war, and statecraft are contests between organizations. They differ only in their weapons or tools of competition."[1]

China has 5,000 years of history in which there were countless military wars although economic competition was weak. On the one hand, it was a tragedy; on the other hand, military decision making has even become a kind of "art." Today, when we read the works *Intrigues of the Warring States*, *The Art of War* by Sun Tzu, or *The Romance of the Three Kingdoms*, we may enjoy reading them as a kind of art, and may even acclaim their military decision making as the acme of perfection. Now, there are many Japanese businesspeople, scholars, organizations, and institutes who have been researching military decision making in *The Art of War*, and *The Romance of the Three Kingdoms*, and how to apply those military decisions to today's business "warfare." *The Art of War* is not only listed as a required reading book in quite a few of the top American universities and their business schools (e.g., Harvard University), but also some critical paragraphs of the book are required to be recited from memory. Therefore, researching the ancient Chinese military strategies used in today's business decision making is important for both the Orient and the West.

YIN *AND* YANG *(UNITY AND OPPOSITE)*

The Book of Changes is an ancient divinatory work that was written in the Zhou Dynasty (11th century BC to 221 BC). This extremely amazing book has puzzled people for thousands of years. Professor Chen Chuankang at the Beijing University asserted that extraterrestrials (ETs) had visited Youli town where *The Book of Changes* was created. Professor Chen maintained that the ETs taught the king, Zhou Wenwang of the Zhou Dynasty (1066 BC to 256 BC), modern science. While the king could not understand science, he accepted it as knowledge from The Divine and based *The Book of Changes* on these revelations. Even today, some people still use the book to predict some future affairs. *The Book of Changes* Research Association of Xi'an city actually forecasted the exact date that the former President and General Secretary of the Soviet Union, Konstantin Chernenko, would die. In 1990, Mr. Zhuang Juxing, an expert on *The Book of Changes*, announced the result of his research and predicted the flood of Tai Lack and the Huai River in the summer of 1991.[2]

Since *The Book of Changes* was an ancient divinatory book in China depicting how the Divine would direct and guide people's behavior, this divinatory book has strongly influenced the Chinese people's decision making. *The Book of Changes* is so complicated that ordinary Chinese people are unable to read and understand it. If we must describe the essence of this book in a sentence, we will compare its concepts of the *yin* and the *yang*. Essentially, the *yin* and the *yang* are the two opposing principles in nature. The *yin* is feminine, and negative, and the *yang* is masculine and positive. "One *yin* and one *yang* can be viewed as the governing principle (truth, how and why)."[3] This concept was written thousands of years ago. One *yin* and one *yang*, however, has been a valuable piece of information, just as a positive and a negative force combine to become information in a modern computer. We have previously addressed that the Chinese philosophy of *yin* and *yang* dialectics believes that the origin or essence of the universe is created by two poles. The *yin* and the *yang* can be interpreted as dead and alive, male and female, true and false, hot and cold, positive and negative, etc. As we can see, the *yin* and the *yang* are interdependent of, but opposite to, each other as well. Therefore, based on the idea of the *yin* and the *yang,* the Chinese evolutionally accepted the philosophy of "unity and opposite."

The philosophy of *yin* and *yang* dialectics and the philosophy of unity and opposition had been incisively and vividly used in Chinese military decision making. In the following, we will share some very interesting examples with the readers.

Increasing Soldiers but Reducing Cooking Sites, and Reducing Soldiers but Increasing Cooking Sites

"Increasing soldiers but reducing cooking sites" was a very tricky art of war in ancient China. During a war, when one party intended to withdraw, the issue they were most concerned with was how to withdraw safely. For the enemy side, they would usually consider two issues: Was this a trick or not? If not, how could they follow up a victory with hot pursuit? "Increasing soldiers but reducing cooking sites" was a remarkably successful trick designed for and used by the withdrawing troops in ancient China. Usually, in the first couple of days, one detail for the pursuing troops to check was to count how many cooking sites were in the enemy's evacuated camp to figure out how strong the forces of the enemy were left to cover the retreat. "Increasing soldiers but reducing cooking sites" was a strategy used to give the wrong impression to the pursuing troops that the forces covering the retreat were weaker than in actuality. When the pursuing troops decided to attack, the pursuers might have their victory turned into a defeat due to this deception. According to the book, *Black Snow*, by Ye Yumeng, which described the Korean War, when the United Nations' troops pursued the North Korean troops to the borders of China, and the Chinese army entered Korea to engage in their first couple of campaigns, the Chinese troops successfully used the trick "increasing soldiers but reducing cooking sites," to turn the victories of the United Nations' armies into defeats.

Now we would like to share with our readers a story from *The Romance of the Three Kingdoms* in which Kongming[4] successfully acted in a diametrically opposite way.

Kongming and his troops had won several victories by defeating the forces of Wei State. If Kongming continued his victory, Wei State would be in a serious and dangerous situation.

At about the same time Kongming was rallying his victorious troops to return to Qishan, Li Yan of the city of Yong'an was sending District Commander Guo An off to deliver a shipment of grain to Kongming. But Guo An, addicted to wine, dallied on the journey, arriving ten days past the deadline. Kongming said angrily, "Grain is a vital necessity for an army. Delivery three days late is punishable by death. You are ten [days late]. Have you any excuse?" Kongming ordered Guo An [to be] removed and executed, but a senior adviser, Yang Yi said, "Guo An is in Li Yan's service. He is responsible for getting money and grain to us from the west. Who will see to delivery after you have killed him?" Kongming ordered the guard to remove Guo An's bonds and after eighty strokes of the staff freed him.

Burning with resentment, Guo An fled to the Wei camp with five or six comrades and surrendered. Called before Sima Yi, he prostrated himself and recounted the incident. "All the same," Sima Yi responded, "knowing Kongming's cunning makes your story difficult to believe. But if you could perform a great service for me, I would recommend you to the Emperor for a high command."

"Whatever you require I shall perform without stint," Guo An answered.

"Then go back to Chengdu and spread the rumor that Kongming envies his sovereign and seeks the opportunity to declare himself emperor. Getting your ruler to recall Kongming will be a great service."

Guo An consented and returned directly to Chengdu, where he met with a eunuch [a chamber guard] and started the rumor that Kongming's pride in his achievements would soon lead him to usurp the ruling house. The amazed eunuch went at once to inform the Emperor. The Second Emperor said in astonishment, "If it is so, what shall we do?" The eunuch said, "Have him recalled to Chengdu and reduce his military authority to forestall future revolt."

The Second Emperor thereupon issued a decree summoning Kongming back to court." Jiang Wan stepped forward and said, "Since the prime minister led the army into the field, he has distinguished himself again and again. For what reason is he being recalled?"

"We have certain matters to discuss with him in confidence," the Second Emperor said, and he dispatched an envoy to recall the prime minister.

The envoy went directly to the main camp in the Qishan hills, where Kongming received him. After reading the edict, Kongming raised his eyes to the heavens and said with a sigh, "Some wily minister near the young sovereign must be influencing him. Why should he recall me when I am about to accomplish something important? If I do not go back, it will be an act of disrespect toward the sovereign. If I obey, another chance like this will be hard to come by."

Jiang Wei said, "If the army withdraws, Sima Yi will seize the opportunity to strike us. What should we do then?"

Kongming answered, "I will divide our forces into five groups for the withdrawal. Today we will evacuate this camp. For every thousand men, we will have two thousand fire pits dug; tomorrow, three thousand; the day after, four thousand. With every new day of retreat, we will increase the number of cooking sites as we move on."

Yang Yi said, "Long ago Sun Bin captured Pang Juan by the ruse of decreasing the cooking sites as he increased his manpower. What is the purpose of adding sites for this withdrawal, your Excellency?"

Kongming replied, "An expert strategist like Sima Yi will pursue us once he finds we have left–but wary of any ambush we might leave, he will count the sites in our former camps. The daily increase in the number of fire pits will make him wonder whether or not we have retreated, and whether or not to pursue. A slow and steady withdrawal will save the lives of our men." So saying, Kongming issued the order of retreat.

Sima Yi assumed that Guo An had by now fully carried out his plan and that he had only to wait for the Riverlands troops to withdraw before mounting a general onslaught. While he was waiting, a report came that the Riverlands positions had been evacuated; warily Sima Yi took one hundred riders to the camp to investigate before ordering pursuit. He had the cooking sites counted and then returned to his base camp. The next day he sent troops back into the evacuated camp to tally the number of fire pits; they reported an increase. Sima Yi said to his commanders, "How clever Kongming is, actually adding troops! Pursuit will lead us into his trap. Let us retreat and plan our next move carefully." Sima Yi and his army turned back, and Kongming headed for Chengdu having suffered no losses. Only later did natives of the Wei River area tell Sima Yi they had seen Kongming add sites but not troops. Sima Yi sighed deeply and said, "Kongming did what Yu Xu once did—and he took me in! He is the better tactician!" So saying, Sima Yi returned to the Wei capital of Luoyang.[5]

The above Chinese strategies could be described in many ways: hiding an advance in retreat, and hiding a retreat in an advance; covering an advance with a retreat, and covering a retreat by an advance; advance in form but retreat in essence, and retreat in form but advance in essence; and, finally, seemingly advance but really retreat, and seemingly retreat but actually advance.

In the Chinese reality, these strategies have been used in business decision making. When the Shanghai stock market was opened in 1992, a gentleman called Yang Millionaire, who was the largest individual stockholder, often used these kinds of tricks, seemingly advance but really retreat, or seemingly retreat but actually advance. Namely, if he really wanted to sell a certain share, he would make people believe that he was buying this share. Then many individuals who followed his lead suddenly bought this stock off of him. Or on the contrary, if he was planning to buy a certain stock, he might let people believe that he was selling his shares. When people sold their shares, he would silently buy it. In addition, Mao Zedong used these strategies quite often. For instance, he encouraged people to criticize the Communist Party because of its problems. He advocated the policy, "Let a hundred flowers blossom; let a hundred schools of thought contend," and encouraged people to engage in the "Rectification Movement" for the Communist Party in 1957. When people believed that the Party really needed rectification and began to criticize the Party, his planned movement "Struggle Against the Bourgeois Rightists" was ready for the persons who criticized the Party. Mao Zedong called his trick "luring the snake out of the hole." Another example happened between China and the United States. In recent years, the United States has often criticized China for selling contraband goods to certain countries. In August 1993, the United States believed that the Chinese cargo ship, Yinhe, was delivering the two banned chemicals, thiodiglycol and thionyl chloride, to Iran in the Middle East. But China denied this accusation. When the United States wanted to check the ship, China refused this request. The United States sent its military planes and naval vessels to follow and keep a close watch on the Chinese ship, which drifted on the ocean and could not pull into a port for days. The Chinese ship looked guilty and was seemingly trying to hide something even in the Chinese ordinary people's eyes. When this event had stirred the whole world, and everyone was waiting for the results, China agreed to let the ship to be checked by a neutral international group in a third country's port. The ship was stranded on August 13, 1993. Nothing contraband could be found on the ship. This event put the United States in a very awkward situation. We think this was a classic example of the Chinese tactic of "hiding advance in retreat."

Associating with Those Distant from You and Attacking Those Close, and Vice Versa

These interesting strategies have been used by China in its relationships with the United States and with the former Soviet Union. Before we address these ideas, we need to introduce some historical background facts that will clarify the story. The period from 475 to 221 BC in China was called the Warring States. As the name indicates, there were countless wars among seven main states, Qin, Qi, Chu, Yan, Han, Zhao, and Wei, and some other small states. After more than 200 years of wars, Qin State, the strongest, finally conquered the other states, thus bringing unity to China. During the period of the Warring States, there were many advisers offering their astuteness, resourcefulness, and strategies to the kings of various states regarding how to beat the others and how to win the wars. The Alliance and the Coalition were the two best-known groups. Su Qin was the representative for the Alliance, and Zhang Yi was the representative of the Coalition. The idea of the Alliance was to ally six states, Qi, Chu, Yan, Han, Zhao, and Wei, to fight against the strongest state, Qin. The strategy of the Coalition was to set one state against another among the six states for the sake of the strongest state, Qin. The following is a story about a counselor of the Coalition, Fan Sui, who advised the king of Qin State to "associate with those distant from him and attack those close by":

> One day, when Fan Sui arrived, the king of Qin State welcomed him to his own palace. After they talked a while, the king of Qin State drove his attendants away. When the palace was empty, the king knelt and said, "What would you please instruct me?"
> "Well, well . . ." answered Fan Sui.
> After a while, the king repeated his request. Again, Fan Sui answered, "Well, well . . ."
> When this happened the third time the king, still kneeling, said, "Probably, you would not be happy to advise me?"
> Fan Sui apologized and talked about his worries. . . .
> "Honored sir," exclaimed the king in kneeling, "What are you talking about? Qin State is a remote country, and its king is ignorant. My luck is to have you here–to having your teaching is proof that heaven favors my ancestors and would not forsake me in my isolation. How could you speak this way to me? There is not any important or insignificant issue–regarding all issues, big and small, no matter whether they concern the queen mother or my ministers, you should not doubt my sincere desire to accept all your advice."
> Fan Sui bowed twice, and the king returned the obeisance.
> Fan Sui said, "Your Majesty, surrounding Qin State there are the mountain and the mountain passes Ganquan and Gukou in the north, the rivers Jing and Wei girdling its south, plateau and mountain regions Long and Zu to the right, and chasms and slopes to the left. Qin State has thousands of war chariots and a

million experienced troops. With these brave soldiers and countless riders, you should be able to fight with those feudal lords just like ferocious hounds chasing crippled hares. Then your supremacy would be established. Instead of this, however, you close your passes and do not dare allow your forces to peer into the east of the mountains. This is because Rang Hou[6] is not royal to Qin State, and your plans fall short."

"I would like to hear how my plans fall short."

"Your Majesty, crossing Wei State and Han State to attack the strong state of Qi is not a wise strategy. If you send insufficient troops you could not harm Qi State, but if you dispatch too many forces, Qin State itself would be harmed. I guess you intend to dispatch partial troops of Qin to bring out all the combined forces of Wei State and Han State. This plan doesn't make sense! Now we know that Wei State and Han State are not friendly, but crossing their countries to attack another one–is this proper? I don't think it is wise. Once Qi State attacked Chu State by smashing Chu's armies, killing Chu's generals, and crossing thousands of miles, but didn't get a single inch of territory in the end. Did Qi State not want land? Yes, but they couldn't get it! When some other Feudal Lords perceived Qi's exhaustion and the conflict between its king and its ministers, they raised their troops to attack Qi State. The king of Qi State was shamed, his forces decimated, and the world laughed. The reason this happened is that while Qi State attacked Chu State, Wei State and Han State were fattened. This is called, 'Borrowing a thief's weapon to feed a robber.' Your majesty, it were better to associate with those distant from you [Qi State] and attack those close by. Then, every inch of territory you win would be the king's inch, and every foot the king's foot. Is this not folly to disregard those near you and attack a distant state. . . ?"[7]

All in all, the king of Qin State eventually gained invaluable advice from Fan Sui, "associate with those distant from you [Qi State] and attack those close by," with his kneeling being the price he paid. This advice and a whole package of these ideas from the Coalition helped Qin State crush the other states and unify China.

Interestingly enough, America has also consciously or unconsciously been involved in the strategies of "associating with those distant from you and attacking those close by," or "attacking those distant from you and associating with those close by." The Korean War and the Vietnam War were the consequences of "attacking those distant from you." Chinese history proved that the words Fan Sui used to advise the king of Qin State several thousand years ago could have been invaluable to America. If we replace Wei State and Han State with Korea and Vietnam, but change Qin State to the United States and Qi State to China, then the words of the sage Fan Sui should have advised the American policy decision makers of the Korean War and the Vietnam War. "Your majesty, crossing Wei State and Han State to attack the strong state of Qi is not a wise strategy. If you send insufficient troops you could not harm Qi State, but if you dispatch too many forces, Qin State itself would be harmed. I guess you intend to dispatch partial troops of Qin to bring out all the combined forces of Wei State and Han State. This plan doesn't make sense! Now we know Wei State and Han State are not friendly, but crossing their countries to attack another one, is this proper? I don't think it is wise." Unfortunately, we do not know whether or not the American policy decision makers for the Korean War and the Vietnam War might have had a chance to read *Intrigues of the Warring States*. We doubt it. However, blockading Cuba, invading Panama on December 20, 1989, and invading Haiti in late 1994 were the successful results of "attacking those close by."

Let us talk about the Chinese policy of decision making that recommends "associating with those distant from you and attacking those close by," or "attacking those distant from you and associating with those close by." In the 1970s and the 1980s, the strategy of China was to associate with those distant from China and attack those close by. The obvious examples: China not only politically but also militarily fought with its neighbors, the Soviet Union and Vietnam, but associated with the United States, which is far distant from China.

Today, the concept of "attacking" may not mean a military action that will destroy buildings and kill people, but could imply a trade warfare, a political argument, or a diplomatic conflict. For this reason, diplomatically, politically, or economically "to fight with those distant from you" may imply a new meaning from what is meant when referring to a military attack. Therefore, a nonmilitary "attacking distant from you" could be considered a tactic. We believe that for various reasons, the current Chinese policy on decision making is to associate with its neighbors close by (the members of the former Soviet Union especially Russia, Japan, South Korea, Pakistan, Mongolia, Thailand, Singapore, India, Indonesia, Vietnam, and Malaysia, etc.) but politically and diplomatically fight with the United States, which is distant from China.

While we are writing this section, the Prime Minister of Japan, Tomiichi Murayama, has just resigned. The replacement, Ryutaro Hashimoto, has been viewed as a hard-liner to the United States, while he has been very friendly to China. That is to say, he would be a strategist or politician who has been implementing the tactics of "attacking those distant from you and associating with those close by." Of course, he may change his strategy because of his new role. We can keep our eyes open to see his actions in the near future.

Will You Survive When You Are Put in Deadly Peril?

Dead and alive are another pair of *yin* and *yang* opposites. When people are placed in deadly peril, they may be able to live. This tactic was found and proven in the ancient Chinese wars.

Han Xin[8] and his troops were sent to subjugate Zhao State. An adviser of Zhao State, Li Zuo, suggested that they block a mountain pass where it was so narrow and dangerous that the troops were unable to go through side by side and seize the grain. Of course, without grain Han Xin would have to retreat. But the king of Zhao State did not accept his idea. When Han Xin knew this, he felt very lucky and admired Li Zuo. He ordered his troops not to hurt Li Zuo during the battle, and would award any soldiers who could catch him.

Han Xin laid an ambush with a part of his troops near the camp of Zhao State, attempting to occupy the camp when the troops of Zhao State charged forward into Han Xin's main forces. Then Han Xin sent his main forces to set up camp with their backs to the river. In the ancient art of war, this kind of encampment was taboo because there was no room for retreat. The soldiers of Zhao State laughed at Han Xin's lack of strategic knowledge, placing his troops' backs to the river. The next day, Han Xin ordered his forces to charge, and the troops of Zhao State fought the approaching enemy. After both armies had fought fiercely, Han Xin and his forces feigned defeat and withdrew toward the river. All the troops of Zhao State rushed out of their camp to chase the enemy. Han Xin's army retreated to the river where there was no room for further withdrawal. The only way out was to turn back and fight with the forces of Zhao State. When Han Xin's troops counter-attacked so vigorously, the army of Zhao State could not defeat them and wanted to retreat to their own camp. However, when they retreated in defeat to their camp, they found that their camp had been occupied by Han Xin's hidden force. Han Xin won a great victory. The king of Zhao State and Li Zuo were caught. Han Xin treated Li Zuo very friendly, but Li Zuo was shy, and said, "How could a failed general show so much courage?!"

Han Xin smiled and replied, "If the king of Zhao State had accepted your suggestion, the failed general would be me, not you and him!"

People asked Han Xin, "Setting a camp with its back to a river is a big taboo for a strategist; how could you deliberately break this rule to win a victory?"

Han Xin said, "Yes, you are right. But my way is also mentioned in the *Art of War* by Sun Tzu. Sun Tzu said, 'Place your army in deadly peril, and it will survive; plunge it into desperate straits, and it will come out in safety.'[9] If you throw your soldiers into positions where there is no escape, they will prefer death to flight. If they face death, there is nothing they may not achieve."[10]

There are also some other military stories that are similar to the one above. For example, Xiang Yu[11] broke the cauldrons and sank the boats after crossing a river–cutting off all means of retreat, to win a great victory.

Drawing a conclusion from the stories, the opposite two poles could mutually change into their reverses. For this reason, the philosophy can be and has been used in business reality, and business decision making. For example, give a deadline to state-owned enterprises that have great deficits, and ask them to make up losses and increase surpluses before the deadline; otherwise, they will go bankrupt. This way works quite often, but the problems of the state-owned enterprises are more special and difficult. A deadline is a deadline, and may never become an "alive-line" for some state-owned enterprises. Another example: first declare a trade warfare to another organization or country, but do not completely close the door on negotiations. In other words, put both parties into a hopeless situation first, then create a gap for the way out, for one side or both. But because Western people usually do not have as heavy a load of "face-saving" as the Chinese do, this tactic must be used very skillfully when one side of the conflict is a Chinese organization or comprised of Chinese citizens. The solution for trade conflicts between the United States and China in March 1995 might be viewed as the strategy of "will you survive when you are put in deadly peril."

Mutual Promotion and Restraint Between What is False and What is True

In any game, whether political, economic, military, or sport, "false and true," a pair of *yin* and *yang* poles, are very sensitive and mysterious. As long as you know other's lies and truth, you may know how to make your decision to win. But in many cases, what is false and what is true may not be so easy to distinguish. Very often what is false could be hidden by a truth, or the truth may be hidden by what is false. Let us enjoy an especially interesting story about the strategy of "mutual promotion and restraint between false and true" from *The Romance of the Three Kingdoms*.

Cao Cao, who was the leader of Wei, the strongest of the three kingdoms, fled from Chibi[12] where he and his troops suffered a crushing defeat by the combination of the other kingdoms, Zu and Wu. He had never expected that Kongming was using this strategy to organize ambushes to wait for him.

Kongming had assigned Zhao Zilong and Zhang Fei to place two ambushes in wait to attack the fleeing Cao Cao. After an argument with Lord Guan,[13] Kongming agreed to allow Lord Guan to ambush at a critical place.

... Lord Guan executed the document, saying, "And if Cao Cao does not take that route?"

"I give you a formal commitment that he will!" Kongming answered, to Lord Guan's complete satisfaction, and then added, "But why don't you pile up dry brambles around the trails and hills by Huarong? At the right time, set them afire. The smoke should draw Cao Cao that way."

"Smoke would make Cao Cao think there's an ambush," Lord Guan protested. "It would keep him away."

"Have you forgotten," Kongming responded, "the tactic of 'Letting weak points look weak and strong points look strong'? Cao Cao may be an able strategist, but this should fool him. The smoke will make him think we are trying to create an impression of strength where we are weak and thus draw him to this route. But I must remind you again, General, to refrain from showing him any mercy." Lord Guan accepted this assignment and, taking his son Ping, Zhou Cang, and 500 practiced swordsmen, headed for Huarong Pass to set up the ambush.

* * *

Cao Cao observed that most of his commanders bore wounds. One solider respectfully asked, "There are two roads ahead; which one does Your Excellency think we should take?"

"Which is shorter?" Cao Cao asked in response.

"The main road is fairly flat, but more than fifty *li*.[14] The other is shorter, but narrow and treacherous and hard-going." Cao Cao ordered some men to climb a hill and survey the road.

"Smoke is rising from several places along the trail," one reported back. "But there seems to be no activity on the main road." Cao Cao ordered the front ranks onto the Huarong Trail.

"Those smoke signals mean soldiers," the commanders protested. "Why go down there?"

"Don't you know what the military texts say?" Cao Cao said. "'A show of force is best where you are weak; where strong, feign weakness.' Kongming is a man of tricks. He purposely sent his men to some nooks in the hills to set fires to deter us from going that way, while placing his ambush on the main road. That's my judgment. I won't fall into this trap!"

"Your ingenious calculations are beyond compare," the commanders agreed and directed their troops toward the Huarong Trail.

By now the men were staggering from hunger. The horses could barely move. Some men had burns; others bore wounds from spears or arrows. On they plodded with walking sticks, dragging themselves painfully along, their clothing and armor drenched. No one had escaped unscathed, and weapons and standards were carried in no semblance of good order. Few mounts had gear since the route north of Yiling, when saddles and bridles had been cast aside. It was midwinter, and the cold was severe. Who can fairly describe their suffering?

Cao Cao saw the front line come to a halt and asked why. The report came back: "The hills ahead are rarely crossed; the paths are too narrow, and the horses have bogged down in the ditches after the morning's rains."

In an exasperated tone Cao Cao said, "Are you telling me that an army that forges through mountains and bridges rivers can't get through a little mud?" Then he sent down the command: "Let the old, the weak, and the wounded follow as best they can; the able-bodied are to carry earth, wood, grass, and reeds to fill in the road. The march must resume, and whoever disobeys dies." As ordered, the soldiers dismounted and cut trees and bamboo by the roadside to rebuild the road. Cao Cao, fearing pursuit, had Zhang Liao, Xu Chu, and Xu Huang lead a hundred riders with swords bared to cut down slackers.

At Cao Cao's order, the troops, starved and exhausted, trudged ahead, trampling over the bodies of the many who had fallen. The dead were beyond number, and the sound of howls and cries on the trail did not cease. Angrily, Cao Cao said, "Fate rules life and death. What are all these cries for? I'll behead the next to cry." One-third of the men fell behind; another third lay in the ditches; one-third stayed with Cao Cao. They passed a treacherous slope. The road began to flatten out. Looking behind, Cao Cao saw that he was left with a mere three hundred mounted followers, not a one with clothing and armor intact. Cao Cao urged them forward.

The commanders said, "The horses are spent; they need a short rest."

"Push on. There'll be time for that in Jiangling," Cao answer.

They rode another *li* or two. Cao Cao raised his whip and laughed again. "Why is Your Excellency laughing?" the commanders asked.

"Everyone thinks Zhou Yu and Kongming are such shrewd tacticians," he replied. "But as I see it, neither is especially capable. If they had set an ambush here we would have surrendered quietly." That moment a bombardment echoed. Five hundred expert swordsmen flanked the road. At their head, sitting astride Red Hare, raising his blade the Green Dragon, the great general Lord Guan Yunchang checked Cao Cao's advance. Cao Cao's men felt their souls desert them, felt their courage die. They looked at one another helplessly.[15]

Of course, weak and strong could be a pair of the opposites *yin* and *yang,* but we do not think that this pair of concepts that the translator of *The Romance of the Three Kingdoms* selected could properly describe the essence of Kongming's trick because a weak force would still mean armed men. But Kongming did not send anyone to the main road. Therefore, we believe the concepts "false and true" we chose will be able to indicate the essence of the strategy better. As an aside, "Huarong Trail" has become the symbol of a dangerous way with uncertain false or true steps.

The examples of "mutual promotion and restraint between what is false and what is true" in business reality would be a long list. We would like to share one that we know with our readers. Since the strategy is being used while we are writing this book, and the final results have not been exposed, please excuse us for names and products.

There are two Chinese factories who are friends but also opponents inasmuch as they make the same type of products. The American partners of both, however, are competitors in American and international markets. The Chinese Factory A is going to expand its productivity of a certain product for American and international markets. The Chinese Factory B intends to go into a joint venture with its American partner. Both try to learn each other's plans. Expanding the productivity of a product will involve an investment to import equipment, as well as in market competition in the near future. To become a joint venture will change too many aspects for a state-owned enterprise. The Chinese Factory A exposed its real intention to sound out the Chinese Factory B, but the latter did not believe the former was telling the truth and B's American business partner has a better control of this product in the American market. The Chinese Factory B could not cover its intention of a joint venture, but tried its best to make the Chinese Factory A believe the impossibilities of a joint venture. Factory A accepted the idea of the impossibilities for B to be in a joint venture with its American partner. Thus, B considered A's truth as false; and A believed B's falsehood was true. Factory B received a major shock when it found out that A has been importing machines to manufacture this product. And A was surprised when it learned that B and its American business partner have signed a contract for their joint-venture enterprise. Now both know each other's tactics, but the real results/consequences of their strategies will not be reflected for the next one or two years.

Competition in a market is crude; some lose, some gain; some fail, some win; in a sense, it is just like war. No wonder people have been using military strategies in business decision making. Now that the Cold War has ended, business may be more like war than it was before.

MILITARY STRATEGY AND TACTICS FROM SUN TZU

How similar war and business are could be far beyond our imagination. For instance, we could even find ideas about joint venture and foreign investment in the strategy that Sun Tzu addressed several thousand years ago in his work, *The Art of War*.[16] Sun Tzu said:

> Poverty of the state mandates that an enemy be kept at a distance. Keeping the enemy at a distance causes the people to be impoverished. On the other hand, the proximity of an army causes prices to go up: And high prices cause the people's subsistence to drain away. When their subsistence is drained

away, the peasantry will be afflicted with heavy exactions. With this loss of subsistence and exhaustion of strength, the home of the people will be stripped bare, and three-tenths of their income will be dissipated; while government expenses for broken chariots, worn out horses, breastplates and helmets, bows and arrows, spears and shields, protective mantles, draught-oxen and heavy wagons, will amount to four-tenths of its total revenue. Hence a wise general makes a point of foraging on the enemy. One cartload of the enemy's provisions is equivalent to twenty of one's own, and likewise a single piece of the enemy's provender is equivalent to twenty from one's own store.[17]

No wonder William A. Levinson asked: "Without its violent aspects, how does war differ from business, politics, or statecraft?"[18]

Beside basic similar symbols between war and business, "contests between organizations," there are also many subtle similarities in which the art of war can be used in business (e.g., "There can never be too much deception in war"; "All is fair in war"; "Speed is precious in war"; and "Defeat one's opponent with a surprising move").

The following would be the strategies of Sun Tzu that we would like to discuss in relation to business issues.

Scheming Before You Act

Sun Tzu said:

> Thus we may know that there are five essentials for victory: He will win who knows when to fight and when not to fight; he will win who knows how to handle both superior and inferior forces; he will win whose army is animated by the same spirit throughout all its ranks; he will win who prepares himself, waits to take the enemy unprepared; he will win who has military capacity and is not interfered with by the sovereign. Hence the saying: If you know the enemy and know yourself, you can fight a hundred battles without defeat. If you know yourself but not the enemy, for every victory gained you will

also suffer a defeat. If you know neither the enemy nor yourself, you will succumb in every battle.[19]

The words of Sun Tzu have consummately generalized the essence of scheming before you act. In the following we will discuss several subsections of scheming before you act.

Know Your Enemy Before You Act

There are several means to be used to know your enemy: collecting secondhand or indirect information about your enemy, directly observing your enemy, spying on your enemy, and testing your enemy. The first two, collecting secondhand or indirect information about your enemy, and directly observing your enemy, are very common means; thus, we are not going to explain them.

As for the third one, spying on your enemy, we will only describe the ancient Chinese strategies about spying on the enemy, since we do not really know how these means and strategies have been used in business reality. Sun Tzu addressed five strategies for spying on the enemy: local spies, inward spies, converted spies, doomed spies, and surviving spies.[20] We may need to explain these five strategies one by one.

1. *Local spies* are native or local people used to collect common or general information that was not worth obtaining through a hidden inward spy.
2. *Inward spies* are the persons hidden in your enemy camp that you have hired to be your secret spies. What kinds of people in your enemy's camp could be or should be selected to be your inward spies? They could be listed as follows: capable persons who are not in appropriate and suitable positions (namely the talented persons who are in the lower positions); persons who had been punished for being false; persons who are in power but are avaricious; persons who feel a grievance about something in their positions or situations; persons who are not trusted by authority; persons who desire to show off their abilities; and persons who easily and often switch sides—inconstant persons.
3. *Converted spies* pretend to know nothing about who the enemy's spies are but release false information to them. Also,

to buy off or bribe the enemy's spies to work for you is another way to "convert" spies.
4. *Doomed spies* are spies you send to deliver phony information to your enemy. When your enemy realizes that they have been taken in, your spies, who may or may not have known the information was phony, could be seriously punished or even killed.
5. *Surviving spies* are your spies who would be able to come back. Usually, the spies were sent legally, or with some special means of protection (e.g., diplomatic immunity).

The five ways of spying on your enemy were all successfully used in Chinese ancient wars. Unfortunately, we are unable to discuss them in today's business reality.

We, however, want to focus on the ancient Chinese strategy—"to know your enemy by testing your enemy." Sun Tzu wrote:

> Military tactics are like water for water in its natural course runs away from high places and hastens downward. So in war, the way is to avoid what is strong and to strike at what is weak. Water shapes its course according to the nature of the ground over which it flows; the soldier works out his victory in relationship to the foe he is facing.[21]

However, how can you know your enemy or opponent, who has been attempting to hide his or her weaknesses and strengths, or true intentions? Besides the use of spies, Sun Tzu designed some other ways of testing the enemy to know the enemy better. For instance, probing your enemy, touching your enemy, and pushing your enemy.

First, let us look at probing your enemy. This is to use some small or indirect activities to probe for a reaction from your enemy (reconnaissance by fire, making noises, etc.). There is another vivid Chinese saying about a probing person (e.g., thief or reconnoiterer): "Throwing a stone to find out if the road is safe–what reaction may occur." The point was to test what the potential or possible reactions from your enemy would be so that you could figure out what kind of true reaction might come from your opponent later. This strategy has been used frequently in wars, and it has been very successfully applied to today's business reality. For example, in 1971, people were probably aware that the Thirty-First World Table Tennis Championships ended, but did not know that the table tennis team from the United States would unexpectedly be invited to visit an enemy country—the Peoples Republic of China. Some astute people might point out that since the Korean War, both countries only "associated" with each other by using guns or through verbal attacks. So why, now, did they "attack" each other with a small white ball?[22] As an enemy country, China sent its invitation to the table tennis team of the United States; this was also a reconnaissance by fire or a trial balloon from China to test its enemy's potential reactions. Just this piece of probing opened a diplomatic route between China and the United States. We could say that a small ball turned around the big ball (earth). Using TV commercials or other mass advertisements can also be the way to probe your competition in today's business reality.

Second, touching your enemy was used to test the reaction from your enemy by some actual physical movements. Actual physical actions in a military performance could be a feint attack, a probing attack, a flank attack, or even a sneak attack. Nevertheless, those attacks must be under control so that you are able to decide when and where the physical attack would be continued or be stopped because the essential purpose of this movement was to find out the real reaction of your opponent. In business reality, a Chinese manufacturer found out how to use a new steel material to make wooden industrial cutting blades that would last more than three times longer than the ones using the old steel material, and the cost of making a blade with the new steel material would be less than the cost of making three blades with the old material not including the cost of processing the knives. This technical and economic superiority of the Chinese factory would cause a major change in wooden industrial cutting knives. But the factory did not know what reactions might come from its opponents who were also working on steel material research to improve the quality of their knives, what heavily reducing their prices for competition would do, or if they should simply give up the competition of these products to move their concentrations to plastic industrial knives or some other products? The factory had two options. One was to release this information in various commercials and advertisements to probe its opponents. The other one was to send its new knives to the customers of its opponents as a form of real touching. The manager of the factory figured that the feedback from commercials and advertisements through the customers and through their opponents would be very slow, and might be also unclear and unreliable. He decided that his factory would rather spend the money to make some free knives for the customers of his opponents than spend the money on the various commercials and advertisements. The first results from the feedback of this strategy of touching his opponents were a great many phone calls from the customers of his opponents indicating a keen interest in the new knives. While his factory was preparing a real and major attack, his opponents kept silent since they could not so heavily reduce their prices for this competition and did not know how to adapt to this challenge and change. Then the factory seized this opportunity and followed up a victory with hot pursuit to occupy as much of the market as the factory could before its opponents might know how to meet this challenge. After more than half a year had passed, while we are writing this section, the factory is still expanding its market because its opponents are at their wit's end.

Third, if the way of touching your enemy would not show your real purpose to your enemy, try the way of pushing your enemy's intentions to make your enemy believe you want to fight. To describe it differently, you should create an atmosphere of war to pressure your opponent to find out what his or her real reactions might be, even if you might not really want to fight. Of course, probing your enemy or touching your enemy could use some of the same activities to create an atmosphere of war. The key must be to assume an intimidating momentum toward your enemy. If your opponent did not believe that you were going to war, he or she would not show real reactions. In fact, by use of force, such as a detachment warfare, you could push your enemy as well as with a mere announcement, without the use of force, and might be able to create enough pressure to push your opponent. Essentially, pushing your opponent was just a means; the final purpose was to understand the real intention and reactions of your enemy. Therefore, pushing your enemy should also be in your control. As long as you know the real intention and reactions of your enemy, you know how to implement your next plan. If the situation were out of control, the consequences might go contrary to your wishes. The appropriate level of pushing your enemy is crucial for this strategy. In today's business reality, pushing your enemy has often been used. A typical instance could be the conflict about protection of intellectual property rights between China and the United States in February of 1995. On February 4, 1995, the Clinton Administration imposed punitive tariffs on more than $1 billion of Chinese goods, the largest trade sanctions in American history, and warned of further action if China continued to refuse to crack down on the piracy of American software, movies, and music. The decision to impose 100 percent punitive tariffs on goods ranging from silk blouses to cellular telephones was met almost immediately by an angry Chinese announcement of tariffs against American-made goods (e.g., cigarettes, film, alcoholic beverages, etc.) Along with the tariff on U.S. products, China will suspend negotiations for United States auto companies seeking to set up joint-venture projects, withdraw approval for United States companies and their subsidiaries to set up holding companies, and suspend approval for United States audiovisual manufacturers to open branch offices.[23] Both adopted their own postures for a trade warfare; both were pushing their opponent to let each other believe they were ready for a trade war. However, both also understood that this was a game in which there was no winner. As we will explain in a later chapter, there would be four possible results from this game: (1) China yields, and the United States wins; (2) the U.S. yields and China wins; (3) neither yields, both seem to be winners but are essentially losers; and (4) both yield, and everyone is a winner. After both understood each other's real intentions and reactions by each pushing their opponent, both began to change their strategies for new negotiations. Noticeably, when pushing your enemy is used on the Chinese, the face-saving issue needs to be considered. In the conflict, the American side skillfully controlled the appropriate level of pushing its opponent for the face-saving issue of the Chinese; we will discuss this in detail in the next chapter.

Know Yourself Before You Act

From the last section, we should understand that it is critical to know your enemy before you act. However, your enemy and yourself are mutual opposites; hence, if someone were your enemy, you would be someone's enemy as well. That is to say, as another's opponent, it would also be critical for you to be known by them. Or you can reason it in a diametrically opposite way: Since it is so critical that you be known by your enemy, knowing yourself would be extremely important to yourself. No wonder Sun Tzu wrote, "If we know that the enemy is open to attack, but are unaware that our own men are not in a condition to attack, we have gone only halfway towards victory . . . If you know the enemy and know yourself, your victory will not stand in doubt."[24] Unfortunately, people usually understand the importance of "knowing your enemy," but may often ignore the significance of "knowing yourself." Even if you realize the importance of understanding yourself, there would still be two difficult points for "knowing yourself." One is that when you are a leader, "self" would mean "selves," which includes your subordinates; so, "knowing yourself" could be "knowing yourselves"–your group. The other is that it would not be so easy to understand yourself objectively and appropriately. Let us discuss these two one after another.

First, as a leader, understanding yourselves would imply knowing about "who could do what" among your subordinates. There is a Chinese belief, "Don't choose the person whom you would not trust for the job. As long as the person has been chosen by you for the job, you should never doubt him." These words are easy to be said, but very difficult to be done, even tried. The key is to really know yourselves. We can see a story that before the king of Qin State became Qin Shi Huang, the First Chinese Emperor who united China, was challenged by the issue of "As long as the person has been chosen by you for the job, you should never doubt him."

At that time, the king of Qin sent a general, whose name was Gan Mao, to persuade Wei State to attack Han State together with Gan Mao. After Gan Mao achieved the goal, he sent a person to tell the king of Qin State that the king had better not send him to attack Han State. The king of Qin State felt very strange, he recalled Gan Mao for questioning at Xirang.

Gan Mao said, "Once Marquis Wen of Wei ordered Yue Yang to command an attack on Zhongshan. After three years he took it and returned to claim his honor. Marquis Wen showed him a chest full of defaming letters and Yue Yang bowed down his head to the ground saying 'Your servant gains no honor in this victory; it was accomplished through the power of his master.' Once, when the saintly Zeng Tzu lived in the Bi County, there was another of the same clan who was also called by his name. This one had killed a man, and a neighbor called out to Zeng Tzu's mother, 'Zeng Tzu has killed a man.' His mother did not leave off her weaving but said: 'My son is no murderer.' In a while another cried, 'Zeng Tzu killed a man,' but she continued to weave as before. The third time someone cried out 'Zeng Tzu killed a man,' she dropped her shuttle in fear, leaped over her threshold, and fled. Despite the virtue of Zeng Tzu and his mother's faith in him, when three others had shaken her confidence, she too disbelieved her son.' Your servant's nobility being somewhat less than that of Zeng Tzu, Your Majesty's faith in me being less firm that Zeng's mother's, and my detractors being more numerous than three, I fear Your Majesty will drop the shuttle while I am gone."

"I will not listen to them," replied the king, "I make a covenant with you now that this will be so." They thereupon made a covenant at Xirang. Yiyang was laid under siege for five months but would not fall. Chu Liji and Gongsun Yan did argue before the king who believed them and recalled Gan Mao to accuse him.

Gan Mao asked: "Was there not a covenant at Xirang?"

"There was," replied the king after a little. Then he mustered all his forces, ordered Gan Mao to lead them against Yiyang once more, and shortly thereafter the city fell."[25]

From this story, we can understand how challenging it would be for a leader to "chose a person and trust him!"

Second, people have difficulty understanding themselves objectively and appropriately because it is human nature to overestimate oneself, and then to have a lack of confidence at a crucial moment. Let us enjoy the following interesting story from *The Romance of the Three Kingdoms*, to understand why "knowing yourself" is so important.

Because Ma Su, a general of Kongming, overestimated himself, he lost Jieting, which was a crucial strategic point. As a result, Kongming had to arrange a whole plan for retreat.

After making these arrangements, Kongming took 5,000 men back to Xicheng to move grain and provender. Suddenly a dozen mounted couriers arrived and reported: "Sima Yi is leading a multitude of 150,000 toward Xicheng." At this point Kongming had no commanders of importance beside him—only a group of civil officials–and half the 5,000 in his command had been detailed to move food supplies, leaving a mere 25,000 troops in the town. The officials turned pale at the news of Sima Yi's approach. When Kongming mounted the city wall to observe, he saw dust clouds in the distance rising skyward as the two northern field armies advanced for battle.

Kongming ordered all flags and banners put out of sight and instructed the wall sentries to execute anyone who tried to pass in or out without authority or anyone who raised his voice. Next, Kongming ordered the town's four gates opened wide; at each a squad of twenty, disguised as commoners, swept the roadway. The soldiers had been told to make no untoward move when the Wei army arrived, as Kongming was following a plan of his own. After this Kongming put on his crane-feather cloak, wrapped a band around his head, and, followed by two lads bearing his zither, sat down on the wall. He propped himself against the railing in front of a turret and began to strum as incense burned.

Meanwhile, Sima Yi's scouts had reached the wall of Xicheng. Finding the scene as described, they advanced no further but reported at once to their commander. Sima Yi laughed and dismissed the report. He then halted his army and rode forward himself to view the town from a distance. There indeed was Kongming sitting by the turret, smiling as ever and burning incense as he played. To his left, a lad held a fine sword; to his right, another held a yak-tail whisk. By the gate, two dozen sweepers plied their brooms with lowered heads, as if no one else were about.

Puzzled, Sima Yi turned his army around and retreated toward the hills to the north. His second son, Sima Zhao, asked, "What makes you sure Kongming isn't putting this on because he has no troops? Why simply retreat, Father?" Sima Yi answered, "Kongming has always been a man of extreme caution, never one to tempt the fates. He opened the gates because he had set an ambush. On entering, we would have been trapped. You are too young to know! Hurry the retreat!" Thus the two Wei armies withdrew.

After the retreating army was well into the distance, Kongming rubbed his palms together and laughed; but his officials were amazed. One of them asked, "Why did a famous Wei general like Sima Yi with 150,000 in his command withdraw after one look at Your Excellency?"

"The man," Kongming replied, "assumed I was too cautious to tempt fate. He saw my preparations, suspected ambush, and withdrew. It was not recklessness. What choice had I? Sima Yi is sure to head for the northern hills. I have already told Guan Xing and Zhang Bao to be waiting for him there."

The astonished officials acknowledged his genius, saying, "The very gods could not outwit Your Excellency. We would have abandoned the town!"

"Could I have gotten far enough with 2,500 men," Kongming asked, "to escape Sima Yi?" His explanation made, Kongming clapped his hands and laughed aloud. "But were I Sima Yi, I would not have gone back!" he said. Next, he ordered the people of Xicheng to follow the troops into Hanzhong in view of the expected return of Sima Yi. And so Kongming set out for Hanzhong from Xicheng, followed by the officials, officers, soldiers, and people of the three districts Tianshui, Anding, and Nan'an.

* * *

Meanwhile, Sima Yi was advancing with a fresh detachment; but the Riverlands army had already completed its return to Hanzhong. So Sima Yi led the detachment back to

Xicheng, where he learned from the few remaining residents and some mountain recluses that Kongming had only 2,500 men in the city, no commanders, a few civil officials, and of course, no ambush in readiness. And at the Wugong Hills, the commanders told him, "Guan Xing and Zhang Bao had only 3,000 men each. They came around the hill yelling and drumming to frighten off pursuers, but they had no other forces and no intention of engaging in battle." Sima Yi looked ruefully into the heavens and said with a sigh, "Kongming's the better man!"[26]

Sima Yi looked like he deeply knew his enemy Kongming who "was too cautious to tempt fate," but Kongming indeed not only knew that he himself "was too cautious to tempt fate," but also knew how his enemy Sima Yi would act based on the knowledge that Kongming "was too cautious to tempt fate." As a result, Kongming produced a very famous story, "Empty-city Stratagem," in Chinese history. Therefore, as we have previously indicated: "Since it is so critical that you be known by your enemy, knowing yourself would be extremely important to yourself."

Knowing yourself then, you should know how to cover yourself to puzzle your opponent as Kongming did—to make your weaknesses look like strengths, and make your strengths look like weaknesses.

There is a Chinese saying, "Sometimes a foot may prove short while an inch may prove long—everyone has his or her strong and weak points."

For this reason, by knowing yourself even if you are weak, you should be able to know if you are able to fight using your partial superiority against your enemy's partial weakness, how to fight, when to fight, and where to fight—or whether to simply avoid the fight altogether.

Sun Tzu listed seven perspectives to compare oneself with the enemy to determine whether or not an army could win a victory.[27] These seven perspectives we can also apply to today's business decision making. Their comparisons are listed in Table 6.1.

From these seven comparisons, we can deduce that not only "knowing yourself" and "knowing your enemy" are critical for a victory in ancient military warfare, but also are true and vital philosophies for wise business decision making in today's economic competition.

TABLE 6.1. Tzu's Seven Perspectives Used to Assess the Enemy Applied to Modern Business Decision Making

Seven Perspectives from *The Art of War* by Sun Tzu	Today's Business Decision Making
1. Which of the two sovereigns is sagacious?	Which enterprise's higher authority is wiser?
2. Which of the two generals is able?	Whose administrator is able?
3. With whom lies the advantageous situation?	Who occupies a better location for markets?
4. On which side is discipline most rigorously enforced?	Whose administrative regulations and discipline are strict, impartial, and effective?
5. Which army is stronger?	Whose human resources, material resources, and equipment imply a higher quality?
6. On which side are officers and men more highly trained?	Whose employees have better training and education?
7. In which army is there the greater constancy both in reward and punishment?	In which enterprise is there a fair reward (pay, bonus, welfare) and a just penalty?

Know the situation. In general, when we identify a problem or define a project for business decision making, the information about your opponents and/or yourself will be contained in the situation.

Sun Tzu, however, was more meticulous when he considered the "situation" for his military decision making. First of all, he divided the situation into three parts: *climate, geographic location,* and *people.* Climate implied the political environment, the social atmosphere, the natural conditions, and weather, etc. *Geographic location* included topography, terrain, position, geographical condition, resources, and transportation, etc. And *people* encompassed the will of the people, the quality of human resources, relationships between the people and the army, the quantity and quality of the troops, the ability of the general, the relationships between sovereign, subjects, generals, soldiers, etc.

Second, Sun Tzu furthered his divisions into two categories: One was the enemy's *climate, geographic location,* and *people*; the other was his own *climate, geographic location,* and *people*.

Indeed, Sun Tzu described his concepts in much more detail. For instance, in one of his works, he explained some important points about *geographic location*:

> The art of war recognizes nine varieties of ground: dispersive ground, facile ground, contentious ground, open ground, the ground of intersecting highways, serious ground, difficult ground, hemmed-in ground, and desperate ground. When a chieftain is fighting in his own territory, it is dispersive ground. When he has penetrated into hostile territory, but to no great distance, it is facile ground. Ground which imports great advantage to either side is contentious ground. Ground on which each side has liberty of movement is open ground. Ground which forms the key to three contiguous states, so that he who occupies it first has most of the empire at his command, is a ground of intersecting highways. When an army has penetrated into the heart of a hostile country, leaving a number of fortified cities in its rear, it is serious ground. Mountain forests, rugged steeps, marshes and fens–all country that is hard to traverse, this is difficult ground. Ground which is reached through narrow gorges, and from which we can only retire by tortuous paths so that a small number of the enemy would suffice to crush a large body of men is hemmed-in ground. Ground on which we can only be saved from destruction by fighting without delay, is desperate ground. On dispersive ground, therefore, fight not. On facile ground, halt not. On contentious ground, attack not. On open ground, do not try to block the enemy's way. On the ground of intersecting highways, join hands with your allies. On serious ground, gather in plunder. In difficult ground, keep steadily on the march. On hemmed-in ground, resort to stratagem. On desperate ground, fight.[28]

Though these "nine grounds" were describing military geographic locations, we can easily borrow them to scheme and formulate our business decision making for modern investment, particularly international competition and foreign direct investment in which we must consider location of investment, local human resources, local material resources, transportation, communication, capital, technology, market, etc.

In brief, in terms of Sun Tzu's idea, before a battle you must list and compare each difference between the enemy and yourself; then you would know whether or not you should fight, and if you could win this battle.

Today, if we go back to check the information about the Korean War, the Vietnam War, the military conflicts between China and India, China and the Soviet Union, and China and Vietnam, the results of the comparison, using the way of Sun Tzu, would show us that China had used the ideas of Sun Tzu to help its decision making. We can assume the Vietnam war as an example to be a potential military conflict between China and the United States. In Table 6.2 the symbol * means better, X means bad, = means similar or tied, and ? means unknown.

From the comparison and analysis in Table 6.2, we find that the United States was in a more disadvantageous and worse situation than China in the Vietnam War that was an indirect and potential military conflict between two countries. Certainly, China has been good at using the strategies of Sun Tzu for its military or even political decision making. China, however, has just accepted the ideas of a market economy since 1992; these strategies from Sun Tzu have not been as appropriately applied in today's business reality as in China's political and military decision making. For example, the investment that built the railways between Tanzania and Zambia could be an example resulting in poor economic consequences from not considering the Sun Tzu's ideas of *climate, geographic location*, and *people,* but rather Mao Zedong's political considerations.

Changing as Your Enemy Changes

Wars have always been full of dynamics and variances from the beginning to the end. Very often, any tiny change might cause a larger change just as pulling one hair might cause the whole body to be affected–a slight move in one part could affect the situation as a whole. For example, if the enemy changes commanders, the strate-

TABLE 6.2. Assessment of China and the United States as Enemies in Vietnam War

	China		The United States
	Climate		*Climate*
=	1. Political environment China had good relations with the developing countries, but not the European Socialist countries.	=	1. Political environment The United States had good relations with its allies, but not with the developing countries.
*	2. Social atmosphere People unconditionally supported Mao Zedong during the Cultural Revolution.	X	2. Social atmosphere People were tired of war, and seriously antiwar. Many people were antiracist.
*	3. Natural condition Good for Chinese troops.	X	3. Natural condition Bad for the United States military equipment.
*	4. Weather Good for local people.	X	4. Weather Bad for many American soldiers.
	Geographical Location		*Geographical Location*
*	1. Topography Suitable for the Chinese army.	X	1. Topography Bad for the United States troops.
*	2. Geographical condition At the Chinese border.	X	2. Geographical condition Too far away from the United States.
*	3. Resources The Chinese were used to them.	X	3. Resources They were bad for the United States troops.
	People		*People*
*	1. The will of the people Support.	X	1. The will of the people Many people were antiwar.
*	2. Relations between people and army All right.	X	2. Relations between people and army Some conflicts.
*	3. Quantity and quality of troops Big quantity, adequate quality.	X	3. Quantity and quality of troops Small quantity, adequate quality.
?	4. Ability of generals Unknown.	?	4. Ability of generals Unknown.
=	5. Relations among sovereign subjects, general, and soldiers All right.	=	5. Relations among sovereign subjects, general, and soldiers All right.

gies, tactics, and fighting styles might change as well. Sun Tzu advised:

> Therefore, just as water retains no constant shape, so in warfare there are no constant conditions. He who can modify his tactics in relation to his opponent and thereby succeed in winning, may be called a heaven-born captain. The five elements[29] are not always equally predominant; the four seasons make way for each other in turn. There are short days and long; the moon has its periods of waning and waxing.[30]

Knowing your enemy and knowing yourself comprise the fundamental basis for any initiative or passive changes. Obviously, without knowing your enemy, you would not know whether or not an action from your enemy would mean a change. Furthermore, without knowing your enemy and knowing yourself, you would not know if you should react to a change from your enemy, and/or how to react to this change of your enemy. Therefore, knowing your enemy and knowing yourself are the cornerstones for the strategy "changing as your enemy changes."

There are two kinds of change: initiative change and passive change.

Generally speaking, changing as your enemy changes is a passive change, but it is made to consciously maintain an initiative position, or to change a currently passive situation. Likewise, in business reality, this military tactic of changing as your enemy changes cannot only keep your marketing initiative position, but change your passive situation in an economic competition as well. There is a story about changing as the market changes.

> One day, a Chinese manager saw a foreign businessman was using a calculator with his left hand while he took his lighter to light a cigarette with his right. The manager suddenly had a brainstorm to combine a calculator with a lighter. His new product, a combination of calculator and lighter, had a strong market for quite a while. Then the sales of this product were reduced. Soon he found out the reason was that when the lighter fluid was gone, the combination became a calculator again because of the inconvenience of adding the lighter fluid.

Then he reduced the cost of the calculator by simplifying its functions, and improved the energy of the lighter. As a result, he regained his markets. Nevertheless, he started to lose his American market. The research showed him that American education did not pay greater attention to basic skills, so for involution, evolution, ratio, etc., many Americans must rely on the calculator. In other words, a too simple calculator was not popular in the United States. He increased the calculator's functions for the American people, then his Calcu-Lite regained its American market.

Only by changing as your customer changes would you be able to open and keep your market.

You could also move your enemy by an initiative change that could be either true or false. Sun Tzu wrote:

> All warfare is based on deception. Hence, when able to attack, we must seem unable; when using our forces, we must seem inactive; when we are near, we must make the enemy believe we are far away; when far away, we must make him believe we are near. Hold out baits to entice the enemy. Feign disorder, and crush him. If he is secure at all points, be prepared for him. If he is in superior strength, evade him. If your opponent is of choleric temper, seek to irritate him. Pretend to be weak, that he may grow arrogant. If he is taking his ease, give him no rest. If his forces are united, separate them. Attack him where he is unprepared; appear where you are not expected. These military devices, leading to victory, must not be divulged beforehand.[31]

On the contrary, when the changes from your enemy were to guide you to change to their direction and plan, and you did not need to change at all, the solution was to use nonchange to challenge and adapt to verities. After the event at Tian'anmen Square in 1989, the various Western countries, one after another, changed their policies to deal with China. Next, social transformations happened one after another in the former Soviet Union and Eastern European countries. As many Chinese cadres did not know how to adapt to these changes, Deng Xiaoping gave this advice, "Calm down to watch the changes in the world while continuing our economic reformation and opening." After three years, his tactic of the use of nonchange to challenge and adapt to verities began to produce the desired results. The Western countries canceled their punishments and restored their normal relationships with China. Also, the countries of the former Soviet Union and Eastern Europe began to pay attention to research, and even wanted to learn from the experience of the Chinese economic reformation and opening.

Winning a Victory by Surprise Action

Sun Tzu wrote:

> The difficulty of tactical maneuvering consists in turning the devious into the direct, and misfortune into gain. Thus, to take a long and circuitous route, after enticing the enemy out of the way, and though starting after him, to contrive to reach the goal before him, shows knowledge of the artifice of deviation.[32]

Our enemies or opponents are usually able people; hence, sometimes we may need to win a victory from them with unexpected action or by surprise behavior. There were quite a few unusual but reasonable stratagems in the Chinese art of war, such as to strengthen in order to weaken; to foster in order to eliminate; to assist in order to defeat, etc. We would select the following as some unusual but reasonable stratagems to share with our readers.

To give in order to take. Here, obviously "to give" was a means, and "to take" was the end. "To take" could often reach a goal when people did not realize "to take" was the end. Sometimes, however, "to give" had just been the end. We have previously spoken of General Han Xin, who set up an army camp with its back to a river. Han Xin had experienced the strategies of both: "To give" was just the end, and "to give" was a means, but "to take" was the end.

> When Han Xin was young, he was very poor. One day, a kind lady who was washing clothes at a river saw that Han Xin was hungry. She shared some of her meal with Han Xin. He was moved, and said, "Kind lady, I must repay your kindness someday."

> The lady laughed and said, "How should a man say these words? Do you think sharing my meal with you is to expect your repayment someday? Don't be silly! Eat it . . . ." Han Xin was touched in his mind. After many years, Han Xin, as the best general, help Liu Bang establish the Han Dynasty. He was offered the kingdom of Chu, and returned to his hometown. The first thing he did was to find the lady, and give her a large sum of money to thank her for her kindness.

In short, for the lady, "to give" was her purpose, with no other meaning to Han Xin. Nevertheless, Han Xin experienced another entirely different story:

> Han Xin, as the best general of Liu Bang, had beaten the troops of Qi State and defeated the army of Chu State. At that time he was just a general. In order to conveniently administer the territory of Qi State, which he had just seized for Liu Bang, he needed an official title. So, he sent his request to Liu Bang for a temporary official title, "Temporary King of Qi State." When Liu Bang received the request from Han Xin, he was surrounded at Xingyang by his enemy. He really needed Han Xin, and he worried Han Xin might betray him if he did not approve Han Xin's request. Therefore, he simply offered the formal title of "King of Qi State" to Han Xin, instead of the temporary title. Later, Han Xin and his troops were great in strength and impetus. Some people advised Han Xin to betray Liu Bang. But Han Xin was considerate of the advantage Liu Bang had offered to him, and kept the good impression of Liu Bang in his mind. He refused this advice, and continued to fight with the enemy for Liu Bang. Under his crucial help, Liu Bang eventually built his own kingdom—the Han Dynasty. Then Liu Bang began to get even with Han Xin. First, he divested Han Xin of his military power and also changed Han Xin's official title to the King of Chu State which was not so important. Later, he demoted Han Xin to the position of a local official in his hometown. Finally, Han Xin was drawn to the palace to be killed by a trick of the wife of Liu Bang. Before Han Xin died, he said with a sigh: "I repent that I didn't accept the other's

advice to betray Liu Bang, so that today I was unjustly killed by a woman's hands . . ."[33]

Evidently, to give the formal title of King of Qi State to Han Xin was just a means from Liu Bang; his end was to take away not only the title of King of Qi State but also Han Xin's life. This was typical of to give in order to take.

Interestingly enough, a lady's hand gave food to Han Xin; also a lady's hand took his life away. Of course, Liu Bang was the chief plotter to kill Han Xin. The critical differences between these two stories: the kind lady just gave something without the purpose of taking something; when Liu Bang gave something to Han Xin he had already planned to take something away from him someday.

Very often, many Chinese people may give something to you without a plan to take something from you someday, or at least without a conscious plan to take something from you. But "to give in order to take" has not only been used in military or political fields, but today's business decision making as well. For instance, we have previously mentioned that a Chinese manufacturer decided to spend the money to make some free sample knives for the customers of his opponents rather than spend the money on various promotions and commercial advertisements. This can also be illustrated with another example. A new Chinese restaurant put a one sentence advertisement in a newspaper: "Free meals from this Monday to Friday." Consequently, thousands of people went to get free meals and voluntarily spread the information about the new restaurant to their friends, relatives, and colleagues. Providing free samples could be viewed as the behavior of "to give in order to take." Another way is to provide very low prices on equipment or machines that would continually need unique attachments, or resources that only machine builders are able to supply. A company has been selling the necessities for a home test for diabetes patients in the market. You can pay a very low price, about $50, to purchase the equipment including a box of "test strips." But when you finish your first box of test strips, and you need to buy the second box by yourself, then you would get a big shock to pay almost $40 just for a box of test strips! However, there is no way to avoid buying the test strips, and it becomes a bottomless pit. So the second box of test strips is not the end for you but just the beginning of "taking" by the company. This is a typical tactic of "to give in order to take." Some would argue that in the West, the notion of planned obsolescence would be a Western example of "to give in order to take."

For the past several years, bribery and gift-giving have been mixed together in China. Sometimes you cannot even distinguish which generosity is a bribe, and which one is a gift. In many cases gift-giving behavior usually may not imply an intention of repayment, or without a conscious premeditation of giving in order to take. But bribery behavior absolutely carries a conscious premeditation of giving in order to take. Furthermore, "to take" will not take something from the person who accepts the bribe, but rather illegally and immorally take from somebody else or from the collective.

One point is worth mentioning. With this philosophical thought of giving in order to take, many Chinese people may be willing to give, or allow you to take more profits when they have their first deal (e.g., sharing a bonus, dividing commissions, loyalty, and interests). Indeed, they may want more than you do, at least they want "equal results" in their minds. Many Western people probably do not realize this; they may continue to keep this unequal division of the results for their second deal. If for courtesy or face-saving custom, Chinese people may not advocate equal results on their own initiative. The best or wisest way is to set up an equal and fair way to share the profits. If you continue the first unequal and unfair way, the third opportunity will be gone when the Chinese people have another choice. In brief, with the idea of "to give in order to take," many Chinese people may be willing to stand to lose in their first deal with you. If you think they were stupid, and continue "to take" from them, your business partnership or friendship will be gone when they have the ability to choose someone else.

To be down first in order to be up later. Sun Tzu said, "The rising of birds in their flight is the sign of an ambuscade."[34] The words of Sun Tzu vividly described that an ambush must be quiet in order to surprise the enemy. The skill of "to be down first in order to be up later" also has been applied in the artistic fields, daily life, the political arena, and business decision making.

The sound of a bomb would not surprise you when gunfire licked the heavens, but a firecracker could give you a big start in a quiet situation. The principle is to be down first in order to be up. When we watch the Beijing opera, our feelings may suddenly be elevated because the music surprisingly rises from a sedate or "down" atmosphere. The purpose of being "down" is to relax people and numb their vigilance. Keeping people vigilant would not reach the goal.

In 1989, there were several students from the special classes for "gifted early youth" in the top Chinese universities who, with very high TOEFL[35] and GRE[36] scores came to Miami University in Ohio. All of them transferred to such top United States universities as Yale, Cornell, and Princeton. Their tactic was "to be down first in order to be up later." Of course, Miami University is an institution with high respect and honor, particularly in undergraduate education, but in many people's opinion, particularly in China, its reputation may be a little lower than Yale, Cornell, and Princeton. Those students exposed their strategy to their friends. Since they came from the special classes for "gifted early youth" in the top Chinese universities, the authority at the Chinese schools would not permit them to apply for any ordinary United States college or university. They, however, were enrolled in the top universities as "gifted early youth" in China; thus, they became the target of criticism and a hot topic of public discussion. China has been a society in which the philosophical "golden mean" has been emphasized. A strategy with too strong characteristics would not easily be understood by many people. For these reasons, if they immediately applied for admission to the top U.S. universities, the envy of others might cause resistance, possibly placing invisible obstacles in the students' ways. Moreover, the period after the Tian'anmen Square Event in 1989 was a subtle and sensitive time between China and the United States. Accordingly, in order to go through the formalities more easily, these students first applied to Miami University, which is very well respected but not in the very top level. After they were accepted and enrolled in the United States, they transferred to the more famous top universities. This was their tactic: "to be down first in order to be up later." Was this true? We only know that they came to Miami University first, then went to Yale, Cornell, and Princeton soon thereafter.

In today's business reality, "to be down first in order to be up later" has been used quite often. The Beijing real estate market has been tremendously vigorous in recent years. So many rich people and their firms from Hong Kong, Taiwan, Singapore, and other countries come in swarms to build commercial buildings, complexes, and luxury residence houses in Beijing. The price for one square meter of commercial building once reached as high as $3,000. The "Oriental Square" is the largest project, and has attracted the most attention. Nonetheless, for some subtle and complicated reasons, this project has encountered obstacles. With some changes, the project was recently approved officially, but it has been delayed for more than one year. Based on this lesson, one Hong Kong businessman has successfully applied the strategy of "to be down first in order to be up later" in the Beijing real estate competition. He went through the formalities and applied for approved documents from the governments for his project with a low-key and an unassuming attitude. When everything was ready for his project, he suddenly changed to high-key. If one always yells in a high voice, people may get used to it. But if one suddenly changes from a low voice to a very high pitch at an important moment, it will attract people's attention. For this reason, this Hong Kong businessman suddenly changed his attitude to heighten his project at a critical moment. His buildings have been sold and rented out successfully while others, who were always acting in a high-key manner, still have some problems in achieving their objectives.

Though the Chinese stock market is still in relative infancy, some big shareholders know how to juggle with the tricks of "to be down first in order to be up later" or "to be up first in order to be down later." When they want to buy certain stocks, first they will sell their share to bid down the selling price; then, they suddenly buy it back. On the contrary, if they want to sell a certain stock, they will first buy this stock to make it higher, and then silently sell this stock while other people are buying it.

The two keys of using this tactic are to relax people and lull people's vigilance during the period of being "down," and then one must switch to being "up" at the critical moment. If people are always vigilant, being "up" would not help one attain a goal. On the other hand, if the switch to being "up" is not done at the critical moment—too early or too late—the whole plan will be unsuccessful. To be "up" too early will reveal your plan or secret too early. To be "up" too late may not give you enough time to reach your goal. To effectively use this "to be down first in order to be up later" notion, timing is critical.

To be devious in order to be direct. The sport of boxing provides an example. Drawing back your hand makes for a better punch by straightening your fist later. To describe it differently, when two boxers are holding together they cannot hit each other with heavy punches. Only when they have enough room to draw back their hands, will the opponent have a change to be knocked down. Therefore, drawing back (devious) could be a tactic for a straight punch (direct) either in military battle, a political arena, or in business decision making. Just as Sun Tzu advised, "The difficulty of tactical maneuvering consists of turning the devious into the direct, and misfortune into gain."[37] This can also be illustrated by an American football analogy. A successful coach directs his team to save one or two of their best potential plays for dire situations. For example, if the coach places a wide receiver way off from the ball and the center of the play and never attempts to complete a pass to that wide receiver in the first three-quarters of the game, then the defensive team may be lulled into thinking that they do not have to closely guard against a long pass. Then, in the closing minutes of the game, the offensive team can score a touchdown from a long pass to the receiver to win the game. Of course, "devious" and "direct" might be described or explained in different terminology in various situations. As management theory suggests, the situational circumstances typically make the difference between effective or ineffective decision making.

In the political arena, "devious" could mean to compromise out of consideration for the general interests, to stoop to compromise for a hidden goal, to endure humiliation in order to carry out an important mission, to hide one's capacities and bide one's time, etc. While we know of many high-level political compromises in the United States, let us look to China to help illustrate this expression. There have been so many stories about how the Chinese politicians stooped to compromise for a hidden goal in both ancient and modern history. We would like to select a story from *The Romance of the Three Kingdoms* to share with our readers.

Before Liu Bei was strong enough to be emperor of one of the three kingdoms, he and his two sworn brothers once attached themselves to Cao Cao, who was the emperor of the strongest of the three kingdoms. Liu Bei had to hide his capacities and political ambitions as a very ordinary person; otherwise, he could be killed by Cao Cao as a potential opponent.

> To avoid arousing Cao Cao's suspicions, Liu Bei took to his garden, planting and tending vegetables, keeping his purpose hidden. Lord Guan and Zhang Fei [his two sworn brothers] asked, "Brother, why have you lost interest in the great issues of the realm and given yourself to a commoner's toil?" "This is something you might not appreciate," responded Lie Bei, and his brothers did not ask again.
>
> One day, when Lord Guan and Zhang Fei were away and Liu Bei was watering his plants, two of Cao Cao's generals, Xu Chu and Zhang Liao, led a score of them into the garden. "His Excellency," they announced, "requests that Your Lordship come at once." Alarmed, Liu Bei asked, "An emergency?" "I don't know," Xu Chu answered. "I was told to request your presence." Liu Bei could only follow the two men to Cao Cao's residence.
>
> A smiling Cao Cao greeted Liu Bei. "That's quite a project you have under way at home," he said in a tone that turned Liu Bei's face pale as dust. Taking Liu Bei's hand, Cao Cao led him to his own garden. "You have taken up a most difficult occupation in horticulture," Cao Cao continued.
>
> "Just to while away the time," Liu Bei answered, relieved. "There is nothing else to occupy me."
>
> Sitting opposite one another, the two men drank freely and enjoyed themselves without constraint.
>
> The wine had enlivened their spirits when dark clouds appeared and overspread the heavens: A flash storm was threatening. An attendant pointed to what seemed like a distant dragon suspended on the horizon. The two men leaned against the balcony and watched it. Cao Cao turned to Liu Bei and

asked, "Does my lord understand the dragon's multiform manifestations?"

"Not in great detail," Liu Bei replied.

"The dragon," Cao Cao continued, "can enlarge and diminish itself, surge aloft or lie beneath the surface of the water. Enlarged, it prances triumphant in the upper realm of space. Under the surface, it lurks among the surging breakers. Now, in the fullness of spring, it mounts the season, like men who would fulfill their ambition to dominate the length and breadth of the land. In this respect, the dragon can well be compared to the heroes of the age. You, yourself, have traveled widely and surely must be familiar with the great heroes of our time. Please try to point them out for me."

"How can these eyes of mine sight heroes?" Liu Bei said.

"Set your modesty aside," Cao Cao urged.

"Thanks to Your Excellency's gracious benefaction," Liu Bei responded, "I have succeeded in serving the dynasty. But as for the heroes of the realm, such things are more than I would know of."

"Even if you do not know any personally," Cao Cao persisted, "you should at least have heard of some"

[Liu Bei pointed out almost ten persons.]

Cao Cao clapped his hands and laughed. "Petty mediocrities," he said, "beneath our notice."

"Truly," said Liu Bei, "I can think of no one else."

"Now," Cao Cao went on, "what defines a hero is this: a determination to conquer, a mind of marvelous schemes, an ability to encompass the realm, and the will to make it his."

"Who merits such a description?" Liu Bei asked.

Cao Cao pointed first to Liu Bei, then to himself. "The heroes of the present day," he said, "number but two—you, my lord, and myself." Liu Bei gulped in panic. Before he realized it, his chopsticks had slipped to the ground. Then the storm came on. A peal of thunder gave him the chance to bend down casually and retrieve them.

"See what a clap of thunder has made me do?" he remarked.

"A great man afraid of thunder?" Cao Cao asked.

"Confucius himself became agitated in thunderstorms," Liu Bei reminded him. "How could I not fear them?" In this way, he succeeded in glossing over the cause of his anxiety.[38]

This famous Chinese story where Liu Bei and Cao Cao discuss who were the heroes vividly described how Liu Bei had hidden his capacities and bided his time. The modern Chinese politicians, such as Zhou Enlai and Deng Xiaoping, also had stories about enduring humiliation in order to carry out an important mission. For example, Deng Xiaoping was politically persecuted twice and two times recovered. In order to regain political power to carry out the Reformation and Opening Movement in the future, he did not hesitate to write several letters to Mao Zedong promising he would never reverse the verdict of the Cultural Revolution, even though he did after Mao Zedong died.

During World War II, the Chinese Communist Party's troops, the Chinese Workers' and the Peasants' Red Army, agreed to a reorganization as the Eighth Route Army, and the New Fourth Army, under the leadership of Jiang Jieshi (Chiang Kai-shek). This was a successful political tactic using "to be devious in order to be direct later." After that, not only the troops of Jiang Jieshi (Chiang Kai-shek) had to stop openly encircling and suppressing the CCP's troops, but also had to fight with the Japanese troops directly. As a result, the CCP's troops sprang up very quickly; after ten years the CCP's troops drove the troops of Jiang Jieshi (Chiang Kai-shek) to Taiwan and took control of China in 1949.

For business decisions, "devious" and "direct" may imply going through an indirect answer to find a direct answer. For instance, a Chinese delegation was sent to an American city for marketing research. They found out that there were not any Chinese furniture stores in this city. Then they had a serious argument. One whether, owing to the lack of any Chinese furniture stores, there was no market for Chinese furniture. On the contrary, the other opinion was that since there were no Chinese furniture stores, there would be a potential Chinese furniture market in this city. In general, the latter was right, because the persons who believed there would be a potential market for Chinese furniture found their direct answer through an indirect answer. Recently in the United States, we have seen similar examples, particularly in consumer retailing, of companies who make their direct decisions through an indirect approach.

In ancient China, Lü Buwei successfully played a political business game with the tactic of "to be devious in order to be direct later," so that he finally became the Prime Minister of Qin Dynasty.

Lü Buwei was a rich businessman. One day he met the son of the king of Qin State who was kept as a hostage in Zhao State. With the sharp sight of a businessman, Lü Buwei found out the tremendous potential worth of the son of the king of Qin State even as a hostage. Then he went home to discuss it with his father.

"How much return profit could you make from farming?" Lü Buwei asked.

His father said, "Ten percent."

"How about the jewelry business?" he asked again.

"One hundred percent!" his father responded.

"Now, how about supporting a king who will be in power?" Lü Buwei continued to question.

His father screamed, "My god! Countless! Countless! . . ."

Then they formulated their political business decision making, and spent a lot of money to carry it out. Finally, the son of the King of Qin State successfully returned to Qin State to be in power. Later, Lü Buwei also became the Prime Minister of the Qin Dynasty.[39]

Obviously, the political business tactic of Lü Buwei was typical "to be devious in order to be direct later."

To release in order to catch. In many cases, "to release in order to catch" means to physically "release," but mentally or psychologically "catch." The most typical example in Chinese culture and literature was the story about Kongming catching Meng Huo seven times but releasing him seven times from *The Romance of the Three Kingdoms.*

In order to concentrate on the battles with the strongest enemy Wei State and Wu State, Kongming must put down and control the southern rear area where the king of the tribes, Meng Huo, often led riots. Kongming and his troops had caught Meng Huo six times and released him six times because Meng Huo was not convinced in his mind to follow Kongming. Then Kongming and his army caught Meng Huo for the seventh time.

Kongming ordered that Meng Huo be brought before him. Meng Huo knelt down, and Kongming had his bonds removed. To ease his fear, he had food and drink provided to the captured king in a separate tent. Finally, Kongming gave certain instructions to the commissary officer.

Meng Huo and Lady Zhurong, Meng You, and the chief of Dailai Hollow, together with their clansmen and adherents, refreshed themselves. Suddenly an officer entered the tent and said to Meng Huo, "His Excellency was too embarrassed to see you, my lord, and has ordered me to release you. Go home and rally your forces for another trial of strength. Quickly, my lord." But Meng Huo, tears falling, replied, "Seven times captured, seven times freed! Such a thing has never happened! Though I stand beyond the range of the imperial grace, I am not utterly ignorant of ritual, of what propriety and honor require. No, I am not so shameless!"

Having thus spoken, Meng Huo, his brother, his wife, and his other clansmen crawled to Kongming's tent. The chastised king knelt and exposed the upper half of his body, betokening his readiness to receive punishment. "Your Excellency's divine prestige ensures that the south will not rebel again," Meng Huo declared.

"Then you submit?" Kongming responded.

Weeping with gratitude, Meng Huo said, "For generations to come, our children and theirs after them will gratefully acknowledge your all-protecting, all-sustaining love, deep as Heaven, vast as earth. How can I not submit!"

Kongming invited Meng Huo into his tent, where he held a feast confirming the king as chief of the hollows in perpetuity, and he relinquished to him all territories seized by the Riverlands troops. Meng Huo and his people, as well as the warriors of the other Man nations, acclaimed his generosity, leaping and vaulting in unbounded excitement.

Senior Counselor Fei Yi entered and protested: "Your Excellency's campaign deep into the wilds has subjugated the Man region, and their king has tendered his allegiance. Is it not now appropriate to establish districts and officials so that we can rule together with Meng Huo?"

"That poses three problems," Kongming replied. "First, if outsiders stay behind, troops must stay with them. But how are we to feed those troops? Second, the defeated Man have suffered grievously, losing fathers and brothers. To leave outsiders here without troops is bound to lead to trouble. And third, the Man nations have always been so politically unstable–the result of jealousies and suspicions–that they will never trust outsiders. If we leave no one, however, and ship no grain, we will find ourselves at peace with them for want of any cause of trouble."

These arguments persuaded the commanders. In gratitude for Kongming's benevolence, the Man people set up a shrine at which offerings were made every season; the prime minister became known among them as "the kindly father." Each of the nations rendered tributes of pearls and precious metals, cinnabar, lacquer, medicinal herbs, water buffalo, and warhorses for military use. And the Man vowed not to rebel. Thus, the south was finally pacified.[40]

From the above story, we can see that the tactic of Kongming was to conquer Meng Huo and his clansmen spiritually and mentally, not to just physically trap him and his men.

The Xi'an Incident in 1936 was a critical event in Chinese history. This event might even have changed Chinese modern history. People cannot imagine that without the Xi'an Incident in 1936 what today's China would be. Even historians will get headaches trying to answer this question. The Xi'an Incident in 1936 reflected the strategy of the Chinese Communist Party, "to release in order to catch."

In 1930s, China was in a chaotic and critical situation in which the Chinese Communist Party fought with the Kuomintang which was under the leadership of Chiang Kai-shek; various warlords were under the leadership of Chiang Kai-shek in name, but conflicted with the Kuomintang in reality; and Japan had been invading China and occupied the three Chinese northeastern provinces (Manchuria). Chiang Kai-shek wanted to squelch the Chinese Communist Party first, and fight with Japan later. He ordered the warlord Zhang Xueliang and his troops who withdrew from Manchuria, and the northwestern warlord, Yang Hucheng and his army, to encircle and suppress the Chinese Communist Party and its Chinese Workers' and Peasants' Red Army. The Chinese Communist Party persuaded the warlords, Zhang Xueliang and Yang Hucheng, to resist the Japanese invasion, but not to fight with the Chinese. Zhang and Yang accepted the idea of the Chinese Communist Party. When Chiang Kai-shek came to the front line to urge and supervise the warlords' troops to encircle and suppress the Chinese Communist Party and its army, Zhang and Yang instigated a mutiny to catch Chiang Kai-shek. All of this stirred the Chinese into various groupings. Some supported this movement; some complained; some, including the group closest to Japan, wanted to kill Chiang Kai-shek in this chaos; and some urged the release of Chiang Kai-shek. At this critical moment, the sworn enemy of Chiang Kai-shek, the Chinese Communist Party, unexpectedly persuaded Zhang Xueliang and Yang Hucheng to release Chiang Kai-shek, but an important condition was to stop the civil wars and lead all of China to fight Japan. The situation was so extremely critical that Chiang Kai-shek had to accept the condition. Accordingly, Chiang Kai-shek was released, but Zhang Xueliang and Yang Hucheng were captured. Chiang Kai-shek began to lead the Chinese forces to resist the Japanese invasion, and the troops of the Chinese Communist Party were reorganized as the Eighth Route Army and the New Fourth Army to carry out the tactic of "to be devious in order to be direct later," which we have previously addressed.

Historians ponder several possibilities for the Xi'an Incident in 1936: if Chiang Kai-shek was killed; if Chiang Kai-shek and the warlords put down the Chinese Communist Party before they resisted Japan; if Zhang Xueliang and Yang Hucheng did not release Chiang Kai-shek; if the Xi'an Incident did not happened in 1936 . . .

The potential possibilities could vary, but the reality was merely that, although Chiang Kai-shek was physically released, he was trapped into the scheme of the Chinese Communist Party.

During World War II, it is true that the Chinese troops could not stop the invasion of the Japanese forces. On the other hand, giving up so huge a territory to the Japanese troops could be viewed, in a sense, as a tactic of "to release in order to catch." That is to say, when Japanese troops occupied such huge lands, they were carrying a very heavy burden as Kongming's words described:

> First, if outsiders stay behind, troops must stay with them. But how are we to feed those troops? Second, the defeated Man have suffered grievously, losing fathers and brothers. To leave outsiders here without troops is bound to lead to trouble. And third, the Man nations have always been so politically unstable—the result of jealousies and suspicions—that they will never trust outsiders.

In today's economic reality, business decision making that allows customers to return for refund the products which they are not satisfied with is the strategy of "to release in order to catch." By doing this, the customers who return the goods seemingly have been released by the stores in a way; essentially, most of them who return the goods have been consciously or unconsciously caught invisibly, mentally, spiritually, and even morally by the stores when they return for new goods. Perhaps the most successful United States retailer in history, Wal-mart, recognizes that much of their success is based on their generous and simple refund (few questions asked) policy.

Your Strength vs. the Weakness of Your Enemy

Using your strength against the weakness of your enemy seems like a very obvious and simple tactic that almost everybody knows how to implement in practice. While this is generally true, it does not always hold true. Theoretically, everyone knows to use their strengths against the weaknesses of their enemy; practically, not so many people do know how to do this. Otherwise there would not be losers in the world. Many Western businesspeople may believe that they understand the weaknesses of Chinese enterprises. But many of them may not realize that Chinese enterprises have their own strengths that the Western enterprises may not understand. In this section, we will focus on the strengths of Chinese enterprises of which the Western business people may not be aware.

Using your partial strength against the partial weakness of your enemy. Obviously, knowing your enemy and knowing yourself is fundamental to applying this tactic of using your partial strength against the partial weakness of your enemy. Sun Bin was a great strategist in ancient China. Many people believe that Sun Tzu who wrote *The Art of War* might be two persons; one was Sun Wu, the other was Sun Bin. Some people believe that Sun Bin was a descendant of Sun Wu. No matter what, the point is that Sun Bin was good at tactics, as has been recorded in Chinese history. Particularly famous is the story about how he applied the strategy of "using your partial strength against the partial weakness of your enemy" to a horse race. In a traditional horse race, each side needed to send three horses to compete with each other. Sun Bin knew that, generally speaking, his three horses were weaker than his opponent's. In order words, his strongest horse was weaker than the opponent's best; his second strongest one was slower than the opponent's second horse; and his worst horse could also not beat the opponent's weakest one. Nobody believed that Sun Bin's side could win the race. Sun Bin, however, not only knew his opponent's situation but also the condition of his side very well. He suggested the tactic of "using your partial strength against the partial weakness of your enemy." He knew that his fastest horse could beat his opponent's second strongest horse; his second fastest horse was better than his opponent's worst one. So his strategy was to send his worst horse to match the other's best horse; but his fastest horse competed with his opponent's second; and his second horse raced with his opponent's worst. As a result, Sun Bin's side lost one game, but won two matches. This is a wonderful example of beating your enemy by the tactic of "using your partial strength against the partial weakness of your enemy."

In Chinese modern history, Mao Zedong was an expert strategist who knew how to use this tactic. We must say that less than 1 million troops of the Chinese Communist Party with very poor weapons defeated 8 million forces of the Kuomingtang with very advanced American weapons after World War II. One of the critical reasons was that Mao Zedong was a great master of using his partial strengths against the partial weaknesses of his enemy.

In today's business practice, the Chinese state-owned enterprises have their own weaknesses, but in quite a few cases, the Chinese governments might operate on the tactic of "using your partial strengths against the partial weaknesses of your enemy" better than many Western enterprises do. One of the reasons is that the Chinese governments–if they so decide–are able to formulate a comprehensive arrangement for the state-owned enterprises and collective enterprises. As for the Western enterprises, because of their individual strategies, usually each does things in its own way. While this may optimize success for a specific Western company, it certainly does not result in optimizing the collective success.

Able to stand a high risk. Sun Tzu emphasized "calculations" before a battle. However, any decision making, either military or business, must stand a certain level of risk. Businesspeople believe the higher the risk, the greater the return (or profit); a lower risk implies a smaller return. Everyone would be able to make a decision without any risk factor. Only able generals and businesspeople can make a decision with their wise "calculations," unusual courage, and resourcefulness, while ordinary people cannot. Generally, when an able person with courage and resourcefulness is sure of having more than 50 percent assurance in his or her "calculations," this person is usually able to make a decision. After the consequences of the Vietnam War, any military decision making must be made very carefully in Western countries. All too often, without 70 to 80 percent certainty, a military decision may not be made because the Western countries have been weakened to stand the risk factors. If an able person with courage and resourcefulness should make a decision when he or she feels more than 50 percent assurance in his or her calculation, but the Western countries only make a military decision when they have 70 to 80 percent of certainty, will this imply the Western counties may lose about 30 percent of their opportunities? For example, China is able to stand a very high risk involving a conflict such as trade warfare. But when the risk goes higher and higher, and the governments in Western countries have to withstand more and more pressure from various sides, they would usually be unable to stick with their original positions. So, the gap between a higher risk China can stand and a lower risk the Western countries can stand could create the opportunities of victory for the Chinese side.

The Communist countries can take very high risks in either military or business because of their social system. In the past thirty years, Cuba and North Korea have taken business and economic risks in which the odds were not favorable. Their leaders had the power to be able to wage a comeback in the event their plans were not successful. Sometimes their general or manager can make a decision even when they feel it has less than a 50 percent chance of certainty. On the one hand, they could lose because of a lower assurance. On the other hand, they would gain more opportunities to win if their calculations were correct. This could be one of the reasons that the Communist troops could win in a military arena such as China, Korea, Vietnam, and Kampuchea. If the Chinese managers of the state-owned enterprises or collective enterprises can "calculate" better, they will have more chances to win in the business arena because of their ability to stand higher risks. Of course, "have more chances to win" only means "chances." A victory in reality will also depend on numerous other elements, such as the seven factors of Sun Tzu we have addressed in an early section of this chapter.

Can easily concentrate a superior force. For the following explanation we will cite, in detail, the words from Sun Tzu that describe concentrating a superior force. He wrote:

> By discovering the enemy's dispositions and remaining invisible ourselves, we can keep our forces concentrated, while the enemy's must be divided. We can form a single united body, while the enemy must split up into factions. Hence they will be a whole pitted against separate parts of a whole, which means that we shall be many to the enemy's few. And if we are thus able to attack an inferior force with a superior one, our opponents will be in dire straits. The spot where we intend to fight must not be made known; for then the enemy will have to prepare against a possible attack at several different points; and his forces, being thus distributed in many

directions, the numbers we shall have to face at any given point will be proportionately few. For should the enemy strengthen his van, he will weaken his rear; should he strengthen his rear, he will weaken his van; should he strengthen his left, he will weaken his right; should he strengthen his right, he will weaken his left. If he sends reinforcements everywhere, he will be weak everywhere. Numerical weakness comes from having to prepare against possible attacks; numerical strength, from compelling our adversary to make these preparations against us. Knowing the place and the time of the coming battle, we may concentrate from the greatest distances in order to fight. But if neither time nor place be known, then the left wing will be impotent to succor the right, the right equally impotent to succor the left, the van unable to relieve the rear, or the rear to support the van. How much more so if the furthest portions of the army are anything under a hundred *li* [about 0.3107 mile] apart, and even the nearest are separated by several *li*![41]

The words of Sun Tzu were so detailed and vivid that any explanation from us is unnecessary. Here, we only want to emphasize that concentrating a superior force is a method to create partial strength. This was how Mao Zedong, using less than 1 million troops with very poor weapons, defeated the 8 million forces of Chiang Kai-shek during the Chinese Civil War (1945-1949).

China is a developing country. Per capita production is very low, even lower that many African countries. China, however, is a Socialist country that will be able to "concentrate a superior force" to compete with any huge Western corporation if it wants. For instance, if China really wants to win a bid from the competition with the Western corporations, China could win it with the support of the whole country's resources. Therefore, in some or many cases, "concentrating a superior force" may be an advantage to China in today's business decision making since most corporations and governments are separated in the Western countries, but the Chinese government is the legal representative of the state-owned enterprises and collective enterprises. The economic principles of size and economy of scale hold true for most major business projects, whether capital or labor intensive.

Can make many important decisions without so much restrictions. We have previously expressed the belief that, since the Chinese state-owned enterprises could stand higher risks, they would have more opportunities to win in a competition environment. The capacity to make important decisions without many restrictions could be another advantage to win a competition. For the Western public enterprises, any important change, sometimes even a less important decision, must be approved by the board, or even a meeting of stockholders, whereas many Chinese managers could decide on their own immediately. For example, during an investment competition, when the price is either higher or lower than normal levels, the Western public corporations must report to their headquarters or their boards and await advice. While they could not get through to their operators for a long-distance call, or were off sending their faxes, a Chinese enterprise might already have made its decision. Of course, in many cases because of the constraints of the bureaucracy and political process, Chinese business decision making could be very slow as well (as discussed in an earlier section).

The above points illustrate some of the key strengths of the Chinese state-owned enterprises and/or collective enterprises. Or examining it from the other perspective, these points may be the vital weaknesses of the Western business corporations.

"THICK" AND "BLACK"

A Chinese gentleman, Li Zong-wu, wrote a book, *The Theory About Thickness and Blackness*,[42] in the 1920s. This book caused a sensation in China, and was banned by all the governments including various warlords', the Kuomintang's, and the Communists'. The author believed that there were some things in the world which you can say but not do; on the reverse side, there are some things in the world which you can do but not say. For example, very often, friends speak some dirty words to each other–those ideas they can only say but not act upon. Likewise, a husband and wife make love, which they generally do without discussing with others. The theory about thickness and blackness was the secret to help you to be successful in those things you can only do, but not talk about openly.

Thickness means thickskinned, brazen, cheeky, impudent, or shameless. Blackness implies black-hearted, evil-minded, cruel, wicked, and merciless. The theory was to uncover the "secret" that would make only the persons with thickness and blackness successful in the world. The author believed that there were three commercial and business stages. During the first stage, commodities were essential goods without a good package. In the second stage, the merchandise was essentially bad but with a beautiful package. During the third stage, goods would be essentially wonderful with a matching package. He thought China was in the second stage since the commodity economy had shown its tortuous life-style and development in China. After 1949, a market economy was prohibited until 1992 when the Chinese government officially and openly accepted it again. We believe that in many cases China is still in the second stage in which imitations, fakes, and piracies are bothering many either domestic or foreign customers and manufacturers. Therefore, we add this special section for our readers. Some of them may have a chance to experience the unusual thickness and blackness in their real lives.

In *The Theory About Thickness and Blackness*, Li Zong-wu pointed out that people who were successful in Chinese history had "thick-skinned faces" and "black hearts."

Cao Cao and Liu Bei were the two most important role models—they were two kings of the three kingdoms during the Three Kingdoms period. Cao Cao had a "black heart," and Liu Bei had "thick skins." Cao Cao had a personal motto: "Better to wrong the world than have it wrong me!" Therefore, in order to reach his goals, he would hurt or kill anybody, even his friends, relatives, seniors, and subordinates, without any guilt.

One day, Cao Cao–who had not been in power yet–failed to murder the Prime Minister, Dong Zuo; then, Cao Cao escaped. Chen Gong, who was a magistrate, caught Cao Cao, but he believed Cao Cao was an honest man and ran away with him.

> After three days' riding, they came to a place called Chenggao. The hour was late. Cao Cao pointed with his whip to a deep grove and said, "Somewhere around here lives a man, Lü Boshe, who once swore an oath of brotherhood with my father.

Let's go there and get news of my family and a night's rest." Chen Gong gladly agreed, and the two men rode to the farmhouse where they found Lü Boshe.

"They say the court circulated a warrant for your arrest," Lü Boshe said, "They applied so much pressure that your father left the Chenliu area. How did you get here?"

Cao Cao related the recent events and continued, "If not for the magistrate, I would have been reduced to mincemeat."

Boshe saluted Chen Gong and said, "Your Honor, the Caos would have been exterminated but for you. Here you may relax and sleep in the back cottage."

Lü Boshe rose and went inside. Eventually he returned and said he was out of wine and had to go to the next village to buy some. Then he hopped on his donkey and was off. Cao Cao and Chen Gong sat a good while. Suddenly behind the farmhouse they heard the sound of knives being whetted. "You know, Lü Boshe is not a close relative," Cao Cao said, "There's something suspicious about his leaving. Let's look into this."

The two men stole behind the cottage and overheard someone mumble, "Let's tie'm up an' kill'm."

"I thought so," Cao Cao whispered. "If we don't strike first, we'll be caught." Cao Cao and Chen Gong entered at once and killed everyone, women and men, eight in all; only then did they see the trussed pig waiting to be slaughtered.

"You were too suspicious," Chen Gong said. "We've killed good folk." The two men hurried from the farm, but before they had ridden half a mile they met their host on his donkey with two jars of wine suspended from the pommel and fruit and vegetables hanging from one hand.

"Dear nephew and honorable sir," he cried, "why are you leaving so suddenly?"

"Marked men can't remain anywhere for long," answered Cao Cao.

"But I told my family to slaughter a pig for your dinner," Lü Boshe said earnestly. "Don't begrudge us the night, nephew, nor you, good sir. Turn back, I pray."

But Cao Cao spurred his horse on. Then he turned and dashed back, his sword drawn, calling to Lü Boshe, "Who's coming over there?" As Boshe looked away Cao Cao cut him down, and he fell from his donkey.

Chen Gong was astounded. "What happened at the farm was a mistake–but why this?"

"Had he gotten home and seen them he would never have let it lay. He'd have brought a mob after us and we would've been done for."

"But you murdered him knowing he was innocent–a great wrong," Chen Gong asserted.

"Better to wrong the world than have it wrong me!" Cao Cao retorted.[43]

Mr. Li Zong-wu did not categorize Cao Cao as having thick skin, but we think he did. Cao Cao had not only a black heart but a thick skin as well. Please consider the following examples:

. . . maintaining the siege was proving a heavy burden for Cao Cao's army; it required vast stores of grain, but the surrounding districts, stricken by dearth, could offer no aid. Cao Cao presented his army for battle, but General Li Feng kept within the walls. After another month, Cao Cao, faced with dwindling supplies, borrowed one hundred thousand bushels of grain from Sun Ce. But he did not distribute it.

During the emergency, Wang Hou, who served under Ren Jun, administrator of rations, petitioned Cao Cao: "There is too little to feed so many. What shall we do?"

"Distribute shorter rations," Cao Cao commanded him, "to tide us over."

"And if they complain?" asked Wang Hou.

"I have provided for that," Cao assured him.

The office gave out reduced rations as ordered. Meanwhile, Cao Cao sent his men around to the camps. From them, he learned that soldiers were accusing him of cheating them. Cao Cao then summoned Wang Hou and said, "You have something I would like to borrow to quiet the soldiers. I hope you will not begrudge it."

"What do I have," Wang Hou answered, "of use to Your Excellency?"

"Your head," Cao replied, "to show the men."

"But I have committed no fault!" the officer cried in fright.

"I know that," Cao said. "I must act, or the army will revolt. I will see after your family personally, so have no concern on their account." Before Wang Hou could say more, the executioners were already pushing him out. They cut off his head and hung it from a pole with a signboard reading, "Wang Hou: Duly Punished by Military Law for Purposefully Assigning Short Rations and Stealing from the Granary." This measure improved the troops' morale.

* * *

Leaving Xun Wenruo in the capital to supervise military operations, Cao Cao directed the main army's advance. The wheat was ripe along the way, but the peasants, frightened by the soldiers, would not work in the fields. Cao Cao circulated a formal letter of assurance to the village elders and local officials: "I hold the Emperor's decree to chastise the rebels and protect the people; for reasons beyond our control, we have to march in a harvest season. We shall execute any officer–high or low–who tramples crops while crossing a field, and enforce military law without mercy or exception. Let no one fear or doubt us."

The peasants welcomed the order with open praise and crowded round the approaching armies to pay their respects. Passing through the fields, the officers dismounted and carefully held aside the wheat stalks with their hands.

One day, a turtledove flew up and caught the eye of Cao Cao's horse. The horse bolted onto a field and ruined a swath of crop. Cao Cao summoned his first secretary and proposed that his crime be punished. The officer said, "How can we condemn Your Excellency?" "If I violate a law I myself made," Cao Cao declared, "how can I hold my men to it?" He raised his sword to his throat. The soldiers and officers stopped him.

Guo Jia said, "According to Confucius' *Spring and Autumn Annals*, 'the law shall not apply to those in the highest positions.'"

Cao Cao brooded silently. Then he said, "Since the *Spring and Autumn Annals* so specifies, we may waive the death penalty. Let this stand for my head." He cut off his hair with his sword and threw it down for all to see.

"The prime minister," messengers explained, displaying Cao Cao's hair, "deserved to die as an example to all for destroying the wheat. In this case, his hair has been cut off instead." The entire army was stricken with fear, and regulations were meticulously observed.[44]

Those examples showed that the mind of Cao Cao was extremely cruel and brazen. He "borrowed" other's heads so dispassionately, but cut some of his own hairs to get through his own difficulty. This same Cao Cao, however, finally became the Emperor of the strongest of the three kingdoms.

As for Liu Bei, the author of *The Theory About Thickness and Blackness* thought that, because of his thick-skinned face, Liu Bei could become an appendage one after the other to Cao Cao, Yuan Shao, Lü Bu, Liu Biao, and Sun Qun, who were mutual enemies, before he established his own kingdom. Liu Bei was good at crying. When he faced a difficult situation, he would cry his heart out to his enemy, his subordinates, men or women, old or young—whoever he needed to. Then he might turn a defeat into a victory. Accordingly, as the saying went, "The state power of Liu Bei stemmed from his cry." He and Cao Cao were matchless in China. With a thick-skinned face, one was brazen; with a black heart, one was cruel. They could not beat each other. So, as we have addressed previously, when they were drinking to discuss who was the hero, Cao Cao pointed first to Liu Bei, then to himself. "The heroes of the present day," he said, "number but two—you, my lord, and myself."

After Cao Cao and Liu Bei died, Sima Yi controlled the Wei State of Cao Cao, and Kongming shielded and sustained Liu Bei's son. Some of the stories about these two rulers we have related several times in this chapter. Because Sima Yi was as cruel as Cao Cao and as brazen as Liu Bei, Kongming, who was extremely intelligent but lacked a black heart and a thick-skinned face, was unable to conquer Sima Yi. After Kongming's death, Simas defeated the other two kingdoms and unified China.

Li Zong-wu also considered that the same thing happened when the Han Dynasty was established. At that time, many people tried to seize China, but Liu Bang and Xiang Yu were the two persons who were most likely to conquer China. Xiang Yu, who was very brave and good at fighting, beat Liu Bang in every battle; however in his first, and also last and only failure to Liu Bang, he committed suicide. Why did Xiang Yu finally lose to Liu Bang? Li Zong-wu believed it was because Xiang Yu had as kind a mind as a lady, and a thin-skinned face. Xiang Yu once inveigled Liu Bang to dine at a banquet where they would sit side by side. Xiang Yu could have killed Liu Bang directly with a finger, but he could not do it. His general, Xiang Zhuang, took his sword and pretended to perform a dance to try to kill Liu Bang. Xiang Yu only needed to nod lightly, then he would be the Emperor of the Han Dynasty. But he was not cruel enough, and Liu Bang escaped because of his hesitation. There are two popular Chinese sayings from this story: "Hongmen Banquet–covering a malicious intention with a party," and "Xiang Zhuang performed the sword dance as a cover for his attempt on Liu Bang's life–acting with a hidden motive." For his last fight, he could have returned to his hometown to reorganize his troops, but he said, "I led eight thousand young men from my hometown, but now none are left alive except myself. I have no face left with which to see my hometown people even though they might forgive me." Then he committed suicide. The author of *The Theory About Thickness and Blackness* believed that there was no reason for men who wanted to be successful politicians to address "face" and "conscience." In other words, with a thin-skinned face and a good conscience, a politician could fail to seize state power.

Liu Bang, however, had a very evil mind. When his father was caught by Xiang Yu, who threatened to kill Liu's father and cook him in soup if Liu Bang did not give up, Liu Bang said, "You can go ahead and cook him, but please share a cup of soup with me." When Liu Bang was being chased by Xiang Yu's troops, in order to reduce the weight of the chariot and escape faster, he pushed his own children out of the chariot. After he gained China and strengthened his power, he killed his subordinates who had rendered outstanding service to him, such as Han Xin, and Peng Yue, etc. He was not only cruel but also brazen to perform such impudent acts in order to reach his goal. Finally, Liu Bang, who had an evil mind and a shameless face, beat all enemies and potential opponents including his subordinates to be the Emperor of the Han Dynasty.

His general, Han Xin, had a thick-skinned face. Before Han Xin was successful, he was looked down upon by others. One day, a young butcher who was fierce and tough stopped Han Xin on the street and insulted him by saying, "Han Xin, you are big, and you carry a sword, but I think you are a coward. If you dare to stab me with your sword; you will be viewed as a true man, and I will let you go. Or, I am sorry, you must crawl through my legs!" Han Xin thought a while, and then silently bent down to crawl through the butcher's legs. Everyone on the street laughed thinking that Han Xin was weak and incompetent. After Han Xin became a general, he recruited the butcher to be the captain of his bodyguards. As we can understand, Han Xin reasoned that if he was not brazen enough to crawl through the butcher's legs, he would have had to physically fight with the fierce and tough butcher. The result would be the death of Han Xin before he could achieve his ambitions to be a well-known and talented general. Han Xin, however, was not cruel and evil. If Han Xin had been cruel enough to betray Liu Bang when he controlled the largest troops of Liu Bang, he would have been the Emperor of the Han Dynasty, not Liu Bang. However, he was brazen but not cruel; he could not be as successful as Liu Bang.

Meanwhile, Fan Zeng, who was the best adviser of Xiang Yu, was very cruel but not brazen. He failed as well. Catching Liu Bang's father and threatening to cook him in soup in order to force Liu Bang to give up was a scheme invented by Fan Zeng. This made it evident how cruel Fan Zeng was. But he was not brazen. When Liu Bang successfully drove a wedge between Xiang Yu and Fan Zeng, Fan Zeng could not stand these great grievances and was very angry. He left Xiang Yu to return to his hometown, and died soon. If Fan Zeng had not left, Xiang Yu might not have failed. The author of *The Theory About Thickness and Blackness* commented, "How could a person who could not indulge any grievances be able to achieve his great ambition?" If Fan Zeng had been able to control himself, it is hard to say who would be the Emperor of the Han Dynasty. Fan Zeng gave away his life and Xiang Yu's future because of his thin skin.

Li Zong-wu pointed out that a face was just several inches wide; a heart was not big enough to fill a hand. However, the skin of a face could be endlessly thick; and a heart could be a matchless black. The fame, gains, statues, money, palace, and empresses all came from these small things–a face and a heart.

The author of *The Theory About Thickness and Blackness* argued that there were three levels of "thickness" and "blackness." The first level was as thick as a wall, and as black as coal. The second level was a solid thickness and a bright blackness. The third level was thick but unstructured, and black but colorless. This was the highest level, in which people were unable to feel your brazenness and were unable to realize your cruelty. To explain: when you were brazen, people felt you were noble; when you were cruel, people thought you were kind. So, people accepted your brazenness as nobility, and took your cruelty as a kindness because your thickness and blackness were unstructured and colorless.

Outside of Chinese history, we can find that thickness and blackness have also acted on the international stage, as in diplomatic conflicts, military warfare, political fighting, and business and economic competition. Adolf Hitler, the leader of the German Nazis, was a typical international thick-and-black ruler who could lie as brazenly as he wanted, killing thousands of Jews and others through various means. Interestingly enough, you would find that by comparison, the history of Adolf Hitler unbelievably reflects Li Zong-wu's theory and philosophy about thickness and blackness.

We could also discover that thickness has been present in U.S. national elections. In the U.S. presidential year-long campaigns beginning every four years, an odd collection of presidential hopefuls rise up and scurry around the American countryside in their individual quest for the ultimate position of power. In the jockeying for power among the individual rivals, one or more subsets of the candidates engage in negative mass-marketing tactics to degrade their competitors and reduce the number of contestants still enduring the race. On a more local level, all around the various political boundaries, we see smaller-scale but just as intense competitors fighting for positions such as mayor, council member, or school board member–often fulfilling their ambitions for intrinsic rewards, not for direct monetary compensation.

Li Zong-wu believed that his theory had some sort of connection with *The Art of War* by Sun Tzu. For example, Sun Tzu wrote, "In battle, there are not more than two methods of attack–the unusual and the standard."[45] Sun Tzu also said, "In all fighting, to directly deal with the enemy use the standard method; to win a victory use the unusual method."[46] Li Zong-wu believed the so-called "unusual method" was his theory about thickness and blackness.

In our opinion, "thickness" could be given a commendatory meaning in quite a few cases, one of which could be the traditional "enduring humiliation in order to carry out an important mission." Just as in the Chinese saying, "A great scheme would be hurt if you are unable to control yourself over some minor stimulation." Therefore, in a sense, when the Chinese people make a decision, thickness might be encouraged in today's diplomatic conflicts, political struggles, and business competitions. On the contrary, though "blackness" implies boldness, it is immoral to go against traditional Chinese ethical standards. For this reason, the book *The Theory About Thickness and Blackness* was prohibited until a couple of years ago and has not been encouraged by any of the Chinese governments.

In business reality, Zeng Xianzi had experienced many stories about thickness before he became the biggest and best Chinese tiemaker.

> One day, Zeng Xianzi brought two boxes of ties when he visited the owner of a store. He smiled as he opened the boxes, and attempted to show his ties. The owner of the store randomly swept over the ties, and then said frostily: "Do you want to make money with this stuff? Do you call these 'ties'? Give me a break! You don't know how terrible you are? Go away! Leave me alone!"
>
> Zeng Xianzi did his best to control his tears until he left the store. The next day, he returned to the store. He said to the owner, "Boss, thank you so much for your criticism yesterday. Today, I am coming back to offer my special thanks to you. I am a new maker of ties. I don't really know what is good or what is bad. In the coming days, I will make some new ties. If it is convenient for you, I will be very honored to invite you to point out the problems that you saw with these ties."

After several days, Zeng Xianzi came back with two boxes of new ties. He said, "Boss, thank you so much for pointing out my problems. I just knew a little bit about ties. After your advice, I learned something. Under your instruction, I have made some new ties. Please check whether or not I have made a little progress. Boss, it doesn't matter if you buy the ties or not. I only want you to point out the good or bad aspects, and teach me how I can improve. Of course, if you are satisfied with even a few of them, it will be really great. All in all, if only you are satisfied, I will be happy. If you bought my ties but could not make money from them, I would feel guilty."[47]

When somebody not only does not care about your abuses but also continues to appreciate your invectives, what can you do? You, on the contrary, may feel helpless in this situation. The owner of the store had no alternative but to deal with the thickness of Zeng Xianzi, and he finally accepted him. Often times, open frankness can be a positive thing. In business, an open confrontation before decision making can uncover key facts that need to be weighed in the decision making process.

The lesson for success we learn from Zeng Xianzi is to control yourself until you reach your goal no matter how you have been insulted. Otherwise, success will always go to others, not to you. Whether operating in a purely free, competitive, and democratic business system or in a controlled state-dominated system, results/output/ performance is what counts in business.

As for blackness in today's Chinese business reality, it has attracted people's greater attention. For instance, so many people died in the Guangxi Zhuang Autonomous Region of China because some businesspeople sold liquor that had been mixed with industrial alcohol. Of course, imitations, fakes, and piracies in China have been hurting many domestic and foreign customers and manufacturers. Evidently, as an element, blackness has influenced some Chinese businesspeople's decision making. This is true whether we are examining pre-1949, 1949 to 1992, or post-1992 decision making.

DISCUSSION QUESTIONS

1. The United States usually changes its head of state every four or eight years through a popular election process. Business seems to continue without major changes no matter who the new U.S. president may be. How and why is China so different?
2. In the West the influence held by the executive branch of government is tempered by many things (checks and balances). How does China differ?
3. Discuss how the role of Christianity influences decision making in the West.
4. Is the "one person, one vote" system a necessary political prerequisite for Chinese success in business and economics? Why or why not?
5. Did the spring of 1989 event at Tian'anmem Square have an impact on business? Was the reaction of Western governmental policy a factor?
6. Compare and contrast (with particular attention to the decision making process) the relationship between the CEO and the board of directors in China with that of the West.
7. In China the Party/government has more influence on business than in the West. Why?
8. Over the past decade, major political topics such as MFN and GATT, the 1997 status of Hong Kong, and the recent activities involving the political future of Taiwan, have all had an impact on trade with the West. How have these issues affected individual business enterprise in China? Cite an example (real or hypothetical) to illustrate your answer.
9. Changeability affects all decision makers. It could be argued that change will have more impact in the next decade on Chinese decisions than in the West. Agree or disagree? Why?
10. Give a couple of business decision making examples to illustrate the Chinese philosophy of *yin* and *yang*.
11. Discuss the potential influences of people and events such as the breakup of the Soviet Union, human rights activist Harry Wu, Hillary Rodham Clinton, and the summer 1995 International Women's Conference in Beijing.

12. What are some practical implications of "complexities" in business decision making?
13. "While business decision making in China is very complicated, it can be very simple as well." Agree or disagree? Why?
14. By Western standards, some past strategic decisions (such as the "Great Leap Forward") seem illogical. Would you anticipate the Chinese political leadership to continue to carry out illogical decisions in the future? Are major business decisions made differently so that the likelihood of an illogical decision is much less than the likelihood of a major illogical political decision?
15. Use an example to illustrate the meaning of "The Golden Mean."
16. Differentiate between thick and black? Use examples from both China and the West to explain this terminology?

REFERENCE NOTES

1. William A. Levinson, *The Way of Strategy*, (Milwaukee, WI: ASQC Press, 1994), xxi.
2. Wenbo, "Science? Superstition? Pondering the craze of *The Book of Changes*," *East West Forum*, No. 2, April, 1992, 46-49.
3. "The Book of Changes," in *Concise Edition of the Chinese Philosophy*. (Beijing: Chinese Publishing House, 1993), 578.
4. Kongming also had another name, Zhuge Liang, and was the prime minister of Zu State, and a strategist in that period of the Three Kingdoms (220-265 AD). Today, he has become a symbol of resourcefulness and wisdom among the Chinese.
5. Luo Guanzhong, *The Romance of the Three Kingdoms*, trans. Moss Roberts, (Berkeley and Los Angeles: University of California Press, 1991), 776-777.
6. Rang Hou was the king's uncle–the brother of the king's mother.
7. Liu Xiang, *Intrigues of the Warring States*, Ed. Zang Lihe (Hong Kong: Shangwu Publishing House, 1962), 44-48. We referred to the translation of *Intrigues of the Warring States*, by J. I. Crump Jr., (Oxford: Clarendon Press, 1970); however, we kept our own understanding and interpretation.
8. Han Xin was a famous strategist who helped Emperor Liu Bang establish the Han Dynasty (206 BC–220 AD).
9. Sun Tzu, "The Art of War," in *Concise Edition of the Chinese Philosophy* (Beijing: Chinese Publishing House, 1973), 179.
10. Yuan Lin and Shen Tongheng, Eds., *The Stories of Chinese Idioms* (Shenyang: Liaoning People's Publishing House, 1981), 28-29.

11. Xiang Yu was the main opponent of Liu Bang, the first Emperor of the Han Dynasty, in unifying China.

12. Chibi was a place which was strategically located at the northern bank of the Yangtze River. Now it has become a well-known place of historical interest, and a scenic spot.

13. He was also called Guan Yu, or Guan Yunchang. Since he was very loyal to his friends with his just behavior, today he has become a symbol of justice and righteousness among the Chinese. The Temple of Lord Guan has been broadly spread in China.

14. One *li* is equal about 0.3107 mile.

15. Luo Guanzhong, 1991, 377, 382-383.

16. Sun Tzu was a great strategist during the Spring and Autumn Period (770-475 BC) in China. He generalized his thirty years of military experience into his work, *The Art of War*, in which there are thirteen chapters existing to date: Laying Plans, Waging War, Attack by Stratagem, Tactical Dispositions, Energy, Weak Points and Strong, Maneuvering, Variation in Tactics, the Army on the March, Terrain, the Nine Situations, the Attack by Fire, and the Use of Spies. The words of Sun Tzu we cited were from "The Art of War," in *Concise Edition of the Chinese Philosophy*. When we translated the words of Sun Tzu into English, we referred to the translation from Mr. Lionel Giles, but kept our own understanding and interpretation.

17. Sun Tzu, 181.

18. William A. Levinson, *The Way of Strategy*, (Milwaukee, WI: ASQC Press, 1994), 217.

19. Ibid, 162.

20. Ibid, 182.

21. Ibid, 171.

22. Huang Quanyu, Richard Andrulis, and Chen Tong, *A Guide to Successful Business Relations with the Chinese: Opening the Great Wall's Gate* (Binghamton, NY: The Haworth Press, 1994), 24.

23. This information was from an article about the conflict of protection of intellectual property rights between China and the United States in *The Cincinnati Enquirer*, February 5, 1995.

24. Sun Tzu, 177.

25. Liu Xiang, 1970; but kept our own understanding and interpretation.

26. Luo Guanzhong, 1991, 734-736.

27. Sun Tzu, 159.

28. Ibid, 178-179.

29. The five elements, water, fire, wood, metal and earth, were held by the ancients to compose the physical universe. Later, they have been used to explain various physiological and pathological phenomena in traditional Chinese medicine.

30. Sun Tzu, 171.

31. Ibid, 159.

32. Ibid, 173.

33. Yuan Lin and Shen Tongheng, Ed., 1981, 675-676.

34. Sun Tzu, 179.

35. TOEFL means Test of English as a Foreign Language—a test foreign students from non-English speaking educational systems must take in order to enroll in American colleges and universities.

36. GRE means General Record Examination—most students (except business, law, and medical), either foreign or American, need to take this test in order to enroll in American graduate schools.

37. Sun Tzu, 159.

38. Luo Guanzhong, 1991, 164-165.

39. Yuan Lin and Shen Tongheng, Ed., Liaoning People's Publishing House, 1981, 453.

40. Luo Guanzhong, 692.

41. Sun Tzu, 170.

42. The copy of *The Theory About Thickness and Blackness* which was published by China Overseas Chinese Publishing House in 1994.

43. Luo Guanzhong, 1991, 37-38.

44. Ibid, 137-139.

45. Sun Tzu, 167.

46. Ibid, 167.

47. Xia Ping, Li Yi, "The Biography of Zeng Xianzi," *The People's Daily*, March 24, 1995.

PART III: THE ELEMENTS THAT IMPACT CHINESE DECISION MAKING

The elements that impact Chinese decision making usually contain traditional culture (including moral ideas and value judgments), modes of thinking, the social system, political factors, and geographical situations, etc. When we discussed organizational structures and the operation of decision making, we have addressed how the social system and political factors influenced decision making in China. Therefore, in Part III, we will mainly focus on two vital elements that impact Chinese decision making: traditional culture and modes of thinking. In Part I, we talked about "*What* are the organizational structures in China?" We discussed "*How* is business decision making operated in China?" in Part II. In Part III, we will analyze "*Why* is business decision making influenced by traditional culture and mode of thinking?"

Chapter 7

Traditional Culture

SAVING FACE

Most people, no matter whether Western or Oriental, probably spend most of their time and energy adorning their faces as opposed to other parts of their bodies. That is to say that we may tolerate some stains on our bodies, but we would certainly clean any spots on our faces. Moreover, as we know, four of the five human senses—seeing, smelling, hearing, and tasting—are centered together on the face. No wonder the face is so important to most races of people. Therefore, we may be able to say that Westerners and Orientals are the same in that both are so strongly concerned with having regular facial features.

Even though people, both Western and Oriental, are so strongly aware of having regular facial features, Americans, interestingly enough, often comb their hair or adorn their faces in public, while feeling completely at ease. But many Chinese people would not comfortably adorn their faces even in a restroom if anybody suddenly walked in. We believe that there must be some deep cultural roots behind these differences. Such as Americans generally acknowledge "original sin" while Chinese people believe in human nature as good, which we will explain later. However, it is definitely true that the Chinese are more strongly concerned about their "face."

The Chinese people have many unusual words, phrases, and sayings about face: a person needs face as a tree needs bark, losing face, saving face, being concerned about face-saving, casting aside all considerations of face, having a respected face—enjoying due respect, having a "big" face—people have to check his or her facial expression (consider his or her willingness) before making a decision, giving him or her a face could indicate at least two meanings (1) to provide a favor to somebody; or (2) to give one an out to saving his or her face. From these unusual sayings, we can see how important a "face" is to the Chinese.

Mr. T. J. Underhill, president of Underhill Knife Company, visited China with the author, Huang Quanyu, in October 1994. One deep impression made on Mr. Underhill was that so many people carried cellular telephones in restaurants that when a phone rang, nobody knew whose was ringing. According to *People's Daily*, with almost one billion yuan volume of business and paying more than 83 million yuan in taxes, China's Motorola branch has the best economic results among the foreign enterprises in Tianjin Economic and Technical Development Zone. The headquarters of Motorola made an initial investment of $120 million followed by a second investment of $160 million in China. Now Motorola is applying to Tianjin City government to add an additional $360 million.[1] As many people know, the biggest cellular phone system was started on February 2, 1995 in China, through which several million people have been using their cellular phones. One of the reasons that Motorola is so successful in China is that a cellular phone symbolizes a person's social status, thus brightening one's face.

Owning a fancy car as an indication of social status shows the Chinese concern about brightening their faces as well. Dr. Richard Andrulis and Dr. Huang Quanyu spoke at a Chinese university in Nanning City in Southern China in November 1994. After the lectures, the Chinese university invited them to visit Beihai Port. As they rode down the highway, Dr. Andrulis sighed with feeling to Dr. Huang, "So far we have been on the road about an hour but I have counted at least eight Mercedes. Compared to the not very well developed industrial and agricultural bases which you can see from both sides of the road, it's just unbelievable . . ."

Why are the Chinese more strongly concerned about "face" than Westerners?

Mr. Hu Wenzhong and Mr. Cornelius L. Grove believed one of the two principal reasons was the following:

> China over the centuries has been an extraordinarily stable society. The Chinese have had little opportunity to move away

from the locality of their birth and have tended to spend their entire lives in the company of the same friends, neighbors, and relatives. When one is attached for life to a given group of people, maintaining harmonious relationships among all its members becomes of paramount importance. Consequently, face-saving behaviors take on great significance; they maintain harmony, avoid conflicts, and protect the integrity of the group.[2]

We believe that there could be thousands of reasons why face has such high importance for the Chinese; there are not one or two principal or essential roots. In order to find a solution for the question "Why are the Chinese people so strongly concerned about face?" we must expose and analyze its roots in traditional Chinese culture.

First of all, most Westerners, particularly Christians, acknowledge "original sin," but the Chinese are very strongly influenced by the Confucian idea of the "fineness of human nature." The first sentence of *The Three Characters of the Confucian Classics* reads, "At the beginning, human nature was good and honest." Almost every Chinese who has even a little bit of education will know it. Before 1949, it was even the first sentence that every elementary school pupil needed to remember. Acceptance of "original sin" is to admit that there is a human ugly side. Since one recognizes the human ugly side, he or she would have to give serious thought to how the human ugly side can be remedied. Based on this philosophy of faith, people are completely at ease dressing up their faces when they think their faces need to be fixed. This is analogous to one who dares to recognize his or her mistake in public and is willing to correct it.

However, since the Chinese do not accept "original sin," they would not dare or would not be willing to face the ugly side of human nature. As a result, they always must hide their deficiencies. Here, we must explain that "to not recognize something" does not mean to "not know it." For example, one who knows that he is not a very smart businessman might or might not recognize it. Those who know and recognize their deficiencies will face them completely at ease; those who know but do not recognize their deficiencies will always try to cover them up. An interesting illustration is of a clown and a beauty pagent contestant. A clown on stage is a person who knows and recognizes his deficiencies; he is happy to show his ugliness and is funny to please his audiences. However, a beauty queen on a competitive stage is a person who knows but does not recognize her deficiencies; she always tries to cover her deficiencies. The Chinese are like the beauties competing on stage who know but do not recognize their deficiencies. This is why many Chinese people would not very naturally adorn their faces in public or even in a restroom if anyone suddenly entered. Furthermore, since most Westerners believe in God, they usually pray to beg forgiveness from God for their sins. The Chinese tradition advocates self-cultivation to achieve the perfect human life. These two understandings of human nature—one as evil and therefore dependent on an external God for salvation, and the other good and therefore dependent on self-cultivation for the achievement of a state of spiritual happiness—illustrate why many Chinese people would not very naturally adorn their faces in public places.

A person who always tries to cover up his or her deficiencies will be very strongly concerned about his or her face. In other words, he or she will be very sensitive to whether he or she can save face, and whether or not a certain behavior may make him or her lose face.

Second, it is common sense that before a person acts a role on stage, he or she must put on makeup. However, traditional Chinese culture praises social roles but strangles the self so that Chinese people usually act various social roles rather than being themselves. Due to Chinese culture, people very often "perform" their actions on the social stage. As a result, when they make a decision, they usually do not consider "Whether or not I should do this" but "How will others view what I am doing?" Essentially, to consider "How will others view what I am doing?" is a concern about face-saving. A role could be perfect, but the self, as an individual, cannot possibly be perfect. To understand that a role could be perfect, we need to analyze it from two angles. One is a role on stage directed by a playwright. An actor's role is not a depiction of reality; he can freely act on stage what he cannot nor would not do or say in real life. The other angle is the social role. Role expectations and norms could be perfect while performance may not. For example, the role expectations and norms of "sales manager" could be written perfectly in a company's handbook even though a sales manager is not perfect in reality. Interestingly, when a Chinese person associates with someone in reality, he or she always thinks and acts a role such as a manager, or as an official. He or she usually does not act as an individual. Therefore, he or she often tries to be perfect or to behave perfectly. If one always tries to be perfect or to behave perfectly, he or she will be strongly concerned about face-saving. As we can see, this mode of thinking is subtly similar to the previous point that "the Chinese are like the beauty queens on the competitive stage who know but do not recognize their deficiencies." We will address how the Chinese traditional idea about "social role and self" influences decision making later in this chapter.

A third reason why the Chinese are concerned with saving face is the customary arrangement of society in order between senior and junior. China is a society where stratification and seniority are emphasized. A junior must respect and obey his or her seniors. In America, we can often see a family conflict in which, when a father asks his child to stop watching TV and go to bed, his child then asks a question in reply, "Why do I have to stop watching TV and go to bed, but you don't?" In China, the father's words are usually an unconditional and unquestionable order. Confucius said, "One, as a son or younger brother, must give presents to his parents at home, and must respect his seniors in society."[3] Obedience from juniors is unconditional, and therefore, offers a respected face–enjoying due respect is what seniors experience either at home or in society. A junior has responsibilities to save a senior's face, but does not have the right to make a senior lose face. But a senior has not only his or her own responsibilities but also the right to save face. However, a person, in a sense, could always be a senior. For instance, I am a son at home, but I am a teacher in my school; you are a student in the school, but you may be an elder brother in your family. People can be a senior in certain situations in which they must not lose face. Interestingly enough, even when you are a junior, you need to save your face too. Why? First of all, Chinese people do not accept "original sin" so they try to cover up their deficiencies. Second, the Chinese often do not consider "Whether or not I should do this" but "How will others view what I am doing?" Even when they are juniors such as students, they will try to behave with a whole set of student's expectations; otherwise, they still think they will lose face.

Moreover, traditional Chinese collective ideas, which we will address next, also make the Chinese concerned about face-saving. These traditional Chinese cultural roots mutually encourage the Chinese people to try to save their faces no matter whether they are juniors or not.

A fourth element of face-saving is collective, rather than individual, thinking. We will discuss how the balance of the individual and the collective influences decision making in China in the next section. Here we focus on how the Chinese collective idea relates to face-saving. When one represents oneself, he or she may be concerned about face-saving; when one represents a collective, a group, a community, a school, a nationality, and even a country, he or she may be strongly concerned about face-losing. Since the individual concept has been weakened for thousands of years in Chinese culture, Chinese individuals usually consciously or unconsciously think they are representing a collective. For example, study is not viewed as an individual but a collective affair. When a child starts to go to school, he or she will think that because he or she is being sent to school by family, he or she should study for his or her family. If a Chinese person studies in a foreign country, he or she may study for his or her home university, or may even feel he or she represents China. There was a perfect example from the article "My Daughter Played the National Anthem of China on the Piano" in the *People's Daily* (August 2, 1995). The author, Xiaoming Zhang, told the story about how her daughter studied in a Japanese school. The daughter, who was a first grade pupil, came to Japan without knowing any Japanese. The parents worried that she could not adapt to changes in the Japanese school system. The girl made great achievements after only six months. The girl often said to her parents "If I cannot do a good job, they (her Japanese classmates) will think that Chinese people are unable to achieve. I must gain a respectful 'face' for our Chinese people." Let's forget the contents of the story. We are only interested in how the parents and the daughter, who was just seven years old, thought an individual might and should represent a collective or even a country–China–and how an individual should "gain a respectful 'face' for our Chinese people." From numerous facts such as this example, we can easily find that individual study is often an affair that relates to collective honor and reputation. No wonder! Representing a collective is a strong pressure that makes people more concerned about face-saving or face-losing.

Fifth, distinguishing between inside and outside could be a cause of face-saving, but might also be a result of face-saving. Chinese culture pays greater attention to stratification and seniority, with a strong influence from the philosophy of *yin* and *yang*; Chinese culture also emphasizes the differences between inside and outside. In China, a father's parents are called grandparents, but a mother's parents are called "wai" grandparents and the mother's family is called a "wai" family. Cousin and cousinship are called "biao" relatives. A foreign country is called a "wai" country and a foreigner is called a "wai" country's person. The Chinese "wai" and "biao" mean "outside." In brief, anything or anyone that is not from a direct relation is called "wai." Here we will not discuss how the patriarchal system impacts the mother's family. We will focus on how the differences between inside and outside impact Chinese face-saving.

It could be human nature that one may dress or behave differently inside or outside of his or her house. But Chinese people more strongly stress the differences between inside or outside than others. The Department of State in the United States is in charge of foreign affairs which are handled by the Ministry of Foreign Affairs in China. Does this mean that China particularly emphasizes the differences between inside and outside? Maybe not! There are Ministries of Foreign Affairs in many countries, e.g., Britain. But there is a Ministry of Foreign Economic Relations and Trade and a Ministry of Domestic Trade in China, which many countries such as the United States and Britain, do not have. In many instances, the Americans use "international," but Chinese use "foreign." For example, "International Education Office" in an American university is called "Foreign Affairs Office" in a Chinese institution; Americans say "international business" but Chinese say "foreign trade." Please remember that "foreign" means "wai" (outside) in Chinese. "International" implies a large area that includes everyone, even oneself. For instance, when American people say "international family" it contains America, and when an "International Invitational Tournament" is held in America, the United States is included, but "foreign" does not include oneself. It only means others. Since Chinese culture so strongly stresses distinguishing between inside and outside, Chinese people have a whole set of behavioral norms for differences between inside and outside, and the Chinese government makes a whole set of policies to deal with inside affairs and outside affairs. As ordinary people, we may tidy up our messy house before a guest visits; we may also dress up and cook some special food that we may not normally serve. These behaviors may be similar to Americans to some extent. Nevertheless, many Chinese people do not allow their children to eat with their guest(s), nor would they allow their children to eat the special foods prepared for the guest(s). This obviously differs from typical American behavior. The special distinctions between inside and outside behaviors have extended to governmental policies to open many "friendship stores" and hotels that sell special goods and provide special services for only foreigners, not for the Chinese in China. And some developed cities and counties are open to foreigners, but some poor areas will not allow foreigners to visit. This may be similar to closing our messy rooms to our guest(s). "Domestic shame should not be made public–don't wash your dirty linen in public." There is a very famous aphorism among foreign affairs personnel: "There will never be any insignificant affair among foreign affairs." To state it differently, anything that relates to foreign affairs will be so important that it may make the country lose face. In one instance, in 1986, Huang Quanyu, as a Chinese tutor, invited his "student"–the American visiting scholar, Dr. Keith Peterman–to his home for dinner as a guest. A lady from the foreign affairs office advised Mr. Huang very seriously, "Don't offer a meal that will exceed our standard! Otherwise it may put the institution in an extremely awkward situation."[4] It should be a friendly but very common behavior for Mr. Huang to invite Dr. Peterman for dinner; however, the office worried that if Mr. Huang was too hospitable to offer a meal of a quality higher than the institute daily cooked for Dr. Peterman, the institute would lose face.

How has face-saving affected decision making in China?

Face-saving is extremely important and, in some cases, even has a crucial impact on Chinese decision making. When a person, a group, a nationality, or a state is only concerned about face-saving, consequences may be ignored. We realize that many wars have resulted from face-saving in Chinese history, such as the Opium War, the bush fire between China and Vietnam, etc. We can also find many consequential results from face-saving. "The Strategy for Gold Medals" is a policy to formulate a whole set of measures and plans for Chinese athletes to win more gold medals in the Olympic Games or at international competitions. For example, the soccer champion in the Olympic Games could win a gold medal, but the fastest runner could also garner a gold medal. Therefore, it would not be as profitable to foster the eleven best soccer players to win one gold medal as it would be to train the eleven fastest runners, swimmers, or skaters to win eleven gold medals and thus make China "look good." As a result, while the amounts of gold medals China has won in the Olympic Games or other international competitions put China among the best three or four countries in the world, the collective sports, e.g., volleyball, soccer, basketball, are suffering. Another example regarding Chinese face-saving is mountaineering, particularly climbing Mount Qomolangma of the Himalayas, the highest peak in the world. This is a comprehensive reflection of a country's highly developed science, technology, and economy. While the well-known mountaineering party of Britain failed seven times, the very young Chinese climbing party reached the top of the highest mountain in the world on May 25, 1960. Why was China, regardless of any conditions and consequences, insistent on climbing this mountain at this time? There were so many special elements that were concerned with face-saving: putting down the rebellion in Tibet, a natural calamity, the failure of the Great Leap forward, and the break in relationships between the Soviet Union and China. Some other instances, caused by face-saving to some extent, which were very inharmonious to the Chinese scientific, technological, and economic bases, were the researching and manufacturing of A-bombs, the developing of space technology, etc.

Face-saving has strongly influenced business decision making in China as well.

Concerning business decision making, there are at least two issues in marketing that need to be considered. One is what and how individuals want to consume; the other is how business decision making can meet the consumers' needs. However, in order to answer these questions, "What and how will individuals want to consume?" and "How can business decision making meet consumers' needs?" we must further ask "Why will individuals want to consume in a certain way?" "Why will consumers want to buy certain goods?" and "How can we meet consumers' needs if we provide a certain good or offer a certain service?" Obviously, "face-saving" is one of the appropriate roots to be explored for a solution.

In 1988 the author, Huang Quanyu, had told his American student, Tom, who was very interested in China and whose father was a millionaire builder, "If you want to conduct a great business in China, you need to persuade your father to invest in an indoor building materials business in China. Though China is still providing houses to each employee at low rent, China must reform its housing system to allow people to purchase private homes soon. Based on the Chinese situation, people cannot choose location, size, and style. But, as you know, Chinese people are strongly concerned about 'face,' so the only thing Chinese people can do to have a respected face–enjoying due respect–is to make the inside of their houses as beautiful as possible when they personally own their own homes. If one percent of the Chinese buy one square yard of carpet from you, the carpet can link Shanghai to San Francisco. That is to say, 'face-saving' may have covered a huge market!" After seven years now, the Chinese people are busily improving their homes for face-saving. And Tom is still thinking about Chinese face-saving.

There is a successful example of going through Chinese face-saving to discover a special market. One was a result from a survey to indicate that pupils above fourth grade in Taiwan would choose any other drink rather than regular water if they had a choice because drinking regular water made them feel as if they were losing face. In terms of this survey, there would have been a business opportunity for people with sharp eyes. Now there are various kinds of drink available in Taiwanese schools, and most pupils drink at least a can or box of a drink each day.

But Chinese face-saving may confuse American businesspeople as well. A Chinese couple applied for their credit cards many times, but they were still not successful even though they had more than $60,000 in their bank account, and had about $70,000 gross annual income. The sole reason that various credit card companies have denied their applications is that they cannot find this Chinese couple's credit history. Outwardly, it seems to be ridiculous: If you have not offered a credit card to this Chinese couple, how can they have a credit history? Deeply exposing it, we can find out that there is a conflict between Western and Chinese consumer ideas that relates to the "face" issue of Chinese culture. Borrowing money can be viewed as losing face for many Chinese people. Therefore, if it is possible, they will do their best to avoid borrowing money. Now, the silly but conflicting questions can be raised. You have not offered a credit card to the Chinese couple, so how can they have a credit history? With $60,000 in savings and $70,000 gross annual income, why do they need to borrow money from credit card companies? If you do not need to borrow money from credit card companies, why apply for a credit card? Both parties need to analyze these conflicts. No matter how much money a Chinese person has, he or she needs to show his or her moral integrity to return the loan. American credit card companies must understand the "face" issue in Chinese culture in order to expand the credit card business in China. In fact, in a sense, a credit card may be able to, in turn, brighten people's faces in China because a credit card is a symbol of good credit.

How does one handle the face-saving of the Chinese culture?

Based on the previous explanation and analysis, we offer some suggestions:

1. Try some methods that can save Chinese face. At any time, try not to make the Chinese feel as if they are losing face. When you have a sticky business problem, try to think carefully if it relates to face-saving. Some Chinese cases may seem to be very knotty, but if you can find some way to save Chinese face, the problems can be readily solved, just as the Chinese saying indicates, "A bamboo will split all the way down once it's been chopped open." For example, when the People's Republic of China and the United States were going to establish their diplomatic relations, one thorny issue was that the People's Republic of China insisted upon stating "There is only one China in the world" in the joint communique. The dilemma for the United States was to establish a diplomatic relation with the People's Republic of China while maintaining a very strong nondiplomatic relationship with the Republic of China. But maintaining that there is only one China in the

world would not help the United States to subtly establish a new relationship while maintaining the old one. Finally, the American delegation found a way to solve the problem. (The Chinese people believe that the idea was from Dr. Henry Kissinger.) The idea was to state these words in the joint communique: The U.S. government "acknowledges that all Chinese on either side of the Taiwan Straits maintain there is but one China and that Taiwan is a part of China."[5] This stratagem solved the knotty issue.

2. Give the Chinese a way out. In a sense, the above example about finding the wording of "there is only one China in the world" to state in the joint communique was to find a way out for both sides. Now the emphasis is on giving an opportunity to extricate the Chinese from an awkward position. In other words, when a conflict occurs and you are in an advantageous situation, a wise way to solve the problem is to give the Chinese a chance to get out without making them lose face. When you provide an out, you should not openly state it, such as "Now I will give you a way out to save your face." If you state this, even if you offer this chance, they may not accept it because your words still make them lose face. Chinese people are very sensitive to hints, so you just need to hint very subtly. They will take the opportunity with tacit understanding. For instance, a Chinese company could not provide qualified samples of hinges on time to H.C.K. International. Although one month late, H.C.K. International still could not find a better source. Then Mr. Huang sent a fax to the Chinese company stating, "We have not received any samples of the hinges from you up to now, which might mean your samples may have been lost in the mail. Would you please send your samples again? But we must receive them before this Chinese New Years Eve! Otherwise our customer will not consider your samples anymore." Just one month later, H.C.K. International received the qualified sample of hinges. An out to the Chinese company was provided by H.C.K. International by sending a fax that stated, the "samples may have been lost in the mail." By emphasizing that the samples must be received "before this Chinese New Years Eve", H.C.K. International not only offered an out to the

Chinese company without face-losing, but also set up a deadline with a warning. The problem was solved nicely.
3. Do not miss an out that may be given from the Chinese. When both parties are in a deadlock or a negotiation has reached an impasse, at a point when the Chinese people are not very willing to take the final step, they usually give a final chance of an out to their opponents. This chance may be offered obviously or just by a hint; the opportunity may last a while, or may be just fleeting. If you do not want to go the final step as well, you need to pay attention to every signal from the Chinese side. If the Chinese are in an advantageous position, the signal will usually be obvious, but the chance may not last too long. When the Chinese are in a disadvantageous situation in which they have lost face, the opportunity may last quite a while but the signal or hint could be very weak. We can see a recent example in the negotiations about the protection of intellectual property rights between China and the United States. On February 4, 1995, the Clinton Administration imposed punitive tariffs on more than $1 billion of Chinese goods, the largest trade sanctions in American history, and warned of further action if China continued to refuse to crack down on the piracy of American software, movies, and music. The decision to impose 100 percent punitive tariffs on goods ranging from silk blouses to cellular telephones was met almost immediately by an angry Chinese announcement of tariffs against American-made goods, e.g., cigarettes, film, alcoholic beverages, etc. Along with the tariff on U.S. products, China would suspend negotiations with U.S. auto companies that were seeking to set up joint-venture projects, withdraw approval for U.S. companies and their subsidiaries to set up holding companies, and suspend approval for U.S. audio-visual manufacturers to open branch offices.[6] This was a very serious conflict in which both countries would be deeply hurt. Some famous economists believe that this is a stand-off in which there can be no winner. But we think that this is a stand-off in which neither China nor the United States are winners, but Japan or European countries could be a winner. The whole world was watching as the two huge ships of state almost crashed in the Pacific Ocean. Never-

theless, the United States made a wise step: Each nation's tariffs (which would double the price of the targeted imports) took effect on February 26, 1995. The delay, a common practice in cases of trade sanctions, is intended to assure that goods shipped before the retaliatory tariffs were announced would not be affected. There could be four possibilities resulting from this stand-off: (1) China yields and the United States wins; (2) the United States yields and China wins; (3) neither would yield to each other and both seem to be winners but essentially are losers; and (4) both yield to each other so that everyone is a winner. Let us analyze the four possible results. First, it is impossible to only ask China to yield to the United States without face-saving. Second, it is also impossible to ask the United States to yield to China without reaching its certain goals. Third, if both would not yield to each other, the United States would certainly not reach its goals because the situation of protecting intellectual property rights in China could become worse. Fourth, both can avoid each other's sanctions but the United States would still hold a means to strongly influence China. Obviously, the fourth result is the ideal one. However, as we know, the Chinese people are concerned about face-saving. The ball is in America's court. Are Westerners concerned about face-saving? Of course! When American guests taste the food from their host and hostess, they usually close their eyes and say, "Mmm! So delicious!" They may even think in their minds: "My God! they (the host and hostess) always forget the salt!" Is this face-saving? Why not?! But Americans do not have as deep and painful needs for face-saving as the Chinese do. The United States has occupied the driver's seat. Two days after the "sanctions" had been announced, a letter from China about rethinking the negotiations reached Washington. As we have explained previously, when the Chinese people are not very willing to take the final step, they usually give a final out to their opponents. This is the "chance" we mentioned. And the United States made a very wise step—the trade sanctions would not be effective until February 26, 1995 during which time there is enough room for renegotiating without Chinese face-losing. The American representatives returned to Beijing to reopen negotiations on February 6, 1995 without concern about who will lose what in the game or who should yield to whom. If we just analyze whether or not the American delegation has handled this tough issue by considering Chinese face-saving, the answer is positive, because they left room and caught the final chance from China skillfully.

4. Do not cast aside all considerations of face unless you desire conflict with the Chinese. A story about a new tycoon in Macao, Mr. Xie Shuowen, is a good example. Mr. Xie signed a contract to sell 300 duplicators to a Chinese import/export company, and each one was quoted at 9,000 yuans. The person from the Chinese company was a good friend of Mr. Xie, so when they signed the contract, he said to Mr. Xie: "We are good friends with a respected face, we don't need to state ultimations, such as 'If the seller can't provide goods on time, the minimum penalty will be 30 percent of the total value' in our contract..." But Mr. Xie knew that the buyer put this article on the contracts with the second buyers. Just ten days before the due day, Mr. Xie was informed by his seller that the goods would be delayed one month. Mr. Xie was a friend of his seller as well, so that they did not state the 30 percent penalty in their contract either. He tried to find a new source to solve the problem. Finally, he found a new supplier two days before the deadline, but each machine would cost 11,500 yuans which meant he might lose $750,000 Hong Kong in this whole deal. Mr. Xie was facing three choices: casting aside all considerations of face to his old seller; casting aside all considerations of face to his buyer without a penalty; supplying a new source and losing $750,000 HK. The first choice did not have any meaning but a friend would be lost; the second choice meant he would lose not only friends but also his own honor and reputation; the third one was to lose $750,000 HK to exchange honor and reputation that was invisible but invaluable. He did choose the last. Now Mr. Xie has become a very successful tycoon in Macao. One of the reasons for his success is that he values his honor and reputation and will not simply cast aside all considerations of face to his Chinese connections.

Another example was the Korean War. Let us list several choices: (1) the United States was ready to have a war with China in Korea; (2) the United States did not intend to have a war with China in Korea, but mistakenly estimated that China, who just finished a civil war, would not fight with the United Nations; (3) being aware of Chinese face-saving, the United Nations would not move forward to Yalu river–the border of China. However, the Korean War resulted. Many people believe that the United States did not intend to have a war with China in Korea, but mistakenly estimated that China would not fight with the United Nations. We are not historians; we do not want to assume too many interpretations about history. We only want to offer our advice: If possible, do not make Chinese people take the final step, such as the Korean War, without considering Chinese face-saving.

THE INDIVIDUAL AND THE COLLECTIVE

An interesting parallel about the conflict between the Western culture's emphasis on the individual and the Oriental culture's stress on the collective can be seen in some ball games, especially informal games. In America, communities usually organize children's soccer or other ball games each season. In age groups, children are arranged on different teams. Players and coaches understand that the purpose of these sports activities is to have fun. Since having fun is the essential purpose, winning or losing is not important. This is radically different from the Chinese culture. The most important thing for the Chinese is whether or not the team wins. But the most important thing for Americans is if the individual has fun. Even if the teams already have their uniforms, some individuals may still want to pay an extra $25 for a uniform with the individual's name displayed on it. This is in America! In order to win in China, however, the poorer players sit on the bench, only the best players can play, and they play the position which optimizes the probability of winning. In the United States, in order to have fun, every player will take a turn at every position, no matter how poorly or how outstandingly they play; as long as every individual can participate and can have fun, the goal has been reached. As for winning or losing for their teams, it is not important. Though some American parents told us that having fun was critical, associating with others on a team was another purpose for joining these games. As we can see, "joining to associate with others on a team" is not a collective concept of the team, because its primary starting point is for the individual to associate with others and does not serve the team but the individual.

The traditional Chinese saying about the relationship between the individual and the collective is "The main stream must be high so that the small streams can rise." The essence of this saying is that without the collective, individuals cannot exist. Undoubtedly, human beings are social animals. Maurice Richter believed that one of the crucial reasons for human beings to be social animals was their dependence. A newborn buffalo could travel on its own feet, keeping up with its mother within a few hours; a porcupine baby achieved its independence in about a week, however, "the dependence of a human child on its elders continues longer." As a result, "Prolonged infantile dependence on elders means that humans must inevitably be social animals."[7] This seemingly proves the traditional Chinese idea about the relationship between the individual and the collective that without the collective, individuals cannot exist. But if we view it from another perspective, we may find out that the traditional Chinese idea about the relationship between the individual and the collective has gone too far to one extreme and has neglected the flip side—that without individuals, the collective cannot exist either.

Dr. Huang Quanyu found an interesting linguistic phenomenon and explained it in his dissertation: if you study personal pronouns in Chinese, all of them relate to people except the first person singular pronoun for which the original ancient character was the symbol for an instrument of punishment because Chinese traditional culture thought that the self was equal to selfishness and privacy, which must be punished. Under the influence from Chinese culture, even the Japanese use the Chinese character 私 (selfishness) to indicate the first person singular in Japanese. The first person singular has been avoided for a very long time in China. In recent years, the first person singular has begun to be used as a normal word to some extent. Usually, Chinese people prefer to use the first person plural pronoun "we" rather than the first person singular "I." There are several reasons why people are likely to do so.

1. Since the traditional Chinese idea about the relationship between the individual and the collective was that without the collective individuals could not exist, as a concept, "individual" could not be identified correctly and clearly. Also, "self" was thought to be equal to selfishness and privacy, which were considered the root of all evil and deserving of punishment. Therefore, when people need to use the first person singular in reality, if it is possible, they will consciously or unconsciously use the first person plural pronoun rather than the first person singular. For example, when people want to say, "I like to drink beer when watching football on TV," they may say, "We like to drink beer when watching football on TV." Interestingly enough, in many cases, you will be understood using "we" instead of "I," because "we" absolutely contains "I," but "I" may not represent "we." This interesting linguistic phenomenon could also support the traditional Chinese idea about the relationship between the individual and the collective that without the collective, individuals could not exist.

2. Because "we" can be a group, an organization, a community, a society, a nationality, or even a country, when you use "we" instead of "I," you will feel you are powerful. For example, when you want to say, "I don't think the United States can threaten China during these negotiations about intellectual property copyrights." But you can say, "We don't think the United States can threaten China during these negotiations about intellectual property copyrights." This is a very strong stratagem. First, the words indicate your idea. Second, your expression makes you sound more powerful and strong, because the word "we" can mean a group of people, a professional organization, a Chinese community, or even China. Third, "we" is a tricky word. As long as there is one other individual who agrees with your idea, "we" will be the correct word to use. For this reason, when you use "we," you do not need to worry whether anyone can prove you wrong. If the listener thinks that you indicate the idea of a group of people, a professional organization, a Chinese community, or even China, you can enjoy your "powerful" feeling; if the listener doubts or questions the meaning of the word "we," you can

simply tell this tactless guy, "'We' means my wife and I." Since using "we" can make one feel more powerful than using "I," people prefer to use the first person plural pronoun wherever possible.
3. Using "we" instead of "I" can make you look modest, not pushy or self-important, yet still expresses your meaning. For instance, the sentence "I study English as a second language for my sales training program in China," people would usually phrase, "We study English as a second language for our sales training program in China."
4. Using "we" not only makes you closer to others, but if any error occurs, you may not need to take the blame. Let us take an explanation from Huang Quanyu as our example: "Suppose I am the third party to work on a Sino-American deal, in which the Chinese factory needs a model sample from the American corporation. When I call the American company, I will not say, '*I* need to send the sample to China.' I will say, '*We* need to send the sample to China,' The word 'we' may make the American company feel I am on their side, working on our common interests so that they may magically mix me and the American company together into one party. However, if anything goes wrong, I do not need to take the blame by myself." In China, "I" always stands behind the "we" so that countless losses from individual mistakes, such as failed investments, wrong products, or even huge losses (e.g., the Great Leap Forward and the Cultural Revolution) have been backed by collectives.

A collective is made up of individuals; therefore, without individuals there is no collective. Likewise, individuals are organized into a collective, and without the collective there are no individuals. Individuals and the collective are interdependent, and represent a unity of opposites. Individuals have their own rights and responsibilities, collectives have their rights and responsibilities, too. Four kinds of conflicts can occur between the individual and the collective: (1) individual rights vs. collective rights; (2) individual responsibilities vs. collective responsibilities; (3) individual rights vs. collective responsibilities; and (4) individual responsibilities vs. collective rights. Since traditional Chinese culture emphasizes the collective and ignores the individual, very different and strange decision making results may occur when Chinese people encounter the above four conflicts. Before we analyze these four conflicting relationships in detail, we would like to share a very interesting story.

Ms. He Zhili, who was the former World Cup Table Tennis Champion of China, beat all Chinese players to win the Championship of the 12th Asian Games for Japan on October 13, 1994. This sweep shocked the Chinese people. However, it originally resulted from Chinese decision making based on emphasizing the collective and ignoring the individual.

Ms. He Zhili, as a member of China's Women's Table Tennis Team, played for the 39th World Cup Table Tennis Championships. On February 18, 1987, the women's singles for the Geist Prize got into the semi-finals stage (from eight to four). The situation in the A group was: Chinese Guan Jianhua vs. Li Fenji (from Chinese phonetic of pronunciation) of North Korea; Chinese He Zhili vs. Chinese Chen Jing. The Chinese coaches had a meeting, and thought that if Guan Jianhua could not beat Li Fenji of North Korea, it would be wise to let He Zhili play against Li Fenji of North Korea. The coaches decided that Chen Jing would lose to He Zhili. But the coach who needed to inform Chen Jing about the decision of the coaches was so busy that he forgot. When Chen Jing won the first set 21:19, He Zhili was so worried that she frequently hinted to the coach to remind Chen Jing to lose. The coach suddenly recalled this decision, and informed Chen Jing during a rest. Then Chen Jing lost to He Zhili very soon. No one knew that Guan Jianhua beat Li Fenji of North Korea, and would play with He Zhili to enter the finals. However, in the B group Chinese Dai Lili would play with Liang Yingzi (from Chinese phonetic of pronunciation) of South Korea. Who would have a better chance to win against Liang Yingzi of South Korea? There were different thoughts among the Chinese coaches. After much discussion, the Table Tennis Association of China made the final decision that Guan Jianhua would play with Liang Yingzi of South Korea. One of the reasons was that

He Zhili had just lost to Liang Yingzi of South Korea in the Asian Games. When the coach told He Zhili to lose to Guan Jianhua, Ms. He was silent and did not indicate any disagreement. Guan Jianhua knew the decision; she was going to save energy to play with Liang Yingzi of South Korea, and stay very relaxed in her playing. In the first two sets, He Zhili won twice 21:7. In the third set, He Zhili still played very seriously. Guan Jianhua realized that Ms. He had decided to ignore the decision of the coaches and the Table Tennis Association of China. But it was too late for Guan Jianhua to win. In the B group, Liang Yingzi of South Korea beat Chinese Dai Lili. A player refused the decision of the coaches. This was a first-time occurrence among Chinese players. All members of China's delegation were shocked by Ms. He's behavior. Nevertheless, everybody was silent because of an order from the Table Tennis Association of China. Nobody bothered He Zhili. If she could beat Liang Yingzi of South Korea, the championship still belonged to China. On the evening of March 1, 1994, He Zhili beat Liang Yingzi of South Korea to win the Geist Prize (the women's singles).

That was a game where, barely had one wave subsided, when another arose—one problem followed another. Since the Chinese player eventually won the championship, and He Zhili was very young to show her strong potential ability, the coaches did not seriously criticize her but educated her about collectivism and patriotism.

However, a conflict finally occurred between He Zhili and China's Table Tennis Teams. Before the Olympic Games were held in Seoul, South Korea in 1988, table tennis had been picked as a sport for the Olympic Games. Chinese people are very crazy about table tennis, which is called the "national sport," and were extremely anxious to win the table tennis championships at the Olympic Games. Who would be selected to be a member of China's Women's Table Tennis Team? People began to worry about Ms. He's behavior in the 39th World Table Tennis Championships. In order to handle it with great care, the coaches met five times. He Zhili did not even get one vote. The Table Tennis Association of China called dozens of table tennis coaches from the whole country together; they had the same idea as the coaches of China's Table Tennis Teams. The Table Tennis Association of China decided to give up He Zhili and choose Chen Jing as a member of the China's Women's Table Tennis Team for the 24th Olympic Games.[8]

Later, He Zhili left China to emigrate to Japan. When she beat all the Chinese players to win the championship for Japan in the 12th Asian Games in 1994, it again shocked the Chinese people. People began to have different opinions on how to view her behavior. We can use this example to analyze the following four conflicts.

1. *Individual rights vs. collective rights.* When the Chinese people face this conflict, they may have several choices. First, as individuals, when the conflict does not relate to their own interests, most of them may make a decision based on collective rights. That is to say that they may believe that He Zhili should do whatever she could do for a championship for China, not just for her own gain or loss. Because the conflict does not relate to an individual's self-interests, their interests may become "collective rights," such as the championship of China. Moreover, they believe that "conceding games" of table tennis is similar to the tactics of "changing players" in football, basketball, volleyball, or soccer. Since each individual player has different characteristics, who plays which positions to the best advantage against different opponents is critical decision making. Since the 1960s, many excellent table tennis players have conceded games or given up their individual gains in order to win collective honors. This is one of the important reasons that China's Table Tennis Teams have won so many championships at international competitions. Nevertheless, there is evidence that some people are beginning to think about individual rights, particularly in recent years.

Second, when the conflict relates to an individual's own interests, there could be two situations to face. (1) When the individuals do not have the authority to be involved in decision making, they usually can or have to give up their individual rights for collective rights. (2) If individuals do have the authority to be involved in decision making, and they can wisely cover up when they hurt the collective rights for their individual rights, individuals might do something for their individual rights. Of course, many individuals may still be able to give up their individual rights for the collective right. It may depend on how seriously the collective rights will be hurt, and how heavy the individual rights are. Most people would not make a decision when the collective will lose millions of dollars at the expense of having a couple of dollars for the individual.

2. *Individual responsibilities vs. collective responsibilities.* There is a very interesting and popular story about the issue of individual responsibilities vs. collective responsibilities. There was a monk who lived in a temple that was located on a very high mountain. The monk must descend the mountain to a brook to tote two buckets of water on a shoulder pole for daily use. He had to rely on himself, since there was nobody to complain to or help him. He was happy by himself. Later, another monk was sent to the temple. The two monks had to share the responsibility of carrying water. They carried one bucket of water on a pole between their shoulders. They began to rely on each other, and complained to each other. But they were still all right even though they had to climb the mountain to carry water many times each day because only one bucket of water was carried each time. When a third monk was sent to the temple, the three monks had no water to drink. They relied on each other; they complained to each other. One monk could tote two buckets of water on a shoulder pole; two monks could carry one bucket of water on a pole between their shoulders. How should three monks carry water to the temple? A wanted B and C to carry water; C wanted A and B to carry water; B wanted A and C to carry water . . . This is a very bitter satire that can, in a way, explain the Chinese idea about individual responsibilities and collective responsibilities. Since traditional Chinese culture stresses that the individual cannot exist without the collective, collective responsibilities were emphasized more than individual responsibilities in many cases. In the West, an individual signature from a general manager of a corporation can be a symbol of the authority of the organiza-

tion. But in most cases in China, only a seal of the organization can imply the authority of the organization. No individual responsibilities can be detected from this seal, only collective responsibilities. Relying on collective responsibilities rather than individual responsibilities was one of the reasons that Chinese people accepted the Socialist system only thirty years after Marxism was first introduced to China. When a decision must be made in which either individual responsibilities or collective responsibilities need to be involved, collective responsibilities will usually be chosen. For example, it was decided that He Zhili should concede the games to Guan Jianhua so that Guan Jianhua would play with Liang Yingzi of South Korea in order to win a championship for China. This decision implied a very high risk. Therefore, this was the collective responsibility of the group of coaches and the Table Tennis Association of China to render this decision. Since the individuals who are involved in the collective decision making generally do not need to individually withstand any responsibilities or mistakes, they may not consider elements of risk too much. As a result, decision making from a collective can withstand very high risks. The projects of the Three Gorges on the Yangtze River can be an example of withstanding a high risk by the collective decision making.

3. *Individual rights vs. collective responsibilities.* In China, individual rights are so strongly excluded, and collective responsibilities are so strongly emphasized that individual rights are mixed into collective responsibilities. For example, if He Zhili wanted to fight for the individual rights for her championship, then people could ask her: "Without the help of the collective, how could you be a champion or even an excellent table tennis player?" He Zhili would have a difficult time answering because "collective help" can have countless meanings to He Zhili. Those "helps"–doctor, coach, and researcher, etc., who earn a salary similar to hers–work for the collective, China, not for her. Of particular importance were those very special "accompanying" players who were selected from the whole of China to play with the members of China's table tennis team because of their unique talents, similar to those of China's

main opponents. For instance, suppose Liang Yingzi of South Korea was chosen as the main opponent for China's team by the coaches and experts. Then the Table Tennis Association of China would check all the players in China to find a player (male or female) who had a similar playing style as Liang Yingzi of South Korea. This player would give up all training or matches to accompany He Zhili or other Chinese players in training. If this player could not be found, a special coach would imitate Liang Yingzi of South Korea to play with the members of China's team. Those special "accompanying" players are called "unknown heroes." For these reasons, a championship has been considered as a collective, not just an individual, quest. As we can see, individual rights are mixed into collective responsibilities. In the business world, the phenomenon that individual rights are mixed into collective responsibilities is obvious as well. Individuals should have the right to own their own houses; but a collective factory or company needs to take care of its employees' housing, even the dining hall, nursery, stores, and hospital.

4. *Individual responsibilities vs. collective rights.* From the above description and analysis of the story of He Zhili, an obvious conclusion can be drawn that individual responsibilities must obey and serve the collective right in Chinese culture. As individual rights are strictly controlled, individuals only have their responsibilities. When they face a conflict from collective rights, the sole choice for them is to obey and serve the collective right. Therefore, He Zhili did not have any other choice; either she must obey and serve the collective right, or the collective responsibilities that had made her a special player would be taken away from her so that she might lose all she had gained and become an ordinary person. When she gave up her individual responsibilities fighting for the collective rights, but won her individual rights, she lost her career opportunity until she emigrated to Japan.

Actually, the idea about the relationships between the individual and the collective of traditional Chinese culture is not only that individual rights are ignored, but individual responsibilities are stressed; collective responsibilities are emphasized, and collective rights are emphasized to the highest degree. Based on this summary, we can also understand how this traditional idea might influence the decision making process in China.

An interesting phenomenon demands our attention. Individual rights are viewed as selfishness. Since the concept of selfishness is almost equal to "the root of all evil," this is a serious factor. Nevertheless, selfish desire is an objective reality independent of the human will. The selfish desire of humans always stubbornly tries to find an opportunity to show itself. In Chinese culture, the selfish desire of humans has recently been finding more and more ways to show itself. An increasingly common way is to use smaller unit collective rights to fight with a larger collective rights. If you are not aware of this subtle phenomenon but only think that Chinese people cannot and would not use their selfishness or their individual rights, you will be unable to make a knowledgeable decision during conducting business with the Chinese.

Encountering the Chinese: A Guide for Americans explains that Chinese negotiators "ultimately represent the interests and viewpoints of the government, frequently the central government in Beijing."[9] Dr. Huang Quanyu pointed out in his book review

> This [idea] may be true to some extent, but there is a famous Chinese saying, '[Where] there is a policy from above, there will be a counter-tactic from below' (*Shang you zhengce, xia you duice*). This means that when Chinese negotiators have a choice involving collective or individual profit, and where they will not violate (at least not seriously) the policies of the central government, they will opt for their individual or collective profits. When readers assume that Chinese negotiators only voice the point of view of the central government, they will be unable to negotiate successfully with the Chinese.[10]

This is to say, selfish desire is an objective reality independent of human will. If selfish desire could be wiped out, Chinese culture would not need to control the selfish desires of humans. Chinese people are humans; they are showing their selfish desires in a novel way–in smaller collective rights. For example, there have been quite a few people in the legal arena sentenced as guilty because they have used different understandings of tax policies from the central government to evade taxes. The authors, Huang Quanyu and Chen Tong, once attended a trial in which the court of a minority autonomous region (similar to a province) in Southern China tried to judge whether or not a manager of a motorbike company was guilty of evading taxes. The workers of the factory supported him, and the main leaders of the region tacitly consented to his behavior; however, the tax bureau, at all levels, wanted to charge him. The trial lasted several years. Finally, he was declared innocent, but subsequently he was also not appointed to an important position. Recently, the most shocking case was one in which the president of the Great Wall Electrical Machinery Corporation, Shen Taifu, was sentenced to death. The accusation against him was that he had raised funds for the company with a high profit through illegal means. The court believed that the results of his behavior had upset the financial order in China. In the first case, the manager did not gain special profits for his actions, but the workers of the factory obtained interest. In the second case, the president secured a very huge profit for himself and his family, but the employees of the company received different benefits, too. Those could be typical examples of mixing individual interests into small collective rights to challenge bigger collective rights.

One point we must explain is that there will be a delicate but major difference between an individual who has the authority to make a decision that relates to his or her own interests, and an individual who has the authority to make a decision that only relates to others' individual interests. In the former case, as long as one can skillfully cover what one would do for his or her own interests, he or she is very likely to try this tactic. In the latter case, many decision makers have been doing things for the collective rights.

In summary, collective rights reign supreme as the basis of decision making. However, Chinese culture and the social morals are being strongly pounded by market economic ideas. While individual rights are gradually recognized, selfish desires remain unchecked. Justified individual rights and selfish desires remain integrated into small collective rights.

EQUALITY

"Are all men created equal?" "Are all human beings created equal?" These questions have been challenging human beings for centuries. Equality is a human ideal. However, it is just like a marvelous mirage: when people pursue the mirage, they find only wilderness. Even so, the Chinese people have been pursuing this "mirage" for literally thousands of years.

Mentioning the concept of "equality," we may have to cite an example from the book *A Guide to Successful Relations with the Chinese: Opening the Geat Wall's Gate* to typify how the Chinese would treat what they believed "equality" was.

At a Chinese university, people debated how to award the winner of a "round-the-school" race. The three possible alternatives considered were as follows:

1. Everyone would get a towel as a prize, regardless of sex and age, as long as they participated (even if some only walked to the finish).
2. The names of the contestants would be arranged in the order of the results, irrespective of gender or age, and the awards would follow according to the finishing order.
3. Sixty-year-old females would start ten minutes ahead of the others; sixty-year-old males and fifty-year-old females would start five minutes ahead of time; young boys would start last. Then, according to the order in which people successfully crossed the finish line, prizes would be awarded.[11]

We can generalize the essential point from this example into one question: Should people focus on equal results or equal opportunity? Can you guess how the Chinese answer this question by choosing the way the race was actually judged by them? Interestingly enough, they chose the first alternative. This differs from Westerners who might have chosen the second one. This manner of deciding the awards for the foot race is typical of how the Chinese behave in their economic endeavors in the pursuit of equality.

Equality simply means equal results to the Chinese people. The Chinese people pursue this concept of equal results in their daily lives.

Let us take the personnel administration as an example. In general, the personnel administration, just as the name implies, works with differences among people. In other words, the personnel administration has to screen and divide people into different ranks, recruit, select, place, reward or promote the better, discard or punish the worst, and reeducate or retrain those who demonstrate a need. Our example in which each person is given a towel regardless of the order of crossing the finish line could be an indication. Obviously, reward, promotion, and punishment are very critical, but as the personnel administration has the difficult job of dealing with people and their differences, reward and punishment are confused when hardworking people and lazy people receive similar bonuses. Also, promotions are generally given to people equally according to their seniority or education but not according to how well they have actually performed their duties. For this reason, when hardworking people and lazy people are promoted together, reward and punishment are confused. This confusion also occurs when lazy persons with more seniority or education are promoted but hardworking people without seniority or with less education are not promoted. Getting what one deserves has become difficult since reward becomes punishment, and punishment becomes reward. Several years ago, every new staff member would be directly appointed to various organizations such as a factory, a company, or a bank by the personnel departments of the higher levels of government. Without candidates and selection, recruitment was a trifling matter. Now recruitment has changed, but the recruitment or appointment of cadres has not. Therefore, the personnel administration has been most important, but this difficulty becomes easy when everybody equally gets a "towel." As for compensation, in recent years, employees of different organizations may receive vastly different incomes. But employees who work for the same factory or company that is not a joint-venture or foreign-owned enterprise usually have narrower ranges in their earned incomes.

Equality is a human ideal, but inequality has been a reality. The Chinese people have neglected three preconditions of inequality to pursue equal results.

The first precondition is that the differences in people are eternal. Human physiology, ethnicity, intelligence, personality, socialization, cultural capital, economic condition, and family background do vary. We cannot even discover twins who are entirely identical. For instance, two things, the brain and the hand, are crucial symbols distinguishing human beings from animals. God has given two hands to almost everybody, but some use their right hand, while some use their left. Some can be the weightlifting champions, some can only hold a pen; some can draw beautiful pictures, someone else's writing may look like chicken scratches; some may be multi-millionaires as professional athletes, some are begging for their bread with their hands; some can create such vital documents as the Declaration of Independence, some have to pick garbage with their hands, and some do not even have two hands. In summary, people are not identical by nature or by social construction. Huang Quanyu has pointed out, "People may have a right to legal equality, but since they are themselves unequal, 'having a right to legal equality' will yield unequal result." And just as "any even number plus an odd number will always be an odd number; when eternal inequality is employed to the people who have a right to legal equality, unequal results will appear among them."[12]

The second precondition is that the hierarchical society is an objective existence. We have previously explained the idea of Maurice Richter that human beings are social animals. He also argued,

> And the full utilization of human intelligence as a substitute for natural weapons in the struggle for survival requires group cooperation. Early human hunters, for example, were much smaller, much less powerful, and much slower than many of the animals they hunted—or that hunted them. They could protect themselves and acquire meat only through their greater intelligence combined with a social organization capable of implementing intelligent plans, such as a strategy for hunting or the controlled use of fire to keep marauding animals at a distance.[13]

If social cooperation means a division of labor, different social positions and different economic incomes in class society will result from the division of labor. That is to say, human beings must organize their hierarchical society so that people have different jobs with different incomes, and have different status.

The third precondition is that competition is an objective reality and independent of human will. Human self-interest is a base of competition. However, the law of competition is that one gains, others lose. Therefore, one of competition's effects is to redistribute wealth and power so that some become more wealthy and powerful than others. As long as people with selfish interests compete with each other in a commodity economy, inequality must result.

From the previous description, we ought to be able to make a conclusion: People will be equal if all people are identical, people do not organize society, and people are not selfish. Otherwise, inequality is eternal. Conflicts about equality can be eliminated in a society where the sources are unlimited. For instance, when air is unlimited, people will not complain whether or not it is equal for you to breathe more air than I do. But as we all know from the most basic of economic principles, the material wants of humans far exceed the available resources. When the resources are limited to meet people's needs, the Chinese way is to control human desire. Some may think, "Yes, equal results are ridiculous, but equal opportunity is fair and possible." But we will ask: "When a disabled person and a top-notch runner have an equal opportunity to stand at a starting line for a race with the same rule, is this equal opportunity fair? Is this race possible?" The answer is that no matter whether equality means equal results or equal opportunity, inequality is perpetual. If equality is pursued by means of eliminating inequality, new inequalities will still appear.

In this book, we are not interested in arguing whether the Chinese people neglect the three preconditions of inequality to pursue equality. That is like Don Quixote fighting a windmill. Our interest is to discuss how the idea of equality in traditional Chinese culture influences decision making in China.

The concept of equality may not be simple, but we will treat it from two dimensions.

1. *Political equality.* The Chinese people pursue equality while acknowledging hierarchy. This is a very interesting but complicated topic. Before we talk about political equality, we must address the subtle relationships between pursuing equality and acknowledging hierarchy.

Confucius frequently stressed "distributing wealth equally." For instance, he said:

> We needn't worry that the state is poor, we should worry that the wealth couldn't be allocated equally; we do not need to worry that the people are needy, we should worry that the state is not at peace. If the riches can be distributed equally, it will make no difference whether people live in poverty; if people are at peace, they will not feel their properties are small; if the state is at peace, political power cannot be toppled.[14]

However, he also emphasized the hierarchy. For example, when Qi Jinggong who was the King of Qi state, asked for advice about politics from Confucius, Confucius stated, "Monarchs should have a monarch's manner; subjects should have the behavior of a subject; a father should have a father's air; a son should be a son." Then Jinggong said, "Yes, if a monarch does not have a monarch's manner; subjects do not have a subject's behavior; a father does not have a father's air; a son does not act like a son, even if there is a bumper harvest [in Qi state], how will I be able to enjoy it?!"[15] As we can see, Confucius strongly emphasized a hierarchy among a monarch and the subjects, a father and a son in a state, a society, or a family. Humans are social animals who must organize their society. If there is a society, there must be a hierarchy. In a society there must be various social roles with different social responsibilities and duties, and occupying different social positions. Let us use a primary example.

Families are the cells that construct societies. There are different roles such as father, mother, son(s), and daughter(s) in a family. Different roles have different positions with different responsibilities and duties. Father and mother can have sex, but the son and daughter absolutely cannot have sex with each other; the mother can have the responsibility to breast-feed her children, but a son or daughter cannot breast-feed the mother. In a society, it is impossible for everybody to be the president of the country. Also, it is impossible for every employee to be CEO, even in a small company. People have different social positions with different social responsibilities and duties. This is a fact which is independent from human will.

Therefore, the Chinese people acknowledge, or have to acknowledge, social hierarchy while they pursue equality. However, social hierarchy could mean political inequality even in a democratic country. In the United States, President Bill Clinton could sit on his special plane, get a haircut while blocking a runway for hours, but an ordinary person must hurry up to catch his or her plane at the last minute, or miss the plane. In any country, the CEO of a company could decide a billion dollar deal, but a common worker could not even determine the cost of the equipment he or she is using. In this sense, as individuals, the Chinese people acknowledge political inequality in society while they pursue economic equality.

Interestingly enough, as a country, or when the Chinese people represent or think they represent their country, they will strongly adhere to political equality, particularly when they deal with the West or the so-called superpowers. We can list several reasons that illustrate this. First of all, with the history of a brilliant civilization, China was a superpower in the world. Translating China into English, it means "the central country" in the world. China viewed and treated its surrounding countries as its dependencies that must offer tributes to the Chinese Emperors every year. The Chinese imperial court was viewed as the "Heavenly Imperial Court" by the Chinese. However, the Chinese were awakened from their dream by the boom of cannons during the Opium War in 1840. Following the Opium War, China was forced to sign a series of unequal treaties with Japan, Britain, France, etc. The Western industrial countries have gained power because of China's failures in the wars. Since then, China lost its position as a great imperial country. The Chinese view this period of history as a humiliation. Therefore, when Mao Zedong proclaimed, "The People's Republic of China has been established! From now on, the Chinese people will stand up!" in the Tian'anmen, and the poorly equipped Chinese troops drove the United Nations troops away from the Yalu River, the Chinese people believed that a new strong China had been born. Many overseas Chinese intellectuals who had very good professional positions in the universities or research institutes in the West, including the United States, gave up their favorable incomes and positions to return to China. They wanted to build a strong and great new China. But with the largest population and with the third largest territory in the world, inequality is real for China. Otherwise, China would not need to insist on political equality when they deal with the West. Making an A-bomb, experimenting with satellites, although not suitable to the Chinese economy, could be an example of efforts to build a strong China that would have political equality when dealing with the West or the superpowers. Insisting on political equality when dealing with the West is very important in Chinese business decision making. In May of 1995, the author, Huang Quanyu, accompanied a Chinese business delegation to a worldwide paper industry fair in Germany. The Chinese delegation had signed a one-half million dollar contract with a German company to purchase three grinders. When the Germans tried to sell one kind of special grinding head as an extra deal, they told the Chinese people that China could not make this kind of grinding head, but could only buy it from Germany. The chief of the Chinese delegation refused to discuss this deal any more. He told Huang Quanyu, "China is able to make satellites; I don't believe that I can't find a factory to make this grinding head for me in China . . ." As of yet, they still have not found a factory to manufacture that kind of grinding head in China. In order to have political equality, China and/or the Chinese people may do what they want to do regardless of the consequences when dealing with the West or the superpowers. An example was that China fought with the Soviet Union, regardless of a broken relationship between the two countries, in order to have a feeling of political equality with the Soviet Union.

The second reason the Chinese adhere to political equality with the West could be the "face" issue that we analyzed. Sometimes, equality is impossible but you might need to, or have to, carefully and skillfully handle political equality for the Chinese people. Let us say your company has its 100th birthday celebration. You will receive many congratulatory telegrams from many pleased customers in several countries. You need to publish their names to thank them for their concern and congratulations. If a few of them happen to be Chinese companies, the order of their names will be of concern to the Chinese people. Likewise, if you need to designate the seating positions for the Chinese representatives who attend your company's 100th-year event, this too could be a politically tricky equality situation. However, you would be unable to list every company's name first on the list, or seat every representative in the first row or next to the CEO. Someone must be first; someone last. Some people may not care about this, but the Chinese people certainly do. A wise way is to arrange the list or the positions of the seats is to follow a strict alphabetical order according to the first letter of their names, thus not paying attention to the size of the company or the sales volume of cobusiness with the company. It must pe pointed out that sometimes political equality implies a state in Chinese minds in which the representatives feel they are respected, and not insulted.

Third, collective rather than individual equality must be considered. We have discussed how the balance of the individual and the collective will influence decision making in China. Here we only want to stress that when one represents a collective, a group, a community, a school, a nationality, and even a country, he or she may be strongly concerned about political equality. Since the individual concept has been weakened by thousands of years of Chinese culture, many individuals are ashamed to ask for personal benefits, even when they are reasonable. For example, a Chinese engineer is sent to a foreign company to jointly conduct research or work. As an individual, this engineer may be ashamed to negotiate about wages and benefits, because he or she may not want to be viewed as pursuing self-interests. But when he or she represents an organization or even a country, this person may do so. In 1988, an American university was going to invite the president of a Chinese university to give lectures and do research as a visiting scholar. He told the author, Huang Quanyu, that "As an individual, I don't care how much the American university will pay me. But I will represent my country as an honorable visiting scholar. How much they pay me will symbolize and reflect how high they value our Chinese scholars. Please understand that I am not a selfish person, but for the respect of our country I have to ask them to pay me as much as they pay the other countries' visiting scholars . . ." Examples such as this are frequent, e.g., asking for an office, a hotel room, etc., to match whatever other countries' representatives might have received. On the surface, such requests look like economic benefits, but they are asked under the name of "political equality."

It is no surprise that the Five Principles for Peaceful Coexistence, which are the Chinese government's main diplomatic policies, include "Equality and mutual benefit" and "All countries, big or small, should be equal." In fact, if we label various countries as a "strong economic country" (Japan), a "strong military country" (former Soviet Union), and a "strong scientific and technological country" (the United States), then the People's Republic of China, as one of the five permanent members of the Security Council of the United Nations, could be viewed as a "strong political country." Of course, it will be reasonable for a "strong political country" to emphasize political equality with the West or with the superpowers.

2. *Economic equality.* This topic has been well explained in the book *A Guide to Successful Business Relations with the Chinese: Opening the Great Wall's Gate.* The consciousness of economic equality is imbedded in the roots of Chinese culture. In the more than 2,000 years of Chinese feudal history, the small-scale peasant economy constructed a social structure in which people's living standards did not differ greatly. People were used to, and accepted, the social situation of "low income, small differences."[16] A puzzle that always bothers the reformers in China is that while people gain more benefits from the reformation, they complain about the reformation more. Essentially, this is the deep-rooted concept of economic equality making mischief in people's minds. The Chinese people understand the concept of economic equality to mean "rich together" as "rich equally." So many Chinese people may think: "Yes, I gained a great benefit from the reformation, but someone else has gained a greater benefit than I did." People do not want to have historical comparisons contrasting the current situation with the past. They only like having a horizontal contrast, comparing oneself with peers or others. This is why almost everybody gains a great benefit from the reformation, but almost everyone complains about the reformation. The author, Huang Quanyu, has conducted cultural and business consultation about the idea of economic equality to several American comanagers who need to administrate joint-venture companies in China:

> People may not be happy even if you pay unequal sums but all more than $100 to each; if you, however, equally pay them

$50 dollars each, they would not complain. 'Why can someone have this, and I cannot?' 'Why can someone earn more than I can?' 'Why can so-and-so do that, and I cannot?' The question of 'why' always bothers the Chinese people. Taking the round-the-school race as an example, if the second way of judging the winner of a round-the-school race was chosen, many Chinese people would say, 'I have joined the race, why can I not have a towel?' If the third one was chosen, many Chinese people would not only ask, 'I have joined the race, why can I not have a towel?' but also 'Why can they start five minutes ahead of me?' If a harmonious working environment is most important, economic equality which simply means equal results would be your first choice. If you want an effective and competitive working atmosphere, you need to consider equal opportunity. Of course, you can also think about the third way of judging the winner of the round-the-school.

In international trade, no matter whether the Chinese are your partners or your opponents, they will insist on political equality. However, when they are your business partners, they certainly prefer economic equality where, regardless if the efforts may be different, the results or benefits will be equal. They may not emphasize or may not care about an unequal effort or unequal input which means that they may work more than you do or you may work more than they do, but they would prefer an equal result in terms of commissions, profits, outcomes, or other types of rewards.

HIERARCHY

We have previously argued that the hierarchical society is an objective existence. Therefore, we believe that China is undoubtedly a hierarchical society, just as other places in the world. Nevertheless, we want to highlight that China is not only a hierarchical society but also a society where hierarchy has been especially emphasized. For this reason, the concept of hierarchy in Chinese culture, in some cases, may strongly influence decision making in China.

How would the concept of hierarchy influence decision making in China? We will discuss this issue from two perspectives, internal and external.

First, hierarchy has been emphasized in Chinese internal administration. In other words, the decision making of the internal administration is based on hierarchy. An obvious example is that China carries out the official standard. All of the organizations that include companies, factories, banks, departments of governments, hospitals, schools, and even temples or churches are divided and ranged into different levels. These different levels of organization indicate different positions, privileges, and responsibilities. The heads of organizations with different levels have different social positions, political privileges, and role responsibilities as well. Their salaries, housing, medical benefits, and travel treatment are different. When people are away on official business, they need to buy the appropriate class of plane or train ticket, or stay in a hotel that will match their position.[17] Even what levels of documents or newspapers, and what kinds of books that they are authorized to read are different. For example, there are different so-called "Reference Newspapers" in China. Those reference newspapers could be international, domestic, and local, which ordinary people could not read. Nevertheless, leaders with different levels of political privileges are allowed to know or read different levels of "Reference Newspapers" in which different ranges of secret news are disclosed. Even the famous Chinese classic pornographic novel, *Jin Ping Mei*, was controlled by the director of the library in a Chinese university in the 1980s. Only the persons with an academic title of lecturer (this position is similar to assistant professor in the United States) or above were allowed to borrow and read it.

From another angle, we can again find out that hierarchy is emphasized in Chinese internal administration. Confucius said:

> I am afraid that the Jin state will be destroyed because of its law of being discarded. The government of the Jin state should follow the laws that their forefather, Tangshu, created to rule the common people. The officials ought to obey the orders to contribute their responsibilities so that ordinary people would respect their nobles, and the aristocrats could maintain their properties. The orders between the noble and the lowly must not be ignored. This is the law.[18]

There were several ancient Chinese sayings which indicated that everyone was not equal before the law, and they can still be used to describe today's situation in China to some extent: "The magistrates are free to burn down houses while the common people are forbidden even to light lamps—one may steal a horse while another may not look over the hedge"; "Corporal punishment could not be used on any senior official of feudal China." The situation in which the magistrates are free to burn down houses while the common people are forbidden even to light lamps could be similar to when common workers' monthly salaries were about 40 *yuans* while Mao Zedong was allowed to earn several million *Yuans* in royalties from his works and be the richest man in China during the Cultural Revolution. Ordinary peasants were not even allowed to feed a hen to lay eggs for market, which was labeled as "the tail of Capitalism" and had to be severed at that time. Another example is the condition "Corporal punishment could not be used on any senior official of feudal China." There are three organizations that keep people's behavior within bounds in China. They are the Chinese Communist Party's Central Commission for Discipline Inspection, the Central Supervisory Committee, and the Ministry of Justice. As the name indicates, the Communist Party's Commission for Discipline Inspection is for the members of the Communist Party. The Supervisory Committee is used to control the government departments and their personnel. The Justice Department handles people's legal behavior. It seems that the justice department handles everyone's legal behavior, but in most cases, the justice department is only handling ordinary people's legal behavior. When a member of the Communist Party or an official breaks the law, very often he or she may only be punished by the Communist Party's disciplines; his or her range of position/title would be demoted or even lost instead of a legal punishment. However, when an ordinary person breaks the laws, he or she would be punished by the law. Of course, sometimes when a member of the Communist Party or an official breaks the laws, he or she might be legally punished; in a few special cases he or she might even be legally punished more heavily than an ordinary person. But more often, the Party or administration carries out its own justice. The fact that only "in a few special cases even he or she might be legally punished more heavily than an ordinary person" can be evidence that the Party or administration carries out their own justice. Because if everybody is equal before the laws, everyone should be equally treated by the laws. When someone is punished more severely than others in the same case, this simply means that there is interference from a higher level of authority or a Party decision.

In fact, the official ranges usually are inversely proportional to that of the punishments, i.e., a higher official rank will receive a lighter punishment, and a lower official rank will get a heavier punishment. There has not been any Communist governor or higher official executed by shooting since 1949—no matter how seriously they have broken the law. This situation even applies to the Communist enemy, the so-called "war criminals" of the Kuomintang (KMT). Thousands of Kuomintang's officials with a lower rank were executed by shooting, but almost every one of the Kuomintang's generals or other high-ranking officials who were captured have been treated quite well by the Chinese Communist Party.

Secondly, hierarchy has been emphasized in Chinese external associations. In other words, the decision making of external associations is based on a hierarchy in which people, or organizations, or countries are divided into different groups and ordered with different levels. How should we associate with those people, organizations, or countries? What kinds of relationships will be granted to those people, organizations, or countries? The decisions will be made based on what kinds of groups into which they are categorized and ordered. For example, the world once was divided into three parts by China: the first world, the second world, and the third world. The first world was the United States and the Soviet Union; the second world included the rest of the Western countries and Japan; the third world encompassed the developing countries. The Chinese used diplomatic strategies and tactics to fight with the first world—two hegemonic powers; to win over the second world; and to unite with the third world. China also categorized the third world into different subgroups: the "real" Socialist countries such as Albania, North Korea, North Vietnam, and "Democratic Kampuchea" (the eastern European countries were not considered orthodox Socialist countries); nonaligned countries, and developing countries. Among those developing and nonaligned countries, China further distinguished the countries with a similar ideology or a close relationship to China, and the countries with a similar ideology or a strong relationship with the two superpowers. For instance, the Socialist Republic of the Union of Burma, and Socialist Ethiopia had ideologies similar to China. Pakistan did not have a similar ideology with China, but had a very close relationship with China because of its unique geographical environment, and its political and historical causes. The countries such as South Korea, Singapore, and Indonesia, despite being controlled by dictatorships (which was counter to the American democratic spirit), had a close relationship with the United States. The Democratic Republic of Afghanistan had an ideology similar to China but had a very strong relationship with the Soviet Union. In summary, China based its diplomatic associations on the political levels of the groups or subgroups. As long as the countries were categorized in the first grade or group to China, and their requests and needs were considered necessary by China, China might, regardless of any consequences, do anything for them. The Korean War, the Vietnam War, and the Railway between Tanzania and Zambia could be appropriate examples.

After Sino-American and Sino-Japanese diplomatic relationships had been built, particularly since China has carried out the policies of reforming and opening to the outside world in 1978, China no longer considered only political elements to categorize the levels of groups for its diplomatic associations. In recent years, Japan, the United States, and European countries have occupied the top positions of conducting international trade with China. Economic factors are gradually becoming very important in categorizing and considering the levels of groups for China's diplomatic associations. Ignoring the anger from the North Koreans to establish a diplomatic relationship with South Korea proves that in China the economy has been highlighted. China has no longer provided free economic aid to Albania, Vietnam, Cuba, and many African countries that have been very close to China for political reasons.

Does this mean that China will not consider politics anymore but only the economy to locate and order countries' levels for its diplomatic associations? The answer is "no"! When consideration could be given to both politics and economy, politics would not be given up. Pakistan always supports China in international affairs; Pakistan also has enough money to conduct business with China. In this case, consideration could be given to both politics and economics. When consideration cannot be given to both politics and economics, decision making will be based on the specific case. In order to be granted the Most Favored Nation status from the United States, China might be willing to have a "political deal" with the United States such as releasing several dissidents from prison. However, after Mr. Lee Teng-hui had a permission to have a "private visit" to the United States, the Taiwan issue, namely the "one-China policy," has become the most important political issue for China. The vice prime minister, Mr. Zhu Rongji who is currently and powerfully in charge of the economic works in China, has been sent to Africa to regroup "politically allied countries" to gain support for the one-China policy with special economic aids and business dealings.

We have previously addressed that individuals would play a very special role in decision making in China. For this reason, relationships between country and country, or between organization and organization could, in a sense, imply a relationship between individual and individual. In other words, the level of the private relationship between individual leaders could simply mean their organizational relationship or even a country's relationship. For example, the ideology of Romania was not too different from the other Eastern European countries'. But China had a closer relationship with Romania than most Eastern European Socialist countries because the leader of Romania, Qiozasiku, had a closer private relationship with the Chinese leaders. If there are some troubles between China and America, if President Richard Nixon were alive, he would be able to do something. Of course, in addition to Dr. Henry Kissinger, President George Bush or President Jimmy Carter can do something, because they are categorized at a very high level and maintain a very good private relationship with Chinese leaders.

Recently, an idea of "containing China" has been quite popular in the United States. We do not want to discuss how unwise this point of view is. We only want to point out that if the other countries do not follow the United States to contain China as they did in the 1950s and the 1960s, America will be excluded from its current priority position for the huge Chinese market since decision making of external associations is based on a hierarchy that is governed by political and economic factors ordered with different levels.

Finally, hierarchy implies power and authority in Chinese culture. "Power" and "authority" are central conceptions of administrative thought. In a work by Max Weber, he wrote that "Power is the probability that one actor within a social relationship will be in a position to carry out his own will despite resistance." Authority, in contrast, is "the probability that certain specific commands (or all commands) from a given source will be obeyed by a given group of persons." Also, Weber distinguished three bases of legitimate authority: charismatic, traditional, and legal. Charismatic authority derives from the exceptional personal qualities of the leader. Traditional authority is based not on the quality of the leader's personality but on social custom and precedent. In legal authority, obedience is owed to people neither because of their vision and inspiration nor because they occupy a position venerated by tradition. Indeed, obedience is not owed to individuals at all. Rather, it is owed to a set of legal principles or laws.[19]

When we attempt to understand the two concepts of "power" and "authority" in Chinese culture, we find that there are some subtle differences. Here, we do not want to argue about Weber's concepts of power and authority; we are only going to discuss the subtle differences between these concepts in Chinese culture, and how these concepts relate to hierarchy and influence decision making.

The characters for power in Chinese are 权力, which indicate that in a certain society, laws/legislation and culture grant certain positions to exercise certain rights and/or use certain forces. That is to say, as long as one is appointed to a certain position, regardless if he or she is moral or intelligent, this person has certain powers to exercise certain rights and/or use certain forces. The power could be not only legal power but also cultural power. Legal power is more readily understood, whereas cultural power may not be so easy to understand in American society. Let us illustrate: Laws/legislation do not grant any rights to parents to beat their children in China, but almost every Chinese parent has heavily or lightly beaten their children. Police do not have the right to interfere with parents beating their children unless a child could be killed. Who gives parents the right to beat their children? Society and culture! It is an unbelievable joke in China that American children have the legal right to call the police if they are beaten by their parents.

The characters for authority in Chinese are 权威, which imply a force that can make people obey, and/or a prestige with strong persuasion. Here, authority includes not only power (权力) but also prestige, might, and dignity, etc. (权威). In fact, the Chinese concept of authority is very close to Weber's charismatic authority and legal authority to some extent, but puts the emphasis more strongly on internal influence.

Authority could imply power, but power might not include authority. Authority can make people sincerely convinced, but may also make people afraid; power can cause fear in people, but may not change their minds. Authority can physically, spiritually, and mentally pressure and influence people internally. Power is physical and external. In China, Jiang Qing[20] and her partners once had the power to mentally threaten and physically hurt people, but they did not have the authority to make people internally convinced. As Vice President of the United States, Dan Quayle had strong position power, but he did not have authority in some people's minds since they believed that he was not smart enough to spell "potato" correctly (i.e, without the letter "e" at the end).

If it is an unbelievable joke in China that American children have the legal right to call the police when they are beaten by their parents, it is also an unbelievable joke in China that American teachers have a legal right to spank their pupils in some localities. Teachers have no legal right to physically punish their pupils in China; they can only use their authority to influence their students. Chinese culture does not emphasize "rule by laws," but "ruling by benevolence." Therefore, authority has a uniquely special position in China. People with authority can strongly or even crucially influence Chinese history without having legal power. Yuan Shikai[21] (1859-1916) who was Minister of Beiyang[22] had the most powerful troops in China at that time. In 1908, the new Emperor of the Qing Dynasty, Xuantong, was enthroned. Because Yuan had too much military power and also destroyed the Wuxu Reform Movement in 1898, he was forced to retire on a ridiculous excuse–having beriberi. Even after he had retired to his hometown, Xiang Cheng in Henan province, if any troops were moved, the generals of Beiyang would certainly obtain permission from him. Jiang Jieshi (Chiang Kai-shek) was another president of China. He retired from the political arena on January 21, 1949, and Mr. Li Zhongren became acting President shortly after. But acting President Mr. Li could not make any important decisions. Most officials still reported and listened to Mr. Jiang. Without Jiang's permission, no important decision could be made. The President of China, Mao Zedong (1893-1976), proposed that he become second in command in 1962 because of the failure of the Great Leap Forward in 1959, but he still firmly controlled China. It has been said that "a sneeze from him could make all China catch cold." Now, Deng Xiaoping no longer has any formal title or official position except the honorary chairman of the Chinese Bridge Association. However, any rumor about his health will not only be able to stir up the stock market on the mainland, but also in Hong Kong and Taiwan, etc.

A Hong Kong businessman told us that he especially liked to conduct business with the children of senior cadres who might even be retired. Those children might not be in power, but they could "borrow" their parents' authority to engage in something that others were unable to do. If their parents have retired, their parents might still have the authority to influence their former subordinates (some of them even promoted by these parents).

Power implies a material/physical hierarchy. Authority symbolizes a physical and mental/spiritual hierarchy. Of course, power and authority both can construct a force for decision making. Nevertheless, authority obviously is a very unique force for decision making in the Chinese culture.

SOCIAL ROLE AND SELF

Role is a term of sociology.[23] In order to explain the relationships between role and self, let us try a metaphor. When a real actor is playing a role, he must act and speak what the playwright or director expects or stipulates. Any actor who does not follow the rules will be viewed as unqualified or merely bad. Nevertheless, what an actor portrays and speaks on a stage may not be what he wants to portray or speak, or may even be what he hates to do and say in his real life. Likewise, if society is a big stage, everyone will be an actor or actress in various social roles. How one ought to act and speak are so-called "role expectations" and "role norms" that are formed or shaped by culture and society. With this analogy, no matter whether you act in a dramatic role or a social role, you need to follow certain rules of behavior. It is not very difficult for an actor to control himself to act and speak what he dislikes on a stage, because the period of a role on a stage is short, and what he portrays and speaks on a stage usually will not impact what he actually does in reality. However, it is very difficult for a person to control himself to act in a social role that he dislikes or hates. For example, suppose you opposed the Vietnam War but you were a soldier in Vietnam. Of course, more often than not, people may like the social roles they act in. This is what we called "human duality" in which a human could have a role while at the same time act outside the expectations of the role. The point that we want to stress is that there are differences between social roles and that for each individual. And we want to stress that social roles and the self could exist in harmony or could exist in various degrees of conflict.

G. H. Mead, a famous American scholar, was, in a sense, similar to the Chinese sage, Confucius. Both did not directly write any philosophical works[24] but their students edited their class notes and conversations to create academic works after these men died. Mr. Mead had a famous idea. He argued that the "self" consisted of two parts–an "I" and a "me." In brief, the "I" was the subjective "self" and "me" was the objective "self." We do not want to discuss what we do not agree with about relationships between the "I" and the "me"; we are interested in how different the social role and the self are in Western culture as opposed to Chinese culture.

In order to have a better understanding, an easier and a simpler comparison is to simply think that the "me" is the social role, and the "I" is the subjective "self."

Western culture particularly emphasizes "I," not "me." Interestingly enough, it is incorrect English grammar to say "Tom's friend is me." It is correct to say "Tom's friend is I." Furthermore, the pronoun "I" is always capitalized, whereas the other personal pronouns are only capitalized when they are at the beginning of a sentence. In Western culture there is more attention paid to the "I" than the "me." In a similar way, the West also pays greater attention to the self than the role.

For this reason, when Nora left the "Doll's House" and Helmer said, "Remember–before all else you are a wife and mother." Nora said, "I don't believe that anymore. I believe that before all else I am a human being."[25]

Many Chinese people have never realized that "Who am I?" is a question. Chinese people always consider that they are a role first, as "wife," "mother," and then a human being second. Very interestingly, according to the Chinese character components (similar to English roots and affixes), almost every personal pronoun relates to people. For example, with 你 (you) and 他 (he and him), the character component 亻 means people. Even 她 (she and her) still relates to people, because 女 means female person. Only 我 (I and me) did not mean people, but are instead much more negative in connotation, the symbol for an instrument of punishment 戈 in terms of its origin of character.[26]

Why does 我 (I and me) not mean people? Because traditional Chinese culture thought "self" was equal to privacy and selfishness. So the self was considered the root of all evil, with the belief that the self must be punished.

Confucius said, "Restraining the self to follow the etiquette is benevolence."[27] What is benevolence? Its Chinese character is 仁, and includes two parts: as we know 亻 means people, and 二 means two. Its connotation actually implies a moral relationship between people.

The moral presuppositions of Chinese culture are to smother "self" for others, to throttle the individual for the collective and society. However, Chinese culture has not really been able to strangle the individual. It slyly separated the self and social roles, then belittled the self and praised the social role with a whole set of role expectations and behavioral norms. This praising of the social role can be found in Confucius's maxim, "The monarch should have a monarch's manner; subjects should have a subject's behavior; a father should have a father's air; and a son should be a son."[28]

In summary, Chinese culture uses a whole set of role expectations and behavioral norms to standardize people into various social roles without the independent or antisocial acts of an individual.

Now let us discuss how strengthening the social roles and weakening the self influences decision making in China from several perspectives.

Role vs. Role

Undoubtedly, there must be conflicts between the social role and the self; otherwise, Chinese culture would not belittle the self and praise the social role. However, there are conflicts between role and role as well. These conflicts can occur between the different social roles in which an individual acts. Suppose you were a son and also a subject. In terms of role expectations and behavioral norms, as a son, you need to follow your father, and as a subject you must obey the monarch. When your father asked you to stay at home to take care of your sick parents, but the monarch asked you to fight in a battlefield, you must solve this role conflict by obeying the monarch, or giving up your interests to work for the collective interests of society. The conflict could appear among different social roles that were acted by different individuals. For instance, there could be conflicts between workers and their manager, between trainees and their trainer, or between engineers and workers. When these kinds of conflicts occur, since a whole set of role expectations and behavioral norms are waiting for you, you do not need to ask anyone the answers to questions such as "Who needs to obey whom?" or "What should I do?" The answers will come to your mind immediately to follow cultural moral norms and social value judgment.

Therefore, we, or even our readers, can easily make a conclusion: Since social roles are emphasized and the self is weakened in Chinese culture, people are not encouraged—or even allowed—to have independent thinking or antirole actions. Role expectations and behavioral norms simply replace the individual's decision making. That is to say, you almost do not need to know the individual's decision making, as long as you know what the situation is, and what social role this individual is acting in. Based on role expectations and behavioral norms, you can almost know or at least accurately predict his or her decision.

Role Responsibilities vs. Individual Responsibilities

No matter whether you are acting as a social role or an individual, you should first fulfill your responsibilities. Social role and self are usually the opposites in a contradiction, and rights and responsibilities are often the two poles of a contradiction as well. Therefore, role responsibilities and individual responsibilities rarely conflict with each other, particularly in a society in which social roles are appraised and the individual is neglected. We even have a difficult time picking an example of conflict between role responsibilities and individual responsibilities. In short, if by any chance role responsibilities conflict with individual responsibilities, role responsibilities are always emphasized first. This could also be viewed as a model of decision making for many Chinese people.

Role Responsibilities vs. Individual Rights

Because Chinese culture appraises social role and belittles the self, and emphasizes responsibilities but ignores rights, obviously, in the contradiction of role responsibilities vs. individual rights, social role responsibilities are stressed and individual rights are neglected. Very interestingly, the same action taken by individuals in different social roles could be understood to be fulfilling the responsibility or appealing to individual rights, depending on which person is performing the action. For example, criticizing the other member of the pair could be considered either a role responsibility or an individual right when occurring among friends. When a father criticizes his son, he is fulfilling his responsibility as a father; when the son criticizes his father, he is claiming an individual right. The problem is that because Chinese culture emphasizes the responsibility of one's social role, the son cannot criticize his father. The individual rights might only be respected when it appears between a junior and a senior. Let us take the traditional Chinese moral standard, "respecting senior and cherishing junior" as an illustrative example. As we can see, "respecting senior and cherishing junior" seems to indicate both social role responsibilities, not individual rights. Nevertheless, if we rethink "cherishing junior" carefully, we find that it could also imply individual (senior) rights. But "respecting senior" certainly indicates social role responsibility. In brief, when people make decisions, their social role responsibilities are emphasized while their individual rights are neglected. There is a very popular saying, the individual must play a role as "screw" and "gear" to be placed in the machine (state or society), and can only follow the operation of the machine without any individual and independent action.

Role Rights vs. Individual Responsibilities

When role rights conflict with individual responsibilities, there will not be a clear answer to which option one should obey. But there will be a clue to a typical answer. It will depend on the situation whether it will be advantageous to society and the collective. If, in a situation, one is giving up role rights to keep individual responsibilities and this will be good for society or for the country, then it will be encouraged; otherwise, it would be criticized.

Role Rights vs. Individual Rights

Usually, there are few conflicts between role rights and individual rights. Suppose there is one. From the preceding analysis, we can easily make the conclusion that to confirm the role rights and give up individual rights would often be appreciated.

In summary, role responsibilities are strongly encouraged and emphasized for use in decision making in China even when they conflict with individual responsibilities, role rights, or individual rights.

Undoubtedly, social roles are praised by Chinese culture. However, there are some abnormal elements from social roles that influence people's decision making of which we should be aware. First, let us consider confused social roles. People may often confuse role expectations or mix expectations from different social roles. For example, a Chinese company hired an American as co-manager. When they needed to evaluate this co-manager to decide whether or not to renew his employment contract, people would not only evaluate whether he was a qualified manager, but also whether or not he was a good husband or a good father. That is to say, even if he was able, he might not be granted continuing employment as a manager if he were not a good husband or father. Interestingly, this confusion of role expectations may also influence American people's decision making when they publicly elect a mayor, congressmen, senator, or president.

In addition, evaluation of social roles from others will highly influence one's decision making. Suppose a Chinese manager needs to decide if the company ought to purchase more effective machinery for the purpose of reducing labor (i.e, terminating employees). While explicitly dealing with social responsibility and business ethics are beyond the scope of this book, this decision dilemma is often a reality in today's society either in China or in the West. The point ponders the issue of how others will evaluate this "role action" may strongly influence decision making. The decision maker may consider "how others will evaluate my act" more than "should I act?"

We have addressed typical Chinese behaviors that are shaped by traditional Chinese culture. However, in the past two decades, the commodity economy has heavily and deeply smashed Chinese tradition. Some radical antitraditional behavior has been appearing in China which we must mention to our readers.

As we know, Chinese culture initiates "ruling by benevolence," but not "ruling by law." Chinese society has been maintained by its moral standards, which include appraising social roles and belittling the self. The primary intention of emphasizing social roles and neglecting the self, we believe, was to make every individual serve society and think about others. But one of the objective consequences is that individual mental health (such as independent consciousness and gaining proper self-interests, etc.,) has not been well developed. During these recent decades, the commodity economy has been strongly and deeply eroding traditional Chinese moral constructions that are built into people's minds. Traditional Chinese moral constructions have become shaky and are even tottering for many people. As when pressing a spring, the more pressure you exert, the more force will be returned from the spring. When people face the commodity economy in which self interests are very dynamic, many move toward the other direction, which is radical. Money has made many people forget or give up their role responsibilities to only seek individual profits. This is one of the reasons that corruption, degeneration, and bribery are so rampant in China in the past twenty years.

MODESTY AND IMPLICATION

Comparing Chinese Taiji boxing with Korean boxing, Tae Kwon Do, you will find out that Korean Tae Kwon Do is a kind of attack boxing that is very fierce and tough. Tae Kwon Do emphasizes quick moving, and "gaining the initiative by striking first" (forestalling the enemy). Its boxer usually likes to rush the attacker and attempt, using quick movements, to knock his opponent down immediately. However, Chinese Taiji boxing is very different from Tae Kwon Do. Taiji boxing emphasizes "gaining mastery by striking only after the enemy has struck," beating fast movements with slow motions, using gentleness to conquer, and bringing movement under control by static. Let us examine several actions from Taiji boxing: Stepping Back and Whirl Arms on Both Sides; Waving Hands Like Cloud; Working at Shuttles on Both Sides; Needle at the Bottom of the Sea; Apparent Close-Up, etc. From the above actions, we may have some basic ideas about the characteristics of Taiji boxing, such as circular moving, gentle and slow. A Taiji boxer must not show his real move, or must hide several real movements in an action attracting an opponent to attack or move first, then counterattack the exposed flaws in the attacker's movement. Since we are not experts in boxing, we will not attempt to judge which style is better, we merely want to use Taiji boxing as a metaphor to describe the Chinese characteristics of modesty and implication.

In fact, even if Tae Kwon Do does not exhibit Korean characteristics, Taiji boxing or Taiji sword fighting would have perfectly reflected the Chinese traits of modesty and implication.

Confucius had a famous saying about modesty: "If three persons walk together, there must be one able to be my teacher. I need to learn his strengths, and check and change my weaknesses by comparing his weaknesses."[29]

The founder of a sect of Taoism, Lao-tzu, said:

> Compromise can be for the sake of the overall interest, contraction can stretch, low-lying places can be full, destroy-

ing the old can establish the new, seizing less can gain more, and gaining more would lose. Therefore, the sages advocate the above principles to all people. Do not only be dependent on your own eyes, then you can see clearly; do not regard yourself as infallible, right and wrong can be distinguished more easily; do not praise yourself, then you will be successful; do not be too self-important, then you can be a leader. Just because you do not compete with anybody, nobody can compete with you . . .[30]

Lao-tzu also said:

Less speaking accords with the natural laws. As you can see, a strong fast wind is unable to last a morning; a storm cannot rain a whole day. What makes this so? The natural world! Even the force of nature cannot last too long, let alone a human?[31]

From these words, we can easily explain the characteristics of Taiji boxing or Taiji sword fighting.

Many people misunderstand Chinese modesty and implication to be glossing things over to stay on good terms, or even to be timid and overly cautious. Yes, Chinese people like to gloss things over to stay on good terms, and in a sense they may even be a little bit timid and overly cautious. For instance, many owners of Chinese restaurants or stores in America would not report minor robberies to the police as some other nationalities usually do. They want to make concessions to avoid trouble where they will be involved in numerous legal activities, even having to fight with the robbers in court. No matter what the results would be, it may cause the offending robbers or their comrades to come back and bring more trouble. Yet things often go contrary to their wishes; in this case, the robbers may come back more often because they are not punished for their crimes. Many Chinese Americans also do not want to be on a jury for similar reasons, particularly for trials in which any Chinese people may be involved.

However, we want to emphasize that though the above phenomenon might be true, and Chinese modesty and implication may mean glossing things over to stay on good terms to some extent, they are not simply timid and overly cautious. Let us take fire and water as a metaphor to explain. Fire always burns as hot and fiercely as it can. Fire has never changed its dynamic. But water is different. Water looks as if it is more generous, lenient, and calm because it can withstand almost everything you throw at it without striking back. Water will yield to force or pressure from you. But this does not mean that water will always be calm and gentle. Sometimes water may become violent, as in a raging river, a flood, or fierce waves. If people only consider water to be gentle without understanding its ability to be fierce, they will suffer from their mistakes. In a sense, the Korean War could be viewed as a result of the misunderstanding of Chinese modesty and implication by the West because of the gentle modesty and implication from the Minister of Foreign Affairs of the People's Republic of China, Zhou Enlai (he was also the Prime Minister).

The first Premier of the People's Republic of China, Zhou Enlai, was a typical example of Chinese modesty and implication. You could not see any "horns" (aggressive displays of one's talent) from Mr. Zhou which had been covered by his modesty and implication. During the Cultural Revolution, thousands of Red Guards surrounded the Great Hall of the People, and their representatives were arguing with Mr. Zhou about the Minister of Foreign Affairs, Mr. Chen Yi. Mr. Zhou explained his opinions to the representatives of the Red Guard neither superciliously nor obsequiously. As long as the representatives of the Red Guard could not persuade Mr. Zhou on a certain topic, they changed to another one; nevertheless, no matter what topics they changed or they wanted to change, eventually they were surprised to find out that they still came back to the original issue Mr. Zhou wanted to discuss. After ten hours of arguments, the representatives of the Red Guard fell asleep one after another until Mr. Zhou was the only one who was awake. People jokingly said that Mr. Zhou was playing Taiji boxing by being slow, gentle, but tough with the Red Guard.

From the above analysis, we can find out that the decision making of people influenced by Chinese modesty and implication may have at least three characteristics: hiding true intentions, hinting, and being tough as Taiji boxing.

First of all, to hide almost all "horns" is a result of decision making from Chinese modesty and implication. Many Western sports participants may openly state to the media, "I came here to the Olympic Games just to win the championship; otherwise, I would not have come. I am in very good shape for competition . . ." Almost no Chinese player will state in public that he or she came to the games to win the championship. They may express many modest and implicative words, such as "Friendship first, competition second"; "Winning or losing is temporary, but friendship is lasting"; "To draw on each other's merits and raise the level of competition together"; "I would not be dizzy with success, nor discouraged by failure." They may not show their true abilities before the games. Likewise, many Western businesspeople may state in public, "I do not come to your country for philanthropy (charity). I am here to conduct business to make money; otherwise, I would not come. Of course, I will legally make money, and follow the (game) rules." But Chinese business delegations would not express these kinds of words. They will tell you that they were visiting to help each other, for mutual friendships, and common interests. For example, Chinese companies in Africa would have never said that their visit was just for their own profits. The Chinese negotiations delegation forming the General Agreement on Tariffs and Trade (GATT) would not say that being a member of GATT was just for China's own profits, rather than good for many countries. Even for the American Most Favored Nation status (MFN), the Chinese side usually indicates that maintaining the Chinese status of MFN would be of benefit to both countries, and lack of it would hurt both sides.

Second, hinting could be a result of decision making from Chinese modesty and implication. Sometimes, Chinese modesty and implication may cause a dilemma by disguising the real intention or hiding true facts. Then, hinting must be employed. When a Chinese delegation comes to the United States for import/export business, they will state the purpose of their trip is to make friends, promote cooperation, and seek common interests. Of course, we cannot exclude the possibility of establishing friendships and cooperation to be a goal, or a goal for the first stage. Generally speaking, in this case, friendship and cooperation actually is a means, or a very vital means, to only seek their own interests in the end. Or let us put it another way: Without their own interests, they would not reach their real goal by only establishing friendships and cooperation. This is strategic to reach their actual goal to gain their own interests through establishing friendships and cooperation. In fact, their real end has been hidden under friendships, cooperation, and common interests. The author, Huang Quanyu, has been involved in several translations for and coordinations between the Chinese visiting delegation and the American parties. In 1988, a Chinese educational delegation came to America. Their real purpose, to enroll some American students to study in their university, was hidden under the slated purpose of mutual learning and friendships. During the negotiation, both parties did not have an agreement about the tuition and expenses of studying in China. The American side did not know or at least did not understand the real Chinese goal, and did not catch the hints from the Chinese side. They did not stay on this topic too long since they believed that the Chinese delegation had reached their goals for friendships and mutual learning through faculty exchange programs and visits to each other's campuses. A similar situation also happened to some other Chinese business delegations. Huang Quanyu had to simply tell the American side about the Chinese delegations' real ends. Understandably, both parties were then able to bargain and argue much more effectively.

A third result of decision making from Chinese modesty and implication is being as tough as Taiji boxing. We have previously addressed the characteristics of gaining mastery by striking only after the enemy has struck, beating fast movements with slow movements, using gentleness to conquer, and bringing movement under control by static, etc. Taiji boxing reflects Chinese modesty and implication. Therefore, here, "as tough as Taiji boxing" means that as a Western businessperson, when you deal with China or the Chinese people, you need great patience, which many Westerners have experienced. Without patience, you are unable to perform Taiji boxing. Likewise, without great patience, you are also unable to deal with the people who do Taiji boxing.

Noticeably, Chinese modesty and implication may not mean a weakness, or an incompetence. As we have previously mentioned, a Taiji boxer may hide several real movements in an action to attract an opponent to attack or move, then counterattack the flaws in the attacker's moves. This means that Chinese decision making from modesty and implication may imply hidden fierce counterstrikes. For example, in 1950, Mao Zedong delightedly led a Chinese delegation to visit the Soviet Union. But arrogant Joseph Vissarionovich Dzhugashvili Stalin did not treat Mao Zedong warmly. Mao Zedong had to wait more than four hours in the Kremlin to meet Stalin.[32] However, Mr. Mao did not show his unhappiness. Later, China played Taiji boxing with the Soviet Union for more than ten years until a serious ideological polemic arose in the 1960s, and even led to an armed clash in the 1970s between China and the Soviet Union. Another example, a vice president of an American company wanted to import Chinese pneumatic chairs through H.C.K. International. The author, Huang Quanyu, was not happy with the impolite and arrogant attitude of this vice president. This American gentleman seemingly thought that he was as important as the Savior (Redeemer) so that he could say any words to a supplier. Huang Quanyu decided to "punish" him with the Chinese way instead of advising him to behave himself directly. H.C.K. International did its best to choose and arrange a manufacturer to make samples, but when the American company accepted the quotations and the quality of the pneumatic chairs, H.C.K. told this vice president of the American company to wait until Mr. Huang came back from his vacation. This impolite and arrogant gentleman seemed to forget that he once acted like the Redeemer; he completely changed his attitude. What Mr. Huang used was "gaining mastery by striking only after the opponent has struck." In other words, do not strike back immediately (did not tell him to change his attitude at the beginning), but react to it at a better moment (let him know that in order to conduct business with the Chinese, he needs to change his attitude). Many people think that the customer is "King." We believe that the "customer is King" is a good idea only for sellers. In most cases, if buyers also think they are "King," they may not be wise and prudent business buyers. A vulgar businessperson thinks that the only thing from a buyer's hand is money. But a wise buyer thinks that the things from a qualified supplier are money as well. Therefore, if you are a Western buyer who knows about Chinese modesty and implication, you should know how to make your decision to deal with a Chinese supplier.

People who think that Chinese modesty and implication implies a weakness, or an incompetence may bring a serious consequence to themselves or their businesses.

DISCUSSION QUESTIONS

Saving Face

1. "Saving face" is as important in the West as it is in China. Why or why not?
2. Explain how the American influence of "original sin" differs from the Chinese notion of "fineness of human nature."
3. While "saving face" has important inferences in personal behavior, it has little significance in business dealings between Chinese and Western business organizations. Agree or disagree? Why?
4. "Why worry about saving face . . . a written contract is a written contract . . . it is legally binding." Do you agree with this way of thinking? Why or why not?

The Individual and the Collective

1. Since the late 1970s President Jimmy Carter and all other U.S. presidents since (with the possible exception of Ronald Reagan) have repeatedly talked about making human rights a major portion of their foreign policy. What impact, if any, does the individual versus collective have on the U.S. human rights policy?
2. Do you think the personal pronouns "I" and "we" really matter, or is this merely some quirk of language development thousands or years ago?
3. Discuss the table tennis example. What are its ramifications today?
4. Compare the Chinese connotation of individual versus collective with other parts of the world (e.g., Japan, Germany, Brazil, Saudi Arabia).

Equality

1. Having people of different backgrounds run a race may be interesting, but what does it have to do with business decision making?
2. Can competition among individuals be a motivator in China? Why or why not?
3. How are political equality and social equality related? How are they different?
4. Is it possible to separate "saving face" from issues of "equality?" and "individuality?" Why or why not?

Hierarchy

1. Why is the concept of hierarchy so important in China? How is hierarchy related to terms such as status and importance?
2. Discuss the internal (within the enterprise) and external (among enterprises or between an enterprise and a governmental unit) complexities of hierarchy.
3. What does the term "control" have to do with hierarchy? Is this important? Why or why not?
4. Compare and contrast the terms "power" and "authority." Do they always go hand in hand? Why or why not?

Social Role and Self

1. Discuss the term "benevolence."
2. Compare and contrast role expectations and behavioral norms.
3. Distinguish among terms "roles," "responsibilities," and "rights."
4. When (if ever) do social roles become more important in Chinese culture than individual independent? Discuss the implications for business enterprises.

Modesty and Implication

1. As Westerners, what can we learn about business decision making from the boxing example?

2. Modesty implies "timid and cautious." Agree or disagree? Why?
3. Can modesty be a hinderance to China-West business dealings? Why?
4. Can modesty be an aid to China-West business dealings? Why?

REFERENCE NOTES

1. Chen Jie, "Motorola in China," *People's Daily* (January 20, 1995): 2nd page.
2. Hu Wenzhong and Cornelius L. Grove, *Encountering the Chinese: A Guide for Americans* (Yarmouth, ME: Intercultural Press, 1991), 115, 116.
3. Confucius, "The Analects of Confucius," in *Concise Edition of the Material of the Chinese Philosophy*, The History of the Chinese Philosophy Group of the Philosophy Research Institute of the Chinese Academy of Sciences (Eds.), The Teaching and Research Room of the History of Chinese Philosophy of the Philosophy Department of the Beijing University, 2nd ed. (Beijing: Chinese Publishing House, 1973), 51.
4. In terms of various levels of guests, the governments have policies to fix a "ceiling" of the quality of a meal. At that time, for Dr. Peterman's level, about ten *yuan*, which was equal to approximately 8 percent of a professor's monthly salary, was the standard for his one meal.
5. United States Foreign Policy 1972 (Washington, DC: Department of State Public Action, Number 8699, April 1973), 343.
6. Information was from an article about the conflict of protection of intellectual property rights between China and the United States in *The Cincinnati Enquirer,* February 5, 1995.
7. Maurice N. Richter Jr. *Exploring Sociology,* (Itasca, IL: F.E. Peacock Publishers, 1987), 130.
8. Xia Wa, "Beginning and End–The Whole Story of Disturbance from He Zhili," *China Sport* (November 21, 1994), 6-11.
9. Hu Wenzhong and Cornelius L. Grove, 96-97.
10. Huang Quanyu, Book review of *Encountering the Chinese: Guide for Americans* by Hu Wenzhong and Cornelius Grove, *China Review International.* (1995, Volume 2, No. 1), 76.
11. Huang Quanyu, Richard Andrulis, and Chen Tong, *A Guide to Successful Relations with the Chinese: Opening the Great Wall's Gate,* (Binghamton, NY: The Haworth Press, 1994), 38.
12. Huang Quanyu, *Conceptual Perplexity and Analysis in Chinese Education,* (Oxford, OH: Miami University, 1993), 125.
13. Maurice N. Richter Jr., 130.
14. Confucius, "Confucius," in *Concise Edition of the Chinese Philosophy,* 43-45.

15. Ibid, 46.
16. Huang Quanyu, Richard Andrulis, and Chen Tong, 39.
17. Ibid, 20.
18. Confucius, 66.
19. Emil J. Haller and Kenneth A. Strike, *An Introduction to Educational Administration: Social, Legal, and Ethical Perspectives*, (White Plains, NY: Longman, 1986), 18-19.
20. She was Mao Zedong's wife. She and her partners, Wang Hongwen, Zhang Chunjiao, and Yao Wenyuan were the so-called "Gang of Four." They were in power and did countless terrible things during the Cultural Revolution.
21. Actually, he was the last Emperor of China. After the Qing Dynasty was overthrown by Xinhai Revolution in 1911, Yuan recontrolled his Beiyang Troop, and forced Dr. Sun Yat-sen to abdicate the presidential position to him. He was not satisfied with "President"; he had himself enthroned as an Emperor on the first day of 1916. However, he had to cancel the autocratic monarchy after he was Emperor for only eighty-three days because of political and military pressure from the whole country.
22. In the Qing dynasty, the coastal provinces of Liaoning, Hebei, and Shangdong were called Beiyang.
23. This section has heavily relied on some parts of the dissertation of Huang Quanyu, *Conceptual Perplexity and Analysis in Chinese Education*, (Oxford, OH: Miami University, 1993); and the work of Huang Quanyu, Richard Andrulis, and Chen Tong. *A Guide to Successful Relations with the Chinese: Opening the Great Wall's Gate*, (Binghamton, NY: The Haworth Press, 1994).
24. Many people believe that *The Spring and Autumn Annals* and some other classical works were revised by Confucius. But it must be noted that the most important work of researching Confucius, *The Analects of Confucius,* was written by his second generation students, and not Confucius himself.
25. Henrik Ibsen, "A Doll's House," in *Six Plays by Henrik Ibsen*, trans. Eva Le Gallienne, (NY: Random House, 1978), 77.
26. Gu Xiegang, *A Simple Explanation to the Origin and Development of Characters*, (Beijing: Rong Bao Publishing House, 1979), 408.
27. Confucius, 49.
28. Ibid, 42.
29. Confucius, 55.
30. Lao-tzu, "Lao-tzu," in *Concise Edition of the Chinese Philosophy*, 239.
31. Ibid, 252.
32. Li Zhirui, *The Private Life of Chairman Mao*, (Taibei, Taiwan: Time Publisher, 1994), 210.

Chapter 8

Modes of Thinking

"John Dewey once made a most perceptive distinction between 'thinking' and 'thought.' Thinking, he observed, is an active, vital, dynamic process full of adventure and excitement, while thought is the end of this process, both its fruit and its demise unless the thought arrived at by thinking leads to more thinking."[1] In our opinion, however, thinking is the internal basis of action, while action is the external result of thinking. With this reasoning, a certain way of thinking must relate to a certain way of acting. Therefore, modes of thinking must affect decision making and behavior norms. We will discuss how traditional modes of thinking influence Chinese decision making in this part.

UNITY OF OPPOSITES

As we mentioned previously, the Chinese dialectic of *yin* and *yang* considers that the origin or essence of the universe consists of two poles such as universality and individuality, subject and object, positive and negative, living and dead, male and female. . . . As we can see, the *yin* and the *yang* are interdependent but opposite to each other as well. Therefore, based on the idea of the *yin* and the *yang*, the dialectics of "unity and opposite" were gradually used to view the world–the natural world and human society–by the Chinese people. All their thought is oriented around the idea that everything is a part of a contradictory pair and that the world changes as a result of the regularity of these contradictions. As a certain result, the Chinese people gradually accepted the mode of thinking of "unity and opposite."

Actually, "one divides into two" and "two combine into one" can be viewed as two different ways to understand the "unity of opposites." In other words, one (origin or essence of the universe) divides into two (the *yin* and the *yang*); or two (the *yin* and the *yang*) combine into one (origin or essence of the universe). No matter whether the former or the latter, the Chinese people believe that the *yin* and the *yang* are mutually promotion and restraint, interaction/interconnection and repelling one another; in short, interdependent but opposite to each other. Since the Chinese people have accepted the mode of thinking of unity and opposite, they would not only like to divide one into two, or combine two into one, but they would also like to use the ideas of the changing, developing, and transforming of a contradiction to consider the law of the unity of opposites.

In order to explain it better, let us take a well-known Chinese story, "The Old Man on the Frontier Lost his Mare," as an example:

> There was an old man who lived near the Great Wall. One day, his horse ran way. His relatives, friends, and neighbors came to comfort him. He, however, seemingly did not care about it. He said, "Who knows? Losing my horse may be a good thing."
>
> Not too long after, his horse not only came back by itself, but led a better horse back as well. The people blessed him. The old man said, "I am not sure about that. This could be a bad thing."
>
> After several days, his son broke his leg after falling off the new horse. And then, the people came to comfort him one after another again. The old man said surprisingly, "Who knows? This might bring good luck to me."
>
> Just after he spoke, a war broke out. All of the young people were forced to join the army. Many of them died or were wounded; many families were broken up or scattered. The son of the old man was not forced to joint the army because of his broken leg. The father and son were safe.[2]

The conclusion of this story is that when the old man on the frontier lost his mare, who could have guessed it was a blessing? Misfortune may prove to be a blessing in disguise.

From this story, we can see how the Chinese people would not only like the notion of dividing one into two, or combining two into one, to consider their decisions, but also like the notion of using the ideas of the changing, developing, and transforming of a contradiction to consider the law of the unity of opposites. Namely, anything could imply the two sides: the good and the bad. Moreover, a bad thing could become a good thing, and a good thing could also turn into a bad one.

On the one hand, the mode of thinking with the law of the unity of opposites makes the Chinese people view things completely; on the other hand, it may also make the Chinese people conservative to some extent. For instance, being hardworking and thrifty are popular traditional Chinese ideas. So, most Chinese people prefer to save their money in banks. Why do people save money rather than consume? There are several Chinese sayings that could offer answers. "Be prepared for danger in times of peace," "Fear of disturbance in the rear," "A gain may turn out to be a loss," "The mantis stalks the cicada, unperish," and "Even the wise are not free from error." In brief, when you are in good condition, you should prepare yourself to be ready for any unexpected misfortune that may happen to you. Hence, saving money is for security. Now there are about two thousand billion yuans of the Chinese individuals' savings in the Chinese banks. This is approximately equal to two years of the Chinese gross domestic product (GDP). Obviously, on the one hand, this is very good for China's reinvestments and constructions for thousands of huge projects; on the other hand, those monies could be a dangerous tiger in a cage that might dash out anytime. If people lose their confidence in the banks someday and start a run on them or begin panic purchasing, these two years of work output equivalency could break the Chinese economy. When every household hands its financial securities to the government, the government, in a sense, has been placed in a critical yet subtly dangerous situation.

The philosophy of unity and opposite, particularly the ideas of the changing, developing, and transforming of a contradiction of the law of the unity of opposite has been used in today's business decision making in China. Let us take Wu Shuwang, a former farmer and current successful businessman, as an example. Mr. Wu, who was a poor peasant fifteen years ago, has used the dialectics of unity and opposite from *The Art of War* by Sun Tzu and *The Romance of the Three Kingdoms* to successfully direct his business decision making for more than ten years. Now, he is not only a successful industrialist and tycoon but serves as a guest professor at a well-known Chinese university—Nankai University. His work, *Philosophy and Business Art*, has been published as a text for college students.

One day he was invited to give a lecture about "Briskly Marketing in a Slack Season" in the Philosophy Department of Nankai University. First, he told a story from *The Romance of the Three Kingdoms* about the strategy of Kongming of "attracting the enemy with bait, retreating on one's own initiative." Kongming had merely 3,000 soldiers but was forced to fight with the 100,000 troops of Cao Cao. He assigned several ambushes around the Bowang Mountain where the road was narrow with dry woods on both sides. Kongming ordered Zhao Zilong and Liu Bei to "fight" with Cao Cao's troops, but "to fail, not win" until seeing a signal fire, then turn back upon them. Kongming defeated the 100,000 troops of Cao Cao by fire and his 3,000 soldiers. Mr. Wu said:

> Two years ago, I was in as difficult a situation as Kongming was. Even though I have manufactured new products—'Space Cotton Shirts,' I was short of capital and it was the off season. The cost of a 'Space Cotton Shirt' was 66 yuans, but the price per shirt would be 76 yuans in a busy season. I decided to use the tactic of Kongming, 'attracting the enemy with bait, retreating on my own initiative' to create a 'brisk market in a dull season.' I announced that the people who placed their orders with payments in May could gain a priority price of 60 yuans per shirt; 66 yuans per shirt in June; 72 yuans per shirt in July; 88 yuans per shirt in August . . . I received about 6 million yuans of orders in May. The dull season became a busy season. In that year, I didn't lose any money, but made about 1.5 million yuans of profits! By using this strategy of Kongming, I had turned 'losing' into 'making' . . .[3]

In fact, *The Art of War* by Sun Tzu and *The Romance of the Three Kingdoms* reflected the dialectics and the mode of thinking of unity and opposite. All examples we cite from these two works in different chapters of our book are evidence to support or prove our argument. Particularly, applying the ideas of the changing, developing, and transforming of a contradiction of the law of the unity of opposites was vividly described and exposed in the military battles, diplomatic competitions, and political conflicts in the two works. Along with the development of a market economy in China, we believe that the works about applying ancient Chinese military strategies to the contemporary business field will soon appear with frequency in China.

The dialectics and the mode of thinking of unity and opposite, and the ideas of the changing, developing, and transforming of a contradiction to the law of the unity of opposites (which had influenced or even directed the Chinese ancient military decision making and the art of war) have also been strongly affecting or even ruling Chinese diplomatic, political, and business decision making. For example, we can make a substantially long list of such policy decision making of the unity of opposites:

- while emphasizing the four adherences (to adhere to the Communist Party Leadership, Marxism and Mao Zedong Thought, the Proletarian Dictatorship, and the Socialist Path), carrying out the Movement of Reforming and Opening
- developing the economy while controlling "spiritual development"
- developing a market economy but also paying greater attention to macroadjustment/controlling
- encouraging the special economic zones to develop but being aware of the balance of the minority autonomous regions' development
- allowing individual enterprises to boom and attempt to rescue/ reform the state-owned enterprises
- allowing some of the people to be rich while preventing the gap from becoming too large between rich and poor
- encouraging the cadres to be professionals/experts while requiring their ideological loyalty
- maintaining a good Sino-American relationship but fighting with the United States in many cases

- adhering to the concept of a united mother-land while encouraging "one country with two systems"[4]

Many Western people cannot understand the above "mutually contradicting" policies in China and are at a loss as to how to deal with these contradictions. If you can understand the philosophy of unity and opposite, and the idea of the changing, developing, and transforming of a contradiction of the law of the unity of opposites, you should be able to understand the roots of why and how the Chinese make these kinds of policy decisions.

TWO UNBALANCED PAIRS

The goal of the dialectics of unity and opposite is to reach the level of the golden mean in order to balance the two sides and avoid any radical results. Unfortunately, when the Chinese people apply the dialectics of unity and opposite, they have not always achieved the goal to balance the two sides. On the issue of how to understand the world, the Chinese lose the two critical balances so that many policy decisions have inborn shortcomings.

Stressing Universality and Ignoring Individuality

Chinese people like to view a situation as a whole in which any possible relationship could be considered. Let us take traditional Chinese medicine as our example.

Traditional Chinese medicine considers the human being as an intermediary between nature and society. For this reason, the awareness of physiology and pathology is more than a medical technology, but a way of understanding human beings and nature. When a doctor diagnoses a patient, the doctor must consider the natural condition and the social situation of the patient as part of the "concept of the whole." For example, the five human internal organs are related to the four seasons of nature. That is why on an overcast and rainy day, some people's joints may ache, and a change of seasons may cause some people to become ill. Even the social situation of a patient might stimulate the change of the functions of his or her internal organs. Traditional Chinese medicine thought the heart would be hurt by fear, the liver by anger, and the lungs by sadness. When a social situation caused a patient to be frightened, angry, or sad, the internal organs would have problems adjusting. This was referred to as "treating a person before curing his or her sickness."

This concept of the human body views its various parts as forming an organic whole. Accordingly, the functions of the organs are intertwined by a common cause. A problem within an organ may influence the whole body, and the sickness of the whole body may be caused by one organ. Interestingly enough, the human kidney looks very much like the human ear, but in terms of anatomy, most people think that there is no relationship between the kidney and the ear. However, the Chinese have a saying, "Like attracts like." Much clinical evidence has proven that diseases of the kidneys could influence the functions of hearing and balance. According to the "concept of the whole," all human organs are linked to each other. Hence, traditional Chinese medicine only needs four methods of diagnosis: (1) observation of the patient's complexion, expression, movements, and tongue; (2) auscultation and smelling; (3) interrogation, and (4) pulse feeling and palpation.[5] These methods of diagnosis are quite simple. They do not require surgical operations or X rays that are powerful means for the probing microscopic analysis of the individual, possibly to their detriment by not considering the whole person.

The five elements, metal, wood, water, fire, and earth, were held by the ancients to compose the physical universe. Later, they were not only used in traditional Chinese medicine to explain various physiological and pathological phenomena, but were also applied to construct the governmental organizations in which five main departments control each other just as the principle of mutual promotion and restraint between the five elements: wood promoted fire; fire restrained metal; water restrained fire, etc. Interestingly enough, the government of the Republic of China in Taiwan consists of five main branches: Executive, Legislative, Judicial, Examination, and Control. There are five stars (symbolic for the workers, peasants, soldiers, students, and businesspeople) in the national flag of the People's Republic of China. Many people believe that these "fives" are not coincidences, but some kind of symbolic connection to the five elements.

Generally speaking, to view the situation as a whole is good, but the analysis of the individual, on the other side, must be emphasized. Otherwise, this characteristic way of thinking is unbalanced. The universe is comprised of various individuals. Without the analysis of individuals, we would be unable to understand individuality. Likewise, without understanding individuality, we would be unable to really understand the universe. Furthermore, without understanding individuality, we would be unable to develop science. Obviously, without operations or X rays, people could not really understand the kidney, heart, liver, lungs and the other human organs. This was a technical and scientific tragedy in China that was derived from the way of thinking.

When stressing universality and ignoring individuality has been extended into human social life, this becomes a behavioral norm to emphasize the collective and neglect the individual. In Chinese culture, if one faces an option between public benefits and private profit, public benefits must be emphasized; between society and the individual, society should be chosen. With this mode of thinking and behavioral norms, the policy decision making or business decision making have become unbalanced between the collective and the individuals. For instance, if there is a conflict between a country's interests and individual benefits, the policy decision making would favor the country rather than the individuals. Or when there is a conflict between country construction and individual consumption, policy decision making will favor the former rather than the latter. When there is an opportunity for a loan, for export trade, or for gaining a priority policy between a state-owned enterprise and an individual company, the scale will certainly be inclined to favor the state-owned enterprise.

No wonder there is a Chinese saying that is against the natural law and common sense: "When the main stream is high, the small streams rise; when the main stream is low, the small stream runs dry–individual well-being depends on collective prosperity." Many people believe that in most cases, the common sense opposite is that because the small streams run together to form the main stream, only when the small streams rise are the main streams high, and when the small streams run dry, the main stream is low.

There was an article in the *People's Daily* (February 14, 1996), titled "Officials Force Individuals to Be Rich and/or Force Officials to Make Individuals Rich." Compared with the old policies to ignore individual profits, the title looked refreshing and original, and attracted people's eyes. The paper was to record a special interview with a young scholar who formulated a program, "Officials Force Individuals to Be Rich," for the Jiyuan city government of Henan Province. Essentially, the program intended to force officials to make the individuals rich. Since individuals were being emphasized, the idea of the program seemed quite original; but we feel that the paper was trying to entice the public with claptrap. In fact, the basic idea of the program has not yet broken with the conventions of the traditional Chinese mode of thinking–stressing universality and ignoring individuality. Here, to be rich is an individual affair that must rely on individual will. A country, government, or society only can provide an environment in which individuals find the conditions to be rich. But a country, government, or society is unable to force individuals to be rich. Very simply, if I am not willing to be rich, I can throw your million dollars away. The key point is that a collective, social, or government action will be unable to override individual will. Without analyzing the individual, we cannot understand the individual; without understanding the individual, we cannot value the individual; without valuing the individual, we cannot realize how important it is to respect the individual will. Believing officials can force individuals to be rich is to think that individual will can be changed or controlled by others is not logical. Accordingly, the idea of the program looks fresh, but, in the final analysis, it is still within the Chinese conventions of the traditional mode of thinking.

Emphasizing Imaginative Thinking and Underestimating Abstract Thinking

First, let us understand the two definitions of imaginative thinking and abstract thinking. Based on the definition of "imagination" from *The Random House College Dictionary*, we understand that "imaginative thinking" is reproducing images stored in the memory under the suggestion of associated images, or of recombining former experiences to create new images. According to the definition of "abstract" in the *Modern Chinese Dictionary*, it is merely theoretical and cannot be experienced. Hence, abstract thinking is a theoretical idea that cannot be experienced. As we can see, the delicate "connections" of both are that imaginative thinking needs to "recombine former experiences," but abstract thinking "cannot be experienced."

A famous sinologist in Britain, Joseph Needham, outlined detailed statistics and an analysis of the development of Chinese science and technology in his book *Science and Civilization in China*. In the three areas of theory, application, and practice, Chinese science and technology were further developed in application and practice, but were backwards in theory. We agree with his conclusion. For example, if a patient has a stiff neck, almost every doctor of traditional Chinese medicine knows how to insert two acupuncture needles into the patient's hand and finger to solve this problem in a few minutes. In other words, according to their direct or indirect experiences, they know very well what they need to do and how they should solve the problem. If you ask doctors why this method is effective, they may not really know because they may not think the reason is important. As long as their method works, why do they need to know or care why it works? The traditional Chinese medicine men paid greater attention to practical and applied experiences. Chinese science and technology also followed the same pattern of thought. Many works of science and technology merely recorded the experience or only described the natural event without probing the underlying theory or research. For instance, the appearance of the comet was recorded at least 500 times in China before 1910. These records included the first time Halley's Comet was seen in 613 BC. Interestingly, there were merely records of sightings without any theoretical research. However, in Britain, Edmund Halley discovered the comet's average cycle in the seventeenth century.

Experience is limited by time and space. A correct past experience may be wrong tomorrow, and a temporary effect may not be permanent. A certain procedure may be effective with patient A, but probably would not be effective with every Chinese person, or with an American. Even though experience needs to be raised to the level of theory, this is not the typical way of thinking for the Chinese.

China, an ancient civilization with its four great inventions (gunpower, the compass, papermaking, and printing) and many championships of the world, is presently backward in science and technology. A critical cause was the way in which civilization overemphasized practicality and experience, as exemplified by the practice of acupuncture without scientific theory. In many cases, theory was seen to have little practicality; the law of universal gravitation and other scientific theories are just accidental curiosities.[6]

One of the necessary results of emphasizing experience and despising theory is that experience has become superior as a mode of thought. Furthermore, one of the necessary results of experience being superior is the direction of decision making by experience. From ordinary people to many intellectuals, from businesspeople to politicians, people like to make decisions based on their past successful and effective experiences.

The industry behind "the third line" in China could be an example. What does the expression "the third line" mean? If the military terms frontline and rear are viewed as the first line and the second line, the third line would mean the areas that are behind the rear. In the 1960s and the 1970s, the Chinese leaders believed that World War III would be impossible to avoid. They decided to build modern factories inland and move the coastal area modern manufacturers such as those in Shanghai, etc., to more remote areas, such as Sichuan or Guizhou provinces, the mountain areas in southwestern China.

With the Chinese historical experience, Sichuan was the great rear of China. The troops of Genghis Khan once made a clean sweep of Asia and Europe without any opponent except the Mongolian troops who were blocked in Sichuan for fifty-two years—more than half a century. During World War II, the Japanese army dashed around madly in China, but they were eventually blocked in Sichuan until the Japanese troops gave up and the war ended. With this war experience, the Chinese leaders decided on a great plan to construct the industry behind the third line; unfortunately, the leaders forgot to consider other prominent factors such as transportation, material resources, electrical power, and trained/skilled human resources.

Now the industry behind the third line, on the one hand, is playing a role to close the gap between the coastal area and the interior of China; on the other hand, quite a few factories have become a drain for China to some extent because of the cost component or lack of transportation, material resources, power, and trained/skilled human resources.

This plan for the whole country was called the "Great Third Line." Each province, however, also was required to construct their own "small third line" to build factories in or move the manufacturers from cities to their own mountain or countryside areas. If quite a few factories of the Great Third Line had become a drain on China's economic well-being to some extent, many of the factories of those small third lines of each province or autonomous region became so heavy a drain that the governments have had to abandon them because of market, transportation, material resources, power, and trained/skilled human resources.

Indeed, in modern war, the frontline and rear have not been as clear as in past wars. Moving factories to the rear, dividing big manufacturers into small ones, and spreading factories from cities to the vast countryside were decided from past war policy experiences. In a sense, before an attack from the enemy, China had defeated itself by these strategic choice movements.

The decision of giving priority to the development of the steel industry and heavy industry in the 1950s was to imitate the relatively successful experiences of the Soviet Union. Unfortunately, it did not consider the situation that in China agriculture and the economic base were so poor. Of course, without believing experience to be superior, the idea of giving priority to the development of the steel industry and heavy industry would not have been accepted. Considering experience to be superior has been a problem among many Chinese, including businesspeople and politicians.

When one consciously or unconsciously considers experience to be superior, he or she may not realize this could be a problem. If we question the Chinese for believing experience to be superior, we may not realize that this notion is also quite popular in America. Evidently, many hiring decisions in America are based on experience. We can see that experience has been strongly emphasized as a requirement for a position. You may even receive a letter from an organization which opens with, "... your strong credentials have given us a deep impression. However, you do not have the experience to meet our requirements..." How contradictory this superiority of experience is. First, if every organization requires an applicant to have experience before they can offer a position, how can one gain experience in such a position without an opportunity? In other words, how can I get experience if nobody offers me a position? Many American teenagers can relate to this after being unable to secure a job of their choice. Second, valuing experience without valuing ability is putting the cart before the horse. Not everyone has ability, but everyone can have experience as long as he or she was once in the position. The people with experience may not have ability, but the persons with ability can get experience easily if given a chance. The persons with ability are able to perform well in the position, but the people with experience may not be able to perform well in the position. The business organizations in America make their personnel staffing decisions based on experience. This is just as a Chinese saying, "Keeping the glittering casket and giving the pearls back to the seller shows lack of judgment."

Actually, we have indirectly addressed how the Chinese modes of thinking have affected decision making in the other chapters and sections. Hence, we do not analyze many examples in this section. Believably, the readers can prove our ideas about modes of thinking that influence Chinese decision making by reading examples in the other chapters or sections on their own.

DISCUSSION QUESTIONS

1. Can the idea of unity of opposite be applied to Western decision making?
2. While "The Old Man on the Frontier Lost His Mare" is an interesting story of the past, can we learn anything from it to help Western organization to business with a Chinese enterprise today?
3. *The Romance of the Three Kingdoms* deals with baiting the enemy. Can this story teach a Western decision maker in marketing any tools for baiting the competition?

4. Explain "mutual contradiction." Why might it be useful tool for modern decision making?
5. The five elements (metal, wood, water, fire, and earth) help us to better understand the Chinese modes of thinking. Do you see any parallel in the way the five universal elements which tie to decision making and the marketing 4Ps (product, price, promotion/advertising, and place/distribution) used in Western business decision making?

REFERENCE NOTES

1. Jonas F. Soltis, *An Introduction to the Analysis of Educational Concepts*, (Reading, MA: Addison-Wesley Publishing Company, 1968), ix.
2. Yuan Lin and Shen Tongheng, Eds., *The Stories of Chinese Idioms*, (Shenyang: Liaoning People's Publishing House, 1981), 497-498.
3. Xia Di, "A peasant lectured on the university platform," *The People's Daily*, February 12, 1996.
4. "One country with two systems" is an idea of Deng Xiaoping on how to treat Taiwan, Hong Kong, and Mocao issues. This means one country (China) can contain and maintain two different social systems–the Socialist social system and Capitalist social system, in different regions at the same time.
5. Huang Quanyu, Richard Andrulis, and Chen Tong, *A Guide to Successful Business Relations with the Chinese: Opening the Great Wall's Gate*, (Binghamton, NY: The Haworth Press, 1994), 69-70.
6. Ibid, 68-69.

Epilogue

When we were writing this book, the United State sent one aircraft carrier after another to the Taiwan Strait where China was operating its largest military exercise in close proximity to Taiwan. The U.S.S. Nimitz and the U.S.S. Independence, along with about sixteen warships and more than two hundred planes, comprise the strongest military concentration in Asia since the Vietnam War. The Chinese and U.S. military forces were closer day by day. The financial markets in Taiwan were in chaos with stocks and real estate slumping, people were swarming toward the banks to exchange Taiwan money to U.S. dollars, and huge amounts of funds were being transferred to foreign countries. Another "Bosnia" tragedy? Another "Vietnam War" or "Korean War"? While nobody knew what would occur, everybody knew anything could happen! As we can see, this conflict was occurring under a big political background in which the Chinese leadership was preparing for the pro-Deng Xiaoping era; a special election was being conducted at the crucial moment in Taiwan; and the American election was becoming more complicated and confusing. Even though President Clinton won re-election, the opposition party Republicans hold substantial power at all levels of government. Thus, the future of national policy is not clear as the twentieth century winds down in the United States. Any decision making about this conflict from any of these three groups, such as intended or unintended action to please the electorate, will influence each other, or may bring unexpected suffering to Asia or the world.

On one hand, with our deep concerns we are opening our eyes to watch for decision-making tendencies or developments from this conflict. On the other hand, we are amazed to discover so many strategies and tactics about decision making, which we have discussed in our book, are being used during this conflict. These include:

- hiding an advance in retreat, or hiding a retreat in an advance
- advance in form but retreat in essence, or retreat in form but advance in essence
- associating with those distant from you and attacking those close by, or attacking those distant from you and associating with those close by
- will you survive when you are put in deadly peril?
- mutual promotion and restraint between what is false and true
- knowing the real reaction from your enemy by probing or touching
- giving in order to take
- to be down first in order to be up later
- being devious in order to be direct
- release in order to catch, to lose a battle, to win a war, etc.

This, from another perspective, is evidence that our book is appropriate for publication.

This book addressed the topic of business decision making in China. It was written to be a useful reference volume for Western businesspeople and professional consultants. Additionally, many others, especially Western government leaders and advanced business and economics students, along with their professors, should find the book influential in assisting their understanding of the world's most-populated country. Advanced students and scholars in the social sciences can also benefit from the lessons detailed in this book. All readers should appreciate and directly benefit from the rich illustrative examples, which not only orchestrate Chinese decision making, but also ease in the comprehension of lessons that Westerns can learn regarding the intricacies of successful business activities with the Chinese.

The topics and contents addressed in this book have been directly and indirectly tied to many historical and contemporary events. We have attempted to relate universal truths to present-day business decision making in China. But what about the future? What does it hold for China? We do not propose that we have the answers, for we may not even have the questions. But we can offer some topics for thoughtful consideration that may well become some of the key strategic issues of the future.

Will China continue its market economy experimentation? Undeniably, China will continue to test the market economic system. That is the easy answer; the tougher question about the implementation and time for China's movement toward a free market economic system is much more difficult to answer. While China has decidedly moved toward supply and demand economics in some ways, in others it clearly has not. The SEZs and various experimental plans have varying degrees of success no matter how they are viewed and measured. In short, China is not an isolated country; therefore, the Chinese movements or issues may become the world's issue. Any event in Asia, the Pacific Rim, or the world may relate to China. For example, the current Taiwan issue is one that certainly will repeatedly surface as an issue in the next several years. As we write this epilogue, recent events in Hong Kong have been making headlines in global news. The transition of political and economic-based power has begun. The Chinese government's actions of appointing and influencing the key leadership selection is still in process. The transfer from the British to the Chinese presents not only problems but opportunities for the region. The direction and momentum of change are difficult to predict. Other major potential issues include the 1997-and-beyond future of Hong Kong, the promarket policies of a changing political paradigm in Vietnam, and the political and economic future of North Korea. Lesser, but still salient topics affecting China over the next decade could include the economic progress and political strategic direction that takes place all over the world, but especially Cuba, Singapore and the southeastern Asian region, Russia and its old allied block, India, and Japan.

We have enjoyed writing this volume about decision making in China; we hope it will be useful to those interested in studying China's business structure, decision making, and culture. Additionally, it is hoped that this book will be an asset for anyone interested in the world's economic development as we approach the twenty-first century, and especially those presently conducting and those contemplating doing business in or with the 1.2 billion people of the People's Republic of China.

Index

Abstract thinking, *x*,289,290. *See also* Imaginative thinking
Agricultural Bank of China, 43. *See also* Bank of China; Bank of Communications of China; Industrial and Commercial Bank of China; People's Bank of China; People's Construction Bank of China
Alliance and the Coalition, 156. *See also* Su Qin; Zhang Yi
Amway distribution system, 66. *See also* Multilayered distribution network system of Amway
Analects of Confucius, The, 133
Anti-peaceful-evolution, 114
Aomen, 12. *See also* Macao
April 5th Movement at Tian'anmen Square, 111. *See also* Event at Tian'anmen Square
Armed Police, 50
Art of War of Sun Tzu, The, x,xvii, 149,160,177,211,284. *See also* Sun Bin
Associating with those distant from you and attacking those close by, 155,158,296. *See also* Alliance and the Coalition; attacking those distant from you and associating with those close by; Su Qin; Zhang Yi
Association of Industry and Commerce, 43

Attacking those distant from you and associating with those close by, 155,158,159,296. *See also* Alliance and the coalition; associating with those distance from you and attacking those close by; Su Qin; Zhang Yi

Bank of China, 43,47. *See also* Agricultural Bank of China; Bank of Communications of China; Industrial and Commercial Bank of China; People's Bank of China; People's Construction Bank of China
Bank of China Investment, 43. *See also* People's Bank of China
Bank of Communications of China, 43. *See also* Agricultural Bank of China; Bank of China; Industrial and Commercial Bank of China; People's Bank of China; People's Construction Bank of China
Bank of Shanghai Pudong Development, 43. *See also* People's Bank of China
Bank of Shenzhen Development, 43. *See also* People's Bank of China

299

Battalion political instructor, 6. *See also* Political instructor
Behavior norms, *x*,281. *See also* Modes of thinking; role norms
Beijing, *ix,xviii*,32,44,47,57,58,82, 93,115,188
Beijing opera, 187
"Big secretary," 127. *See also* "Confidential secretary"; "small secretary"; "written secretary"
Bill Clinton, 16,138,139,251
Clinton Administration, 171,231
Birth control education, 3
Black Snow, 151. *See also* Korean War
"Blindly choosing stones to cross a river," 83,84,100. *See also* Movement of Reforming and Opening
*Book of Changes, The, xvii,*150,214. *See also Yin* and *Yang*
divine, 150
Book of Mencius, The, 133
Bridge game, *xiii*
Bush, George, 16,260

Cadres, 1,6,8,23,61,63,84,93,94,138, 139,182,247,285. *See also* Paying tuition
senior cadres, 37,263
Cao Cao, 161,162,163,164,190,191, 192,203,204,205,206,207, 284. *See also* Kongming; Liu Bei; *Romance of the Three Kingdoms, The*
Cargo ship, "Yinhe," 155
CCP, 93,94. *See also* Chinese Communist Party
Central Advisory Commission, 59,60
Central Commission for Guiding Party Consideration, 59,60

Central Committee of the CCP, 61,94,97. *See also* Central Committee of the Chinese Communist Party
Central Committee of the Chinese Communist Party, 56,59,62, 72,73,78,104,105,114,115, 126,127. *See also* Central Committee of the CCP
Central government, 26,37,38,39,47, 56,59,62,65,74,75,77,78,79, 116,244,245. *See also* Central Committee of the CCP; Chinese People's Political Consultative Conference; National People's Congress; State Council
Central Supervisory Committee, 257
Ministry of Commerce, 31
Ministry of Domestic Trade, 225
Ministry of Finance, 46
Ministry of Foreign Affairs, 59,65, 225,272
Ministry of Foreign Economic Relations and Trade, 25,35, 36,39,52,74
Ministry of Justice, 257
Central Military Committee, 61. *See also* Central Military Committee of the Party
Central Military Committee of the Party, 64
People's Liberation Army, 1,61, 93,114
Central Supervisory Committee, 257. *See also* Chinese Communist Party's Central Commission for Discipline Inspection; Ministry of Justice
Chairman of the Central Committee, 61. *See also* Mao Zedong

Index

Changeability, 100,101,104,122,213. *See also* Inflexibility
Charismatic authority, 261. *See also* Legal authority; traditional authority
Chen Tong, *x,xix,xx*,24,82,146,215, 245,278,279,294
Chiang Kai-shek, 90,192,195,196, 201. *See also* Jiang Jieshi
Chibi, 161,215. *See also* Romance of the Three Kingdoms, The
China Association for Promoting Democracy, 58. *See also* Democratic parties; democratic personage(s)
China Council for Promotion of International Trade, *xiv*,56, 57. *See also* Nongovernmental organizations
China Democratic League, 58. *See also* Democratic parties; democratic personage(s)
China Democratic National Construction Association, 58. *See also* Democratic parties; democratic personage(s)
China Zhi Gong Dang, 58. *See also* Democratic parties; democratic personage(s)
China's Table Tennis Teams, 239, 240,242. *See also* Geist Prize
China's Women's Table Tennis Team, 238,240
Chinese Bridge Association, 263. *See also* Deng Xiaoping
Chinese Communist Party, *xv*,1,16,59, 60,61,66,67,71,72,93,97,103, 104,131,137,141,142,192,195, 196,198,258. *See also* Central government (State Council); Chinese People's Political Consultative Conference; Communist Youth League Committee; National People's Congress

Chinese Communist Party *(continued)*
  Central Committee of the CCP, 61,94,97
  Central Committee of the Chinese Communist Party, 56,59,62, 72,73,78,104,105,114,115,127
  Central Advisory Commission, 59,60
  Central Commission for Guiding Party Consolidation, 59,60
  Central Military Committee of the Party, 64
    People's Liberation Army, 1,61,93,114
  Chinese Communist Party's Central Commission for Discipline Inspection, 257
  General Office, 61
  United Front Work Department, 59,62
  Collective leadership of the Party committee, 72
  Constitution of the Chinese Communist Party, 74
  Party leadership, 3,4,8,15,73,100, 146,285
  Party policies, 65,82,97,98,99, 100,103,104,113,115,116, 117,122,125,141,142
  Party principles, 99,103,104
  Party branch, 19,72
  Party committee, 8,9,50,56,60, 72,73,74,94,96,100,115
    Organizational Department, 8,19,20,33,34,40,42,50, 56,62
  Party members, 8,9,11,16,50
  Party secretary, 4,6,71,72
  Propaganda department, 4,19,20
  Standing Committee of the Politburo, 61
Chinese Communist Party's Central Commission for Discipline Inspection, 257

Chinese Constitution, 16,71. *See also* Constitution; Constitution of China
Chinese Peasants' and Workers' Democratic Party, 58. *See also* Democratic parties; democratic personage(s)
Chinese People's Association for Friendship with Foreign Countries, 65. *See also* Nongovernmental organizations
Chinese People's Institute for Foreign Affairs, 65
Chinese People's Political Consultative Conference, 58. *See also* Central Committee of the CCP; Central government (State Council); National People's Congress
Chinese saying, 23,33,76,83,100, 119,139,168,176,208,211, 229,235,244,257,283,288, 293
Chinese Workers' and the Peasants' Red Army, 192. *See also* Eighth Route Army; New Fourth Army; People's Liberation Army
Choosing alternatives and implementing actions, 79
choosing alternatives, 85
Chu State, 21,157,184
Clinton Administration, 171,231
Collecting and analyzing feedback, 101,106,107,122,144. *See also* Collecting and analyzing information
Collecting and analyzing information, 79,81,84,85,86, 87,106,107,108,111,122,126, 144,145. *See also* Collecting and analyzing feedback

Collective enterprises, *x,xiv*,9,10,11, 12,16,29,80,93,95,98,100, 199,200,201,202. *See also* State-owned enterprises
Collective leadership, 61. *See also* Collective leadership of the Party committee
Collectivism, *x*,239
Commercial organizations, 31,51,57
Communist Youth League Committee, 3,5,8,9,13,14,19, 20,25,29,34,40,42,49,50. *See also* Chinese Communist Party
Complexities, *x,xvii*,42,122,214,277. *See also* Simplicity
"Comrade plus brother," 105. *See also* North Vietnam
Concept of the whole, 286,287. *See also* Individuality; universality
"Confidential secretary," 126,127. *See also* "Big secretary"; "small secretary"; "written secretary"
Confucianism, 91,110
Confucius, 108,133,192,206,223, 250,256,264,265,270
 Analects of Confucius, The, 133
 ruling by benevolence, 90,91, 102,142,145,262,269
 Book of Mencius, The, 133
 Doctrine of the Mean, The, 133
 go-between, 133,134,135
 golden mean, *xvii*,82,106, 133,135,146,187,214,286
 philosophy of the doctrine of the mean, 134
 Great Learning, The, 133
 Spring and Autumn Annals, 206
 Three Characters of the Confucian Classics, The, 221
 fineness of human nature, 221,276

Connections, 95,128,233
Considerate, 102,106
Constitution, 97,98. *See also*
　Chinese Constitution;
　Constitution of China
Constitution of China, 59,74. *See also* Chinese Constitution; Constitution
Constitution of the Chinese Communist Party, 74. *See also* Constitution of the Party
Constitution of the Party, 120. *See also* Constitution of the Chinese Communist Party
Containing China, 260
Contracted responsibility system, 60
Control and feedback, 86
Converted spies, 167. *See also* Doomed spies; inward spies; local spies; surviving spies
Cultural power, 261. *See also* Legal power
Cultural Revolution, 6,73,86,87,108, 111,115,120,131,180,192, 237,257,272,279
　Red Guards, 73,272
　Revolutionary Committees
　　representatives of the revolutionary army men, 73
　　representatives of the revolutionary cadres, 73
　　representatives of the revolutionary masses, 73

Daqiu village, 12. *See also* Collective enterprises; Yu Zuomin
Defining project(s), 79,80,81,144
Democracy, 53
Democratic parties, 67. *See also* Democratic personage(s)
　China Association for Promoting Democracy, 58
　China Democratic League, 58

Democratic parties *(continued)*
　China Democratic National Construction Association, 58
　China Zhi Gong Dang, 58
　Chinese Peasants' and Workers' Democratic Party, 58
　Jiu San Society, 58
　Revolutionary Committee of the Kuomintang, 58
　Taiwan Democratic self-government, 58
Democratic personage(s), 57,67. *See also* Democratic parties
Deng Bing, 47,48. *See also* Shen Taifu
Deng Office, 127. *See also* Deng Xiaoping
Deng Xiaoping, 16,37,60,61,64,73, 74,83,89,90,94,95,104,105, 110,111,113,114,115,117, 118,120,128,137,182,192, 263,294. *See also* Pro-Deng Xiaoping era
Divine, 150. *See also Book of Changes, The*
Doctrine of the Mean, The, 133
Doomed spies, 168. *See also* Converted spies; inward spies; local spies; surviving spies

Economic equality, 251,254,255. *See also* Political equality
Economic macro-controlling, 104
Eight Military Commands, 72
Eighth Route Army, 192,196. *See also* Chinese Workers' and the Peasants' Red Army; New Fourth Army; People's Liberation Army
Empty-city stratagem, 176. *See also* Kongming
Equality, *x,xviii*,246,247,248,249, 251,254,277
　economic equality, 251,254,255

Equality *(continued)*
political equality, 249,251,252, 253,254,255,277
social equality, 277
Event at Tian'anmen Square, 94,99, 110,114,118,182,187
Export permission certificates, 38,52. *See also* Import permission certificates; initiative (active) quotas; quotas

Face-saving, *xx*,83,161,171,186,219, 221,222,223,224,225,226, 227,228,229,232,233,234. *See also* Saving face
Fan Sui, 156,157,158
Financial organizations, *x,xv*,31,43, 47
Fineness of human nature, 221,276. *See also* Original sin
Firest in command, 94. *See also* Number one person
First meeting of the 7th National People's Congress, 74,96
Five elements, 181,215,287,288,294
Five Principles for Peaceful Coexistence, 254
Foreign Currencies Administration Bureau, 136,137. *See also* RMB
Foreign-owned enterprises, *x,xiv*,21, 22,23,24,29,37,39,247. *See also* Joint-venture enterprises
Foreign trade organizations, *x*,31,35, 36,37,38,39,51,52,57
Formulating alternatives and schemes, 79. *See also* Formulating schemes and choosing alternatives
Formulating schemes and choosing alternatives, 86,87. *See also* Formulating schemes and choosing schemes

Founder of a sect of Taoism, 270. *See also* Lao Tzu
Four adherences, 98,134,146,285
Communist Party leadership, 146,285
Marxism and Mao Zedong Thought, 146,285
proletarian dictatorship, 146,285
socialist path, 146,285
Four great inventions, 291
Fourth Meeting of the 7th National People's Congress, 141
Free market economy, *ix,x*,297. *See also* Market economy

Gang of Four, 279. *See also* Jiang Qing
GATT, 273. *See also* General Agreement on Tariffs and Trade
Geist Prize, 238,239
General Agreement on Tariffs and Trade, 273. *See also* GATT
General Office, 61
General Secretary, 61,64,74,94,97. *See also* Hu Yaobang; Jiang Zemin; Zhao Ziyang
Generalized System of Preferences, 99. *See also* GSP; most favored nation
Genghis Khan, 291
Go-between, 133,134,135. *See also* Golden mean
Golden mean, *xvii*,82,106,133,135, 146,187,214,286. *See also* Go-between
Gong Sunyang, 109. *See also* Legalists; Shang Yang
Goroug Yao Lee, 90
Governmental organizations, *x,xiv,*23,25,26,32,55,93,287. *See also* Nongovernmental organizations; semigovernmental organizations

Governmental viewpoints, *xvi*,99, 100,116,117,122,125. *See also* Party policies
Government's laws and regulations, 82. *See also* Party policies
Great Hall of the People, 272
Great Leap Forward, *xvii*,86,108, 111,130,146,214,227,237,263
Great Learning, The, 133
Great Third Line, 292. *See also* Small third line
GSP, 99. *See also* Generalized System of Preferences
Guang Da, 43. *See also* Hua Xia; Zhong Xin
Guangdong, *ix*,26
Guangxi Zhuang Autonomous Region, 108,212
Guizhou, 291

Han Dynasty, *xvii*,184,208,209,214, 215. *See also* Liu Bang
Han Xin, 159,160,183,184,185,208, 209,214. *See also* Liu Bang
Handicraft industry bureau, 11. *See also* Second industry bureau
Heaven, 91. *See also* This life and this world
Heavenly Imperial Court, 251
Hierarchy, *x*,*xviii*,249,250,251,255, 256,258,261,263,277. *See also* Equality; social hierarchy
Hillary Rodham Clinton, 113,213. *See also* Bill Clinton
Himalayas, 227
Mount Qomolangma, 227
Hong Kong, 12,26,39,43,89,103, 188,213,233,263,294,297
Hongmen Banquet, 208. *See also* Liu Bang; Xiang Yu
Hu Yaobang, 16,60,61,92,94,97,120. *See also* General Secretary

Hua Guofeng, 91,120. *See also* Mao Zedong
Hua Xia, 43. *See also* Guang Da; Zhong Xin
Huang Quanyu, *x*,*xix*,*xx*,23,24,27,45, 93,103,116,139,146,215,220, 226,228,235,237,244,245, 248,252,253,254,274,275, 278,279,294
Huarong Pass, 162. *See also* Huarong Trail
Huarong Trail, 162,163,164. *See also* Huarong Pass
Human duality, 264

Imaginative thinking, *x*,289,290. *See also* Abstract thinking
Import permission certificates, 38,52. *See also* Export permission certificates; initiative (active) quotas; quotas
Income tax law of Chinese-foreign joint ventures, 141
Income tax law of foreign enterprises, 141
Income Tax Law of the People's Republic of China on Foreign Investing Enterprises and Foreign Enterprises, 141
Individual company, *x*,*xiv*,26,28,288. *See also* Mou Qizhong
Individualism, *x*
Individuality, 277,281,286,288,289. *See also* Universality
Industrial and Commercial Bank of China, 43. *See also* Agricultural Bank of China; Bank of China; Bank of Communication of China; People's Bank of China; People's Construction Bank of China

Inflexibility, x,106,107,110,111,112, 117,120. *See also* Changeability
Initiative (active) quotas, 52,88. *See also* Export permission certificates
Institute of International Relations, 65
Institute of International Studies, 65
Institute for Policies Research, 85
Intrigues of the Warring States, 149, 158,214
Inward spies, 167. *See also* Converted spies; doomed spies; local spies; surviving spies
Ironclad cases, 111,112,118

Jiang Jieshi, 90,192,263. *See also* Chiang Kai-shek
Jiang Jingguo, 90
Jiang Qing, 262. *See also* Gang of Four
Jiang Zemin, 74,104,120,121. *See also* General Secretary
Jiu San Society, 58. *See also* Democratic parties; democratic personage(s)
Joint-venture enterprises, *x,xiv,xix*, 12,16,25,29,38. *See also* Foreign owned enterprises

"Kickback," 23
Kissinger, Henry, 12,230,260
KMT, 258. *See also* Kuomintang
Knowing your enemy, *x*,172,176, 181,198. *See also* Knowing yourself
Knowing yourself, *x*,172,174,176, 181,198. *See also* Knowing your enemy

Kongming, 152,153,154,161,162, 164,174,175,176,193,194, 195,197,207,214,284. *See also* Cao Cao; *Romance of the Three Kingdoms, The*; Sima Yi; Zhuge Liang
Empty-city Strategem, 176
Korean War, 151,158,169,179,234, 259,272. *See also* Black Snow; United Nations' armies
Kuomintang, 195,196,198,202,258. *See also* KMT

Land Reform Movement, 131
Lao tzu, 270,271,279. *See also* Founder of a sect of Taoism
Law of Enterprise, 74
Law of the People's Republic of China on Chinese-Foreign Joint Ventures, 15,18. *See also* Income tax law of Chinese-foreign joint ventures
Law of the People's Republic of China on Foreign-Owned Enterprises, 25. *See also* Income tax law of foreign enterprises
Leading Group for Education of Cadres, 61
Leading Group for Educational Reform, 61
Lee Teng-hui, 90,95,99,120,138,147, 260. *See also* Taiwan
"Left" conservative officials, 115
Legal authority, 261. *See also* Charismatic authority; traditional authority
Legal power, 261. *See also* Cultural power
Legalists, 109
  Gong Sunyang, 109
  Shang Yang, 109
  Xunzi, 110

Leonard, Joseph W., *x,xiv*,24,30,88
"Let a hundred flowers blossom, let a hundred schools of thought contend," 155. *See also* Struggle against the Bourgeois Rightists
Li Zhongren, 263. *See also* Chaing Kai-shek; Jiang Jieshi
Li Zong-wu, 202,205,208,210,211. *Theory about Thickness and Blackness, The*, 202,203,207, 208,209,210,211,216
Lian Chan, 95
Liberation Daily, 114,115. *See also* "Mouthpiece of the Party"
Life and this world, This, 91. *See also* Heaven
Like attracts like, 287
Lin Biao, 73,120
Liu Bei, 190,191,192,203,207,284. *See also* Cao Cao; *Romance of the Three Kingdoms, The*
Liu Shaoqi, 120
Local spies, 167. *See also* Converted spies; doomed spies; inward spies; surviving spies
Logistics department, 4,5,14
Low income, small differences, 254
Lu Buwei, 193

Macao, 12,233. *See also* Aomen
Macro-adjustment/controlling, 285
Macro-control of investments, 116
Macro-economy system, 99
"Manager/director being in charge" system, 72. *See also* Secretary of the Party committee
Manchuria, 196
Manufacturing Organizations, 3
Mao Office, 127

Mao Zedong, *xvi*,61,67,71,72,73,87, 90,91,94,104,105,108,111, 115,120,127,145,154,155, 179,180,192,198,199,201, 251,257,263,275,279. *See also* Free market; planned economy
"Let a hundred flowers blossom, let a hundred schools of thought contend," 155
On the Ten Major Relationships, 72
Market economy, 32,33,44,46,78,80, 81,85,94,95,97,98,99,104, 111,115,118,119,122,131, 134,141,179,203,285,297. *See also* Free market; planned economy
Marxism, 242
Marxism-Leninism, 113
Marxism and Mao Zedong Thought, 146,285
Marxist theorists, 110
Mass organization, 3,19,55,56,57. *See also* Political organization
Member of the Secretariat, 127
Members of the Standing Committee of the Politburo, 61
MFN, 99,138,146,213,273. *See also* Most favored nation
Min-Sheng, 53. *See also* People's Livelihood
Min-Sheng Bank, 44,53
Minister of Beiyang, 262. *See also* Yuan Shikai
Ministry of Commerce, *xv*,31
Ministry of Domestic Trade, 225
Ministry of Finance, 46
Ministry of Foreign Affairs, 59,65, 225,272
   Chinese People's Association for Friendship with Foreign Countries, 65

Ministry of Foreign Affairs *(continued)*
Chinese People's Institute for Foreign Affairs, 65
Institute of International Relations, 65
Institute of International Studies, 65
Ministry of Foreign Economic Relations and Trade, 25,35, 36,39,52,74
Ministry of Justice, 257. *See also* Central Supervisory Committee; Chinese Communist Party's Central Commission for Discipline Inspection
Modes of thinking, x,217,281,293, 294. *See also* Behavior norms
Modesty and implication, x,82,270, 271,272,273,274,275,276, 277. *See also* Taiji boxing; Taiji sword
Most favored nation, 99,138,260, 273. *See also* Generalized System of Preferences; MFN
Motorola, 220,278
Mou Qizhong, 26,121
Mount Qomolangma, 227
"Mouthpiece of the Party," 113. *See also Liberation Daily; People's Daily*
Movement for Agricultural Cooperation, 131
Movement of Joint State-Private Ownership of Individual Enterprises, 131
Movement of Reforming and Opening, 36,37,61,94,110, 111,115,285. *See also* Deng Xiaoping; Hu Yaobang; Zhao Ziyang
Multilayered distribution network system of Amway, 75. *See also* Amway distribution system
Mutual promotion and restraint between false and true, 161, 164,296. *See also* Unity and opposite; unity of opposites; *Yin* and *Yang*
Mutual promotion and restraint between the five elements, 287. *See also five elements*

National People's Congress, 57,58, 64,65,98. *See also* Central Committee of the CCP; Central government (State Council); Chinese People's Political Consultative Conference
First meeting of the 7th National People's Congress, 74,96
Fourth Meeting of the 7th National People's Congress, 141
Nationalism, 53
Needham, Joseph, 290
Science and Civilization in China, 290
New Authority, 92,94,110. *See also* Powerful men
New Fourth Army, 192,196. *See also* Chinese Workers' and the Peasants' Red Army; Eighth Route Army; People's Liberation Army
Nongovernmental organizations, x,xiv,xix,55,57,58,59. *See also* Semigovernmental organizations
North Vietnam, 105,258. *See also* "Comrade plus Brother"

"Number one person," 64,94,95,96, 117,122,123,124,125,128, 137,139,142,143,144. *See also* First in command

Office of Fact-Finding and Research on Policies, 85
Official standard, 256
Old Man on the Frontier Lost his Mare, 282. *See also* Unity of opposites
Olympic Games, 227,239,240,273
On the Ten Major Relationships, 72
One country can accommodate two different social systems, 105. *See also* One country with two systems
One country with two systems, 286, 294. *See also* One country can accommodate two different social systems
One divides into two, 282. *See also* Two combine into one
One-China policy, 260. *See also* Taiwan Strait
Operation of decision making, 69,217
  changeability, 100,101,104,122, 213
  complexities, 42,122,214,277
  inflexibility, 106,107,110,111,112, 117,120
  poor continuity, 138,139,140,141, 142,143,144,145,146
  predictability, 112
  simplicity, 106,129,130
  unpredictability, 118
  timing, 135,137,138,146
Opium War, 226,251
Organizational Department, 8,19,20, 33,34,40,42,50,56,62
Oriental Square, 188

Original sin, 219,221,223,276. *See also* Fineness of human nature
Orthodox Marxists and Leninists, 115

Party branch, 19,72
Party committee, 8,9,50,56,60,72,73, 74,94,96,100,115
Party Committee Collective Leadership, 40
Party leadership, 3,4,8,15,73,100, 146,285
Party members, 8,9,11,16,50
Party policies, 65,82,97,98,99,100, 103,104,113,115,116,117, 122,125,141,142
Party principles, 99,103,104
Party secretary, x,4,6,71,72
Passive quotas, 52,53,88. *See also* Initiative (active) quotas
Paying tuition, 84. *See also* Cadres
People's Bank of China, 43,44,46, 47. *See also* Agricultural Bank of China; Bank of China; Bank of Communications of China; Bank of China Investment; Bank of Shanghai Pudong Development; Bank of Shenzhen Development; Industrial and Commercial Bank of China; People's Construction Bank of China
People's commune, 60
People's Construction Bank of China, 43,51. *See also* Agricultural Bank of China; Bank of China; Bank of Communications of China; Industrial and Commercial Bank of China; People's Bank of China
People's Daily, 113,115,116,142, 224,289

People's Liberation Army, 1,61,93, 114. *See also* Chinese Workers' and the Peasants' Red Army; Eighth Route Army; New Fourth Army
Armed Police, 50
Eight Military Commands, 72
People's Livelihood, 53. *See also* Min-Sheng
People's Republic of China, *ix*,1,6, 43,229,251,254
Philosophy of the doctrine of the mean, 134
Planned economy, *x,xvi*,32,33,46,48, 78,80,85,95,97,104,118,119. *See also* Market economy; socialist planned economy
Politburo, 61
Political commissar, 71,72. *See also* Political instructor
Political equality, 249,251,252,253, 254,255,277. *See also* Economic equality; social equality
Political instructor, 71. *See also* Political commissar
Battalion political instructor, 6
Political organization, 3,19,55,56,65. *See also* Mass organization
Poor continuity, 138,139,140,141, 142,143,144,145,146
Power and authority, *xv,xvii*,261,263, 277
  charismatic authority, 261
  cultural power, 261
  legal authority, 261
  legal power, 261
  traditional authority, 261
Powerful man/men, *xvi,xvii*,61,89, 90,91,92,107,108,111,112, 117, 118,120,121,129,136. *See also* Jiang Jieshi (Chiang Kai-shek); Yuan Shikai; Deng Xiaoping; Mao Zedong

Predictability, 112. *See also* Unpredictability
Private company, 16,27,28,129. *See also* Individual company; privately-owned enterprises
Privately-owned enterprises, 28. *See also* Individual company; private company
Pro-Deng Xiaoping era, 295
Project from a note, 92,93. *See also* Project of a senior official
Project of a senior official, 92,93. *See also* Project from a note
Project of Three Gorges, 85,118,242
Proletarian Dictatorship, 146,285
Propaganda department, 4,19,20

Qi State, 21,157,158,184,185,250
Qin Dynasty, 193. *See also* Qin Shi Huang; Qin State
Qin Shi Huang, 172. *See also* Qin Shi Huang; Qin State
Qin State, 109,155,156,157,158,172, 193
Qing Dynasty, 262,279
  Xuantong, 262
Quotas, 38,39,79,87
  Initiative (active) quotas, 52,88
  Passive quotas, 52,53,88

Railway between Tanzania and Zambia, 259
Reasonable, 102,106
Rectification Movement, 155
Red Guards, 73,272
Reference Newspapers, 256
Reforming and opening, 12,84,113, 114,118,259. *See also* Movement of Reforming and Opening
Reforming and Opening movement, 83. *See also* Movement of Reforming and Opening

Religious Bureau of the State Council, 59
Representatives of the revolutionary army men, 73
Representatives of the revolutionary cadres, 73
Representatives of the revolutionary masses, 73
Republic of China, 287. *See also* Taiwan
Revolutionary Committee of the Kuomintang, 58. *See also* Democratic parties; democratic personage(s)
Revolutionary Committees, 73
Rich equally, 254. *See also* Rich together
Rich together, 254. *See also* Rich equally
RMB, 136,137,147. *See also* Foreign Currencies Administration Bureau
Role expectations, 90,222,264,265, 266,268,269,277
Role norms, 264
Romance of the Three Kingdoms, The, xvii,149,152,161,164, 173,193,214,215,216,284
Ruling by benevolence, 90,91,102, 142,145,262,269. *See also* Ruling by laws
Ruling by laws, 90,91,142,145,269. *See also* Ruling by benevolence
Rural Policy Research Center, 60

Saving face, *xviii*, 82,116,119,219, 276,277. *See also* Face-saving
Science and Civilization in China, 290
Second light industry bureau, 11. *See also* Handicraft industry bureau

Secretariat, 61
Semigovernmental organizations, *x,xiv*,55,58,59. *See also* Nongovernmental organizations
Senior cadres, 37,263
Separation of the Party from the administration, 100. *See also* Party policies
Service organizations, *x*,31,75
SEZs, 82,297. *See also* Special Economic Zones
Shang Yang, 109. *See also* Gong Sunyang
Shanghai, *ix,xvii,*114,131,291
Shen Taifu, 47,121,245. *See also* Deng Bing
Shenzhen, 115,131,147. *See also* Special Economic Zones
Sichuan, 291
Sima Yi, 152,153,154,174,175,176, 207. *See also* Kongming; *Romance of the Three Kingdoms, The*
Simplicity, 106,129,130. *See also* Complexities
"Small secretary," 127. *See also* "Big secretary"; "confidential secretary"; "written secretary"
"Small third line," 292. *See also* "Great Third Line"
Social animals, 235,248,250. *See also* Hierarchy
Social equality, 277
Social hierarchy, 251
Social role and self, *x*,223,263,264, 267,277
  human duality, 264
  role expectations, 90,222,264, 265,266,268,269,277
  role norms, 264

Socialist economy, x,98,119,142. *See also* Socialist market economy; socialist planned economy
Socialist market economy, 113,118, 133,134,142. *See also* Market economy
Socialist Path, 98,134,146,285
Socialist planned commodity economy, 113. *See also* Market economy; planned economy
Socialist planned economy, 113. *See also* Planned economy
Social public ownership, 134. *See also* Collective enterprises; state-owned enterprises
Socialist system, 113,119,134,242
"Southern Orange and Northern Jyy," 21. *See also* Yan-zi
Soviet Union, 1,33,72,73,114,117, 120,150,155,158,159,179, 182,183,213,227,252,254, 258,259,275,292
Special Economic Zones, 115,147, 285. *See also* SEZs
Spring and Autumn and Warring States, 146
Spring and Autumn Annals, 206
Stalin, 60,275
Standing Committee of the Politburo, 61
State Council, 36,44,64,65. *See also* Central Committee of the CCP; Central Government; Chinese People's Political Consultative Conference; National People's Congress
China Council for Promotion of International Trade, *xiv*,56, 65,57
Ministry of Commerce, *xv*,31
Ministry of Domestic Trade, 225
Ministry of Finance, 46

State Council *(continued)*
Ministry of Foreign Affairs, 59,65, 225,272
Ministry of Foreign Economic Relations and Trade, 25,35, 36,39,52,74
Ministry of Justice, 257
State-owned enterprises, *ix,x,xiv,xix*, 3,12,18,29,37,39,41,65,98, 129,142,160,161,199,200, 201,202,285,288. *See also* Collective enterprises
State-owned overseas organizations, 35,36,37,43,51
Strategy for Gold Medals, 227
Struggle Against the Bourgeois Rightists, 86,111,155. *See also* "Let a hundred flowers blossom, let a hundred schools of thought contend"
Su Qin, 156. *See also* Alliance and the Coalition; Zhang Yi
Sun Bin, 153,198. *See also* Sun Tzu
Sun Tzu, 81,165,166,167,168,172, 176,177,178,179,181,182, 183,186,189,198,199,200, 201,211,214,215,216
Art of War of Sun Tzu, The, 149, 160,177,211,284
Sun Yat-sen, 53,90,279. *See also* Sun Zhongshan
Three People's Principles, 53
Surviving spies, 168. *See also* Converted spies; doomed spies; inward spies; local spies

Table Tennis Association of China, 238,239,240,242,243
China's Table Tennis Teams, 239, 240,242. *See also* Geist Prize
Table tennis team of the United States, 169

Tactics of decision making, 149. *See also Art of War of Sun Tzu, The; Intrigues of the Warring States; Romance of the Three Kingdoms, The*
  knowing your enemy, 172,176, 181,198
  knowing yourself, 172,174,176, 181,198
  to be devious in order to be direct, 189,192,193,196,296
  to be down first in order to be up later, 296
  to give in order to take, 296
  to release in order to catch, 193, 195,197,296
  will you survive when you are put in deadly peril, 159,296
Taiji boxing, 270,271,272,274,275. *See also* Taiji sword
Taiji sword, 270,271. *See also* Taiji boxing
"Tail of Capitalism," 257. *See also* Cultural Revolution
Taiwan, 12,39,89,90,95,120,137,138, 147,188,192,213,228,260, 263,287,294,297. *See also* Republic of China
Taiwan Democratic self-government, 58. *See also* Democratic parties; democratic personage(s)
Taiwan Strait, 230,295. *See also* One-China policy
Theory about Thickness and Blackness, The, 202,203,207, 208,209,210,211,216
Third line, 291,292
Three Characters of the Confucian Classics, The, 221
Three People's Principles, 53
Tianjin Economic and Technical Development Zone, 220. *See also* Motorola
Timing, 135,137,138,146

To be devious in order to be direct, 189,192,193,196,296
To be down first in order to be up later, 296
To give in order to take, 296
To release in order to catch, 193,195, 197,296
Traditional authority, 261. *See also* Charismatic authority; legal authority
Traditional Chinese culture, x,221, 222,238,241,243,249,265, 269
Twelfth Asian Games, 240
Two combine into one, 282. *See also* One divide into two
"Two-line struggles," 103. *See also* Chinese Communist Party

Union, 3,4,6,14,17,19,25,40,42,49
Union Law of the People's Republic of China, 14
United Front Work Department, 59,62
United Nations' armies, 151. *See also Black Snow*; Korean War
Unity and opposite, 150,151,281, 282,283,285,286,293. *See also* Unity of opposites; *Yin* and *Yang*
Universality, x,281,286,288,289. *See also* Individuality
Unpredictability, 118. *See also* Predictability

Vietnam War, 140,158,179,199,259, 264,295

War of Resistance against Japan, 107
Warring States, *xvii*,155

[Where] there is a counter-tactic from below, there will be a policy from above, 79. *See also* Party policies
[Where] there is a policy from above, there will be a counter-tactic from below, 76,79,244. *See also* Party policies
Will you survive when you are put in deadly peril, 159,296
Women's Commission, 3,5,6,9,13, 14,17,19,20,25,34,40,42,49, 50
 birth control education, 3
Workshops, 4,14,27,28
World War II, 192,197,198,291
World Women's Conference, 114. *See also* Hillary Rodham Clinton
"Written secretary," 127. *See also* "Big secretary"; "confidential secretary"; "small secretary"
Wuxu Reform Movement, 262

Xi'an Incident, 195,196. *See also* Yang Hucheng; Zhang Zueliang
Xiang, 10,11,17,18,30,47
Xiang Yu, 160,208,209,215. *See also* Liu Bang
Xuantong, 262
Xunzi, 110

Yan-zi, 21. *See also* "Southern Orange and Northern Jyy"
Yang Hucheng, 196. *See also* Xi'an Incident
Yangtze River, 85,118,215,242
Yin and *Yang, xvi,xviii*,106,111,150, 151,159,161,164,213,225, 281. *See also Book of Changes, The;* unity and opposite; unity of opposites
Yu Zuomin, 12. *See also* Daqiu village
Yuan Shikai, 262. *See also* Minister of Beiyang

"Zeng Tzu killed a man," 173
Zhang Xueliang, 196. *See also* Xi'an Incident
Zhang Yi, 156. *See also* Alliance and the Coalition; Su Qin
Zhao Ziyang, 16,60,64,120,121. *See also* General Secretary
Zhong Xin, 43. *See also* Guang Da; Hua Xia
Zhou Dynasty, *xvii*,150
Zhou Wenwang, 150
Zhou Enlai, 16,90,92,192,272
Zhou Wenwang, 150. *See also Book of Changes, The*
Zhu Rongji, 46,47,260
Zhuge Liang, 214. *See also* Kongming

Order Your Own Copy of This Important Book for Your Personal Library!

BUSINESS DECISION MAKING IN CHINA

_____ in hardbound at $49.95 (ISBN: 1-56024-997-8)

_____ in softbound at $24.95 (ISBN: 0-7890-0190-X)

COST OF BOOKS_____	☐ **BILL ME LATER:** ($5 service charge will be added) (Bill-me option is good on US/Canada/Mexico orders only; not good to jobbers, wholesalers, or subscription agencies.)
OUTSIDE USA/CANADA/ MEXICO: ADD 20%_____	
POSTAGE & HANDLING_____ (US: $3.00 for first book & $1.25 for each additional book) Outside US: $4.75 for first book & $1.75 for each additional book)	☐ Check here if billing address is different from shipping address and attach purchase order and billing address information.
	Signature _____
SUBTOTAL_____	☐ **PAYMENT ENCLOSED: $**_____
IN CANADA: ADD 7% GST_____	☐ **PLEASE CHARGE TO MY CREDIT CARD.**
STATE TAX_____ (NY, OH & MN residents, please add appropriate local sales tax)	☐ Visa ☐ MasterCard ☐ AmEx ☐ Discover ☐ Diner's Club
	Account # _____
FINAL TOTAL_____ (If paying in Canadian funds, convert using the current exchange rate. UNESCO coupons welcome.)	Exp. Date _____
	Signature _____

Prices in US dollars and subject to change without notice.

NAME _____

INSTITUTION _____

ADDRESS _____

CITY _____

STATE/ZIP _____

COUNTRY _____ COUNTY (NY residents only) _____

TEL _____ FAX _____

E-MAIL_____
May we use your e-mail address for confirmations and other types of information? ☐ Yes ☐ No

Order From Your Local Bookstore or Directly From
The Haworth Press, Inc.
10 Alice Street, Binghamton, New York 13904-1580 • USA
TELEPHONE: 1-800-HAWORTH (1-800-429-6784) / Outside US/Canada: (607) 722-5857
FAX: 1-800-895-0582 / Outside US/Canada: (607) 772-6362
E-mail: getinfo@haworth.com
PLEASE PHOTOCOPY THIS FORM FOR YOUR PERSONAL USE.

BOF96

NEW · FORTHCOMING · AND · RECENT BOOKS
FROM HAWORTH INTERNATIONAL BUSINESS PRESS

TAKE 20% OFF EACH BOOK! Special Sale!

THE TRANS-OCEANIC MARKETING CHANNEL
A New Tool for Understanding Tropical Africa's Export Agriculture
H. Laurens van der Laan, PhD
Examines the opportunities, problems, and policies of the various channel members.
$49.95 hard. ISBN: 0-7890-0116-0.
Text price (5+ copies): $24.95.
Available Fall 1997. Approx. 269 pp. with Index.
Over 250 Pages!

HANDBOOK OF CROSS-CULTURAL MARKETING
Paul A. Herbig, ABD
Shows you how to sensitize your marketing approaches to the cultural norms and taboos of other societies.
$59.95 hard. ISBN: 0-7890-0154-3.
$29.95 soft. ISBN: 0-7890-0285-X.
Available Winter 1997/98. Approx. 318 pp. with Index.
Over 300 Pages!

GUIDE TO SOFTWARE EXPORT
A Handbook for International Software Sales
Roger A. Philips
Provides a step-by-step approach to initiating or expanding international software sales.
$49.95 hard. ISBN: 0-7890-0143-8.
Text price (5+ copies): $24.95.
Available Winter 1997/98. Approx. 248 pp. with Index.
Features case studies, tables, and appendixes.

BUSINESS DECISION MAKING IN CHINA
Huang Quanyu, PhD, Joseph W. Leonard, PhD, and Chen Tong, MS, MGS
Helps Western readers better understand Chinese decision making.
$49.95 hard. ISBN: 1-56024-997-8.
$24.95 soft. ISBN: 0-7890-0190-X.
Available Summer 1997. Approx. 320 pp. with Index.
Over 300 Pages!

PRIVATIZATION AND ENTREPRENEURSHIP
The Managerial Challenge in Central and Eastern Europe
Edited by Arieh A. Ullmann and Alfred Lewis
Provides penetrating insights into the details of managing in the former socialist countries.
$49.95 hard. ISBN: 1-56024-972-2.
Text price (5+ copies): $29.95.
1996. 358 pp. with Index.
Includes an Instructor's Manual.
Over 300 Pages!

AN INTERNATIONAL ACCOUNTING PRACTICE SET
The Karissa Jean's Simulation
David R. Peterson, and Nancy Schendel, CPA, MBA
The only currently available simulation for international accounting, business and accounting students.
$39.95 hard. ISBN: 0-7890-6004-3.
$14.95 soft. ISBN: 0-7890-6021-3.
1996. 144 pp. with Index.
Includes 42 pp. Instructor's Manual.
NOW IN PAPERBACK

IMPLEMENTATION OF TOTAL QUALITY MANAGEMENT
A Comprehensive Training Program
Rolf E. Rogers, PhD, CMC
Apply these proven methods for implementing TQM training in your workforce.
$39.95 hard. ISBN: 1-56024-996-X. 1996.
$14.95 soft. ISBN: 0-7890-0209-4. 1997. 117 pp. with Index.
NOW IN PAPERBACK

THE EIGHT CORE VALUES OF THE JAPANESE BUSINESSMAN
Yasutaka Sai
$49.95 hard. ISBN: 1-56024-870-X. 1995.
$19.95 soft. ISBN: 1-56024-871-8. 1996. 177 pp. with Index.

INTERNATIONAL NEGOTIATING
Michael Kublin, PhD
$49.95 hard. ISBN: 1-56024-854-8.
Text price (5+ copies): $19.95. 1995. 165 pp. with Index.

EUROMARKETING
Pervez N. Ghauri, PhD
Text price (5+ copies): $24.95. 1994. 361 pp. with Index.
Over 300 Pages!

GLOBALIZATION OF CONSUMER MARKETS
Edited by Salah S. Hassan, PhD, and Erdener Kaynak, PhD, DSc
$74.95 hard. ISBN: 1-56024-429-1.
Text price (5+ copies): $29.95. 1994. 333 pp. with Index.

A GUIDE TO SUCCESSFUL BUSINESS RELATIONS WITH THE CHINESE
Quanyu Huang, PhD, Richard Andrulis, PhD, and Tong Chen
$59.95 hard. ISBN: 1-56024-868-8.
Text price (5+ copies): $24.95. 1994. 254 pp. with Index.
Over 300 Pages!

HOW TO UTILIZE NEW INFORMATION TECHNOLOGY IN THE GLOBAL MARKETPLACE
Edited by Fahri Karakaya, PhD, MBA, and Erdener Kaynak, PhD, DSc
$49.95 hard. ISBN: 1-56024-900-5.
Text price (5+ copies): $19.95. 1994. 270 pp. with Index.
Includes an Instructor's Manual.
Over 250 Pages!

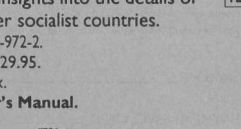

VISIT US ON THE INTERNET!
www.haworth.com

International Business Press
an imprint of The Haworth Press, Inc.
10 Alice Street,
Binghamton, New York 13904-1580 USA

Textbooks are available for classroom adoption consideration on a 60-day examination basis. You will receive an invoice payable within 60 days along with the book. If you decide to adopt the book, your invoice will be cancelled. Please write to us on your institutional letterhead, indicating the textbook you would like to examine as well as the following information: course title, current text, enrollment, and decision date.

INDUSTRIAL PRODUCTS
Hans Jansson, PhD
—*Science Books & Films*
$79.95 hard. ISBN: 1-56024-425-9.
Text price (5+ copies): $24.95. 1994. 229 pp. with Index.

PRODUCT-COUNTRY IMAGES
Edited by Nicolas Papadopoulos, DBA, and
Louise A. Heslop, PhD
Over 400 Pages!
$79.95 hard. ISBN: 1-56024-236-1.
$29.95 soft. ISBN: 1-56024-237-X. 1993. 477 pp. with Index.

MULTINATIONAL STRATEGIC ALLIANCES
Edited by Refik Culpan, PhD
Over 350 Pages!
$79.95 hard. ISBN: 1-56024-322-8.
$24.95 soft. ISBN: 1-56024-323-6. 1993. 351 pp. with Index.

MARKET EVOLUTION IN DEVELOPING COUNTRIES
Subhash C. Jain, PhD, MBA
Over 300 Pages!
$79.95 hard. ISBN: 1-56024-360-0.
Text price (5+ copies): $24.95. 1993. 329 pp. with Index.

CALL OUR TOLL-FREE NUMBER: 1-800-HAWORTH
US & Canada only / 8am–5pm ET; Monday–Friday
Outside US/Canada: + 607–722–5857
FAX YOUR ORDER TO US: 1-800-895-0582
Outside US/Canada: + 607–771–0012

E-MAIL YOUR ORDER TO US: getinfo@haworth.com

VISIT OUR WEB SITE AT: www.haworth.com

THE GLOBAL BUSINESS
Four Key Marketing Strategies
Edited by Erdener Kaynak, PhD, DSc
Over 400 Pages!
$8.95 (was $39.95) soft. ISBN: 1-56024-249-3.
1993. 432 pp. with Index. *(No additional 20% discount on this title.)*

INTERNATIONAL BUSINESS EXPANSION INTO LESS-DEVELOPED COUNTRIES
James C. Baker, DBA
Over 300 Pages!
$79.95 hard. ISBN: 1-56024-201-9.
Text price (5+ copies): $39.95. 1992. 313 pp. with Index.

HOW TO MANAGE FOR INTERNATIONAL COMPETITIVENESS
Edited by Abbas J. Ali, PhD
Over 250 Pages!
$79.95 hard. ISBN: 1-56024-202-7.
$39.95 soft. ISBN: 1-56024-203-5. 1992. 276 pp. with Index.

INTERNATIONAL MARKETING
Edited by Erdener Kaynak, PhD, DSc
Over 300 Pages!
$89.95 hard. ISBN: 0-86656-951-0. 1990.
$24.95 soft. ISBN: 1-56024-989-7. 1996.
387 pp. with Index.

INTERNATIONAL BUSINESS HANDBOOK
Edited by V. H. (Manek) Kirpalani, DSc
Over 600 Pages!
$89.95 hard. ISBN: 0-86656-862-X. 1990.
$39.95 soft. ISBN: 0-7890-0082-2. 1996.
657 pp. with Index.

NOW IN PAPERBACK
TAKE 20% OFF EACH BOOK!
Special Sale!

Order Today and Save!

TITLE	ISBN	REGULAR PRICE	20%-OFF PRICE

- Discount good only in US, Canada, and Mexico and not good in conjunction with any other offer.
- Discounts not good outside US, Canada, and Mexico.
- Individual orders outside US/Canada/Mexico must be prepaid by check, credit card, or money order.
- Postage & handling: US: $3.00 for first book & $1.25 for each additional book; Outside US: $4.75 for first book & $1.75 for each additional book.

NAME_____

ADDRESS_____

_____

CITY_____

STATE_____ ZIP_____

COUNTRY_____

COUNTY (NY residents only)_____

TEL_____ FAX_____

E-MAIL_____
May we use your e-mail address for confirmations and other types of information? ( ) Yes   ( ) No

- MN, NY, and OH residents: Add appropriate local sales tax.
- If paying in Canadian funds, please use the current exchange rate to convert total to Canadian dollars.
- Outside USA, Canada, and Mexico: Add 20%.
- Payment in UNESCO coupons welcome.
- Please allow 3–4 weeks for delivery after publication.

☐ **BILL ME LATER** ($5 service charge will be added).
(Bill-me option available on US/Canadian/Mexican orders only. Not good for subscription agencies. Service charge is waived for booksellers/jobbers.)

Signature_____

☐ **PAYMENT ENCLOSED**_____
(Payment must be in US or Canadian dollars by check or money order drawn on a US or Canadian bank.)

☐ **PLEASE CHARGE TO MY CREDIT CARD:**
  ☐ VISA ☐ MASTERCARD ☐ AMEX ☐ DISCOVER ☐ DINERS CLUB

Account #_____ Exp Date_____

Signature_____

(17) 05/97 BBC97

The Haworth Press, Inc.
10 Alice Street, Binghamton New York 13904-1580 USA